ACCOLADES

Tony Cooke provides a moving account of God's extraordinary works through the history of His church with encouraging and balanced wisdom for us today as we seek to learn from those who have gone before us.

—Craig S. Keener, PhD
Author of *Miracles: The Credibility of the New Testament Accounts*
F.M. and Ada Thompson Professor of Biblical Studies,
Asbury Theological Seminary

My friend, Tony Cooke, takes us on a deep dive into history and brings us to the present in a way that makes not only the Bible come alive, but the God of the Bible come alive for us! His book highlights how God has supernaturally intervened in the affairs of human beings for many generations. It will inform your head and stir faith in your heart!

—Bishop Dale C. Bronner, DMin
Founder and Senior Pastor
Word of Faith Family Worship Cathedral
Atlanta, Georgia

I highly recommend Tony Cooke's book, *Miracles and the Supernatural Throughout Church History*. I am also a student of history, and there is much to glean from our early and modern-day church fathers. This book is a fantastic study of miracles and the supernatural. It is an excellent addition to anyone's library.

—Kenneth W. Hagin
President, Kenneth Hagin Ministries & Rhema Bible Training College
Pastor, Rhema Bible Church

Tony Cooke has done an excellent job of showing how the Holy Spirit continued to work in the church after the death of the twelve apostles and how He continues to work powerfully today.

He has also done an excellent job of showing from example the importance of maintaining a healthy balance between Word and Spirit. Anyone wanting to learn about the Holy Spirit will want to give priority to reading this volume.

—Eddie Hyatt, DMin
Hyatt International Ministries, Grapevine, Texas
Author of *2000 Years of Charismatic Christianity: A 21st Century Look at Church History from a Pentecostal/Charismatic Perspective* and *1726: The Year that Defined America*

Tony Cooke has a written an amazing book about our miracle-working God. *Miracles and the Supernatural Throughout Church History* details for today's believer that we not only serve a God who has done miracles in the early church, but our same Lord is confirming His Word with signs following within the church of today. Tony's detailed study of the Spirit's work, by way of miracles and other supernatural manifestations throughout history, strategically positions him to counsel the church of today to expect the miraculous in our day. This book will bolster your faith and you will find yourself saying, "Oh Lord, do it again in my generation!"

—Bradley Trask, DMin
Lead Pastor, Brighton Assembly of God
General Council Executive Presbyter, Assemblies of God

What Tony Cooke gives us in his book, *Miracles and the Supernatural Throughout Church History*, is masterful. The research of individuals from the early church fathers to this present time who experienced and believed in God's miraculous power is both informative and inspiring. Along with being a brilliant resource on the subject, *Miracles and the*

Supernatural also provides solid instruction for anyone in our day who desires to understand and be used of God in the miraculous.

—Patsy Cameneti
Pastor, Teacher, Author
Logan, Australia

It's clear that we have seen a great increase in the manifestation of the Spirit's power and gifts since the early 1900s, but it's also clear the Spirit never stopped healing and delivering and working miracles throughout Church history. Here, with careful research but in very readable, balanced form, Tony Cooke presents a faith-building survey of the Spirit's work over the past 2,000 years, using the miraculous accounts as teachable moments as well. As you read these pages, culminating with today's worldwide, mighty outpouring of the Spirit, your heart will be stirred to prayer and to action. All things are possible with Him!

—Dr. Michael L. Brown, PhD
Host of the *Line of Fire* broadcast
President of FIRE School of Ministry

My father-in-law, John Osteen, who spent nearly two decades as a Baptist minister, had his life and ministry dramatically altered through seeking and experiencing the Holy Spirit's power personally. Healings, miracles, and supernatural works resulted in his family, church, and ministry serving in foreign lands. He loved telling people his whole life was revolutionized when he realized: "There never was a day of miracles; there is a God of miracles." May the wonderfully researched insights of Tony Cooke's book, *Miracles and the Supernatural Throughout Church History*, usher you into that same transforming reality.

—Jim Graff
Pastor of Faith Family Church
President of The Significant Church Network

As a prolific teacher of the Word, Tony Cooke has blessed thousands of lives all around the world through his written works, his sermons, and his life. This book describes the remarkable outpouring of the Holy Spirit since the first century until today through encouraging and accurate research. This rich, historic background awakens us to the magnificent work God has done through the ages, reinforces our convictions to be doers of the Word, and cheers us up to the living and glorious hope prepared for the Body of Christ.

—Guto Emery
Apostle and President of Verbo da Vida Ministries
Campina Grande, Brazil

Through well-documented and captivating research, Tony Cooke takes his reader on an insightful journey through Church history tracing the supernatural activity of the Holy Spirit as reflected in a variety of chronicled miracles and manifestations. His thorough exploration uncovers inspiring and even surprising firsthand accounts of the charismata since the writing of the New Testament. I highly recommend this book to all who are interested in learning more about the rich heritage of the Spirit's work of which we are not only grateful recipients but also privileged participators.

—Bill Buker, DMin, PhD, LPC
Associate Dean and Professor of Counseling
Graduate School of Theology and Ministry
Oral Roberts University

This is a most refreshing book and an essential read for every believer. It is both history and teaching material. It shows us that after Jesus and His apostles, the miraculous works of Jesus have continued in and through His Church for the past 2,000 years, and they continue even today. Having preached in more than seventy-five countries since

1976, I have seen the dead raised, the lame walk, the blind see. This is because the miraculous is an integral part of the Gospel of Jesus. My experience is that it is normal that miraculous signs always accompany the preaching of the Word of God.

—Christopher Alam
Evangelist and Founder of Dynamis World Ministries

Tony Cooke's latest book provides readers with an understandable and balanced overview of the supernatural ministry of the Holy Spirit in the Church since the first century that will inspire, correct, and instruct Christians as they set about to do the works of Jesus in the 21st century. For those who, like the psalmist of old, have a heart-held conviction that *the works of the Lord* [are to be] *studied by all who delight in them*" (Psalm 111:2 English Standard Version), time spent pondering the historical gems and insights that Tony offers in this volume will be well rewarded.

—Joseph Purcell, MABTS, JD
Missionary to Southeast Asia

This book is a masterpiece, a classic and a must-read for any serious student of the Bible and/or Church history. It is thorough, well-researched, educative, and very informative. It will stir up in anyone a hunger for a closer walk with God and a passion to see His miracle-working power move again today to bless people and glorify Jesus.

—Toks Adejuwon
Preacher, Teacher, International Speaker, Author
National Director of Rhema Bible Training Centre, Nigeria

Tony has a divine passion for leaders to let the supernatural power of God shine through their work. His book, *Miracles and the Supernatural Throughout Church History*, is an extremely timely book that demonstrates the power of God. I highly recommend it to *all* who desire to lead in the ministry.

—Benson M. Karanja, EdD, HSC
President, Beulah Heights University

Tony Cooke has done it again! I believe *Miracles and the Supernatural Throughout Church History* to be by far his most important work to date. The great men and women of God through history had one thing in common—they studied the miracles in the life of Jesus and the lives of the saints, and this book does both! Knowing what God did throughout history will inspire you to believe and expect God to do the same through you today. Tony's documentation of present-day miracles and practical takeaways are worth the entire book!

—Jeff Oliver
Author of *Pentecost to the Present:
The Holy Spirit's Enduring Work in the Church*

MIRACLES
AND THE
SUPERNATURAL
THROUGHOUT CHURCH HISTORY

Harrison House

Shippensburg, PA

Other Harrison House Books by Tony Cooke

Lift: Experiencing the Elevated Life

The Work Book: What We Do Matters to God

Grace: The DNA of God

Your Place on God's Dream Team:
The Making of Champions

Through the Storms: Help from Heaven
When All Hell Breaks Loose

Qualified: Serving God with Integrity and
Finishing Your Course with Honor

Additional Books by Tony Cooke

Life After Death: Rediscovering Life After the Loss of a Loved One

In Search of Timothy: Discovering and Developing
Greatness in Church Staff and Volunteers

www.tonycooke.org

MIRACLES
— AND THE —
SUPERNATURAL
THROUGHOUT CHURCH HISTORY

REMARKABLE MANIFESTATIONS
OF THE HOLY SPIRIT FROM THE
FIRST CENTURY UNTIL TODAY

TONY COOKE

Published by Harrison House Publishers
Shippensburg, PA 17257

Cover design by Eileen Rockwell

ISBN 13 TP: 978-1-6803-1489-2

ISBN 13 eBook: 978-1-6803-1490-8

ISBN 13 HC: 978-1-6803-1492-2

ISBN 13 LP: 978-1-6803-1491-5

For Worldwide Distribution, Printed in the U.S.A.

    3 4 5 6 7 8 / 24 23 22 21 20

DEDICATION

IT is with warmest memories and greatest respect that I dedicate this book to my first Church history professor, Cooper Beaty. In reference to his rapid-fire teaching style, students affectionately called him "Machine Gun Beaty." His zeal and contagious excitement about Church history came out in every lesson. A former Quaker pastor for twenty-nine years and evangelist for seven years, Cooper also taught Church history and other subjects at Rhema Bible Training College for twenty-six years. Having been his student, I was later privileged to become Cooper's colleague and fellow instructor. I was always amazed at his voracious appetite to continually study and his discipline to regularly update his notes—he was always seeking to learn, improve, and grow. He never failed to give his students the very best he could. Cooper joined the great cloud of witnesses at the age of 97 in 2014. The impact and impression he made on his students live on.

No great work has ever been accomplished except through the power of the Holy Spirit, who is the great Executive of God, carrying out the will of God in all things.

–James Gilchrist Lawson

There has never been a time in the history of the Christian church that some of the gifts were not present and effective.... Link upon link, a chain of spiritual Christianity has been fashioned by the Holy Spirit.

–A. W. Tozer

I see no reason why we should not have a Pentecost greater than Peter saw and a Reformation deeper in its foundations, and truer in its building up than all the reforms which Luther or Calvin achieved! We have the same Christ, remember that! The times are changed, but Jesus is the Eternal and time touches him not.

–Charles H. Spurgeon

CONTENTS

FOREWORD

by Rick Renner

AT long last…the book for which I've been waiting for many years! Finally, a book on miracles and the supernatural throughout Church history that totally debunks the naysayers who allege the miraculous work of the Holy Spirit ended with the apostolic age!

I'd like to give you a piece of my own history to tell you why I believe this book is so important. I was raised in a denomination that sincerely believed the age of miracles had ceased. We were "cessationists"—we held the theological position that spiritual gifts and manifestations, such as healing, speaking in tongues, and prophecy, *ceased* with the apostolic age. Perhaps you were reared in a similar traditional church and were taught as I was.

Because our denomination believed the age of miracles and spiritual gifts had ceased, we generally thought that Pentecostals and Charismatics—and wayward denominational people who had been caught up in these groups—were doctrinally off base and that whatever it was they were claiming to experience was nothing more than made-up works of the flesh based on bad doctrine and a mishandling of Scripture.

It is important to have no judgment for those who embrace this view of Cessationism. Based on defective doctrine, ignorance of Church history, or an intellectually dishonest view of Church history that has been perpetuated by theological professors in seminaries, they may sincerely believe the lie that the age of miracles has ceased. I, too, was once part of those who sincerely believe this.

It's safe to assume that somewhere along the way in your own personal journey, you have encountered or will encounter people who do not believe that miracles or the supernatural gifts of the Holy Spirit are for us today. "Those people" may have once even been *you*. Because it is likely you will encounter those who believe this way, it is vital to know what you believe and how to answer those who disbelieve. Perhaps their questioning has affected you and made you wonder if there is any truth to the allegation that the age of miracles has ceased.

Is it true that we are witnessing fewer miracles today than earlier ages witnessed? Have miracles and the gifts of the Holy Spirit diminished throughout the history of the Church? The book you hold in your hand right now will answer those questions. The author systemically goes through 2,000 years of Church history to analyze the *facts* about miracles and the gifts of the Holy Spirit. To do such research requires an honest and brilliant mind. I do not know a person more qualified for such a feat than Tony Cooke, who has a balanced view of the Charismatic world, with no delusions, and has been willing to honestly examine the whole of Church history to obtain a factual account of the truth.

Honesty is *required* to produce a correct analysis—and an honest and correct analysis is what you have in this marvelous book. I am so thankful for it, and I am certain that it will reinforce, based on *historical proof*, your belief in miracles and the gifts of the Holy Spirit. Furthermore, it will encourage you to launch into the realm of the miraculous in your own life!

This book is a treasure produced by the mind of a knowledgeable person who has been willing to give *years* to finding the historical evidence that miracles never ceased and that they have, in fact, abounded throughout centuries. Its academic approach includes actual early writings that have survived from the first centuries of the Church and are filled with marvelous commentary, insights, and testimony that prove the nonstop miraculous work of God though the ages.

Miracles and the Supernatural Throughout Church History is divided into geographical regions to make it easier for you to observe how the Holy Spirit has moved consistently in each place. It will take you into supernatural works of the Holy Spirit in Rome, Northern Africa, Asia Minor, and Europe—all in the earlier centuries of the Church. Then the author takes you into the historical proof of supernatural works of the Holy Spirit that occurred in the *Reformation*, in the ministry of *John Wesley*, in the *Great Awakening*, and even in the ministries of *Spurgeon* and *Moody* (yes, even in *their* ministries!). Last, you are walked into the unparalleled miraculous move of the Holy Spirit from the twentieth century to the present. By the time you are finished reading this book, you'll have all the evidence needed to prove unequivocally *to yourself and others* that the age of miracles *never ceased*.

I am especially thankful for the final chapters in which Tony truthfully scrutinizes the pitfalls that have unfortunately accompanied some of these movements of the supernatural throughout history. He does this not with a critical or negative eye, but with a mind to help us learn what to avoid and to keep the miraculous work of the Holy Spirit advancing in the purest form possible. Then at last, Tony provides sound advice about what to do when it seems the miraculous is not occurring.

This book is *the undoing* of bad doctrine and *a correction* to bad renditions of Church history that have been perpetrated on the minds of God's people for generations. As you read, you'll find yourself standing on a firm foundation if you are among those who believe the age of miracles has never ceased! So get ready for a wonderful experience as you dive into the pages of this treasure trove of information.

I'm thankful Tony has written this book, and I personally count it a privilege to be asked to write the Foreword for such a respectable work!

—Rick Renner
Moscow, Russia
Author, Broadcaster, Pastor, Teacher

PREFACE

THE supernatural? Church history? Why this book?

I first experienced the supernatural power of God in 1977, a few weeks after graduating from high school. John Fenn, a friend I had known since early elementary school, took me to a meeting that was radically different from the traditional church services I had experienced growing up in a mainline, denominational congregation. I saw spontaneity and vibrancy instead of the formalism and ritual I was used to. The people were not excessively emotional—their worship was heartfelt and sincere. Their devotion was reflected in their joyous, radiant faces, hands lifted high toward Heaven, and songs flowing jubilantly and meaningfully from their hearts.

I could not have expected what happened next. The minister asked those with back problems to stand up. I had experienced pain in my lower right back for about two years. It had been a chronic challenge for me, and it especially made playing tennis, something I loved to do, uncomfortable and challenging. My parents had sent me to three different doctors seeking a solution, but nothing had helped.

A gentleman named Charles Hunter prayed for me that evening, and I sensed a tangible power flowing into my body. The only way I know to describe it is that it was like a combination of electricity and warm honey. That sounds like an odd mixture, but it is the best way I know to illustrate what happened to me. There was none of the pain or discomfort associated with an electrical shock. On the contrary, it was the most pleasant sensation I have ever experienced in my life.

After receiving prayer, I found that God had totally healed my back. I was able to bend over and put both palms on the floor with no pain whatsoever—a radical change from the way my back had been. I could relate to the experience of the woman who touched the hem of Jesus' garment, *"she felt in her body that she was healed of the affliction"* (Mark 5:29). To say that I was impressed that God had done that for me is a great understatement; something I assumed only happened in Bible days had just happened in my life!

Later that night at my friend's house, he asked if I had received the Holy Spirit. I had heard of the Holy Spirit as long as I could remember. He had been referred to in my church every Sunday with reverence in the Apostles' Creed and in the Doxology, but I had never thought about the idea of "receiving Him" in a personal way. I had never been told that He wanted to fill and empower me.

My friend showed me several passages in the book of Acts demonstrating that the Holy Spirit is a Person who dynamically impacted the lives of early believers.[1] It was revolutionary to think that the same Holy Spirit I had heard about all my life in church services actually wanted to work in my life and give me power, but that is what I was now reading in the Bible.

John prayed with me that evening to receive infilling the Holy Spirit, and my life has never been the same. With the Holy Spirit's help, I began to understand the Bible, and the Book that had always seemed incomprehensible and confusing now seemed to percolate with life, power, and meaning. I quickly noticed that the Holy Spirit's influence always directed my attention to Jesus and to what Jesus had done for me. As the Holy Spirit continued to work in my life, I began sensing a calling to serve God, and began noticing certain spiritual gifts that were surfacing and working in my life.

Shortly before this experience, I had declined the opportunity to speak at my high school graduation as the senior class president. I simply had no interest in speaking publicly. After being filled with the Holy Spirit, a new desire was birthed in my heart. I wanted to communicate God's truths to others. What God did in my heart eventually led me into a teaching ministry that has allowed me to teach the Bible to groups and crowds of all sizes in more than thirty nations and in nearly every State in the Union. Since that experience in 1977, I have enjoyed His on-going presence and enablement in my life. The Holy Spirit has helped me serve God and serve others. I have seen Him do things that only He could do, things far beyond my ability.

History and Present-Day Similarities

On the history side of the equation, I have long appreciated the historic aspects of the Gospels and the book of Acts. I was raised to believe the Bible was true, and I have always believed that God, through Moses, split the Red Sea. I have always believed that Jesus walked on water, multiplied the loaves and fish to feed a multitude, and that He was raised from the dead. I always believed the miracles mentioned in the book of Acts were true.

However, all those things were ancient history. Miracles, in my mind, were not a present-day occurrence. Because divine healing, miracles, and spiritual gifts were never mentioned in my church growing up, I just assumed that God had stopped doing those things centuries before.

Of course, I reasoned, God could still do a miracle if He really wanted to, but I certainly had never heard of one happening, nor did I ever see anyone express any expectation of anything supernatural happening.

My experience of healing in 1977, and many subsequent experiences, caused me to rethink everything. If I saw Him work supernaturally in my late teens and many times since, maybe He has been doing so all along, and I just didn't know it. Like many Christians, I didn't know much about church history. A few years later in Bible school, I had an excellent class in Church History with an outstanding professor, but much learning was yet to come.

Teaching the Bible and working in ministry has given me the privilege of traveling to many places in the world, including lands referenced in the Bible. I have been all over Israel, to Egypt, Greece (Corinth, Athens, Philippi, Thessalonica, Patmos, etc.), Turkey (Ephesus, Colossae, Laodicea, Miletus, etc.), Rome, Lebanon, Cyprus, Malta, and Crete. Walking in the steps of Jesus, Paul, Peter, John, and others really helped biblical history come alive to me.

In addition, I have also had the joy of visiting many of the locations related to great church leaders through history. These include sites—churches, homes, and/or burial sites—of people including Jan Hus, Martin Luther, Ulrich Zwingli, John Calvin, John Wesley, George Whitefield, Charles Finney, Billy Sunday, C. S. Lewis, and Billy Graham. Visiting these various sites has given me a profound appreciation for our spiritual forefathers—for those who have gone before us and were used so mightily by God.

After visiting several of the Luther sites in Germany a few years ago, I was inspired to embark on a more formal study of Church history and earned a Master's degree in Theological Studies with a Church History cognate. Through this intensive study, I became all the more impressed with vast numbers of men and women who were used by God through the centuries, who preached the gospel and were anointed by the Holy Spirit.

I had heard stories over the years about the Holy Spirit manifesting Himself powerfully at different times through Church history, but through both formal and personal study, I have been absolutely amazed to learn far more details about the wonderful outpourings of the Spirit, revivals, and manifestations of spiritual gifts that have taken place over the centuries.

I am persuaded from Scripture—and from abundant evidence throughout history, even in modern time—that God never intended His people to be devoid of the Holy Spirit's power or gifts. I invite you, in the following pages, to journey with me through Scripture and through history, discovering God's wonderful, supernatural workings in and through the lives of His people.

Endnote

1. Here are some of the references in the book of Acts, and one from Ephesians about "receiving" or being filled with the Holy Spirit: Acts 2:4; 4:8,31; 6:3,5,8; 7:55; 8:14-17; 9:17; 10:44-46; 11:24; 13:9,52; 19:1-6; Ephesians 5:18.

INTRODUCTION

IN the Preface, I described my personal journey. In this Introduction, I share helpful thoughts about this book that I trust will enable you get more benefit from its content. Attempting to address any topic over nearly 2,000 years of Church history is a daunting task, much less addressing the supernatural works of God that have taken place for and through His people. As a result, I had to be very selective in what I covered. At times during the research and writing process, I felt like I was trying to fit the ocean into a gallon container. This volume is neither comprehensive nor exhaustive; it is more like a rock skipping across a pond; I was just able to hit some highlights.

You may wonder why I included some notable figures but not others. There are many people who were mightily used of God whom I did not include in the following chapters. This is why I have included a Recommended Reading section at the very end of the book. I have benefited greatly from the studies and writings of others. Through these types of works, interested readers can learn about some of the other wonderful servants of God who were not included in this work.

I use the words *Pentecostal* and *Charismatic* somewhat interchangeably throughout this book. These terms may conjure up many various ideas and images in the minds of different readers. I am not referring to a denomination per se, or to any specific congregation. Nor am I referring to any of several misconceptions or stereotypes sometimes associated with the Pentecostal and Charismatic monikers, such as styles of preaching delivery, music, or type of dress. I am also not referring to any particular socioeconomic status or degree of emotionalism displayed during worship. When I use these terms, I am referring to believers who identify with and embrace the types of beliefs, practices, and experiences that are seen throughout the book of Acts.

This book is laid out in three sections.

The first section is comprised of only two chapters and is titled The Biblical Basis for Supernatural Works. I hope that most readers are at least fairly familiar with the biblical accounts of miracles and supernatural works, especially in the four Gospels and in the book of Acts. It was not my intention to cover in detail everything that happened in those five books of the Bible, but to give a brief overview and to provide meaning of that content relative to what continued happening after the New Testament era.

The second section constitutes the bulk of the book, and this material deals with Historical Accounts of Supernatural Works beginning after the death of the apostle John and coming up toward modern times. The more I studied the individuals who are covered, the more I admired and respected their faith and their love for the Lord Jesus Christ. They were all human, and some of them had glaring flaws in their lives. Like all of us, each of them was a work in progress. None of them were infallible or omniscient; they were all growing and learning throughout their journeys. Some of them changed their views about different topics as their faith evolved and matured.

For example, in the last couple of years of his life, Augustine (covered in Chapter Five) revisited his massive literary works and wrote about things that he would say differently at that later point in his life. Another prolific writer, Thomas Aquinas, (not covered in this book) was asked a couple of months before his death if he was going to continue writing; he said, "I can write no more. All that I have written seems like straw." What was it he saw in his latter days that caused him to describe his former writings that way?

With all of this in mind, we are humbled at our humanity, and we realize that only Scripture is infallible. Still, *"we know in part and we prophesy in part,"* and we still *"see in a mirror, dimly"* (1 Corinthians 13:9,12). But thank God for what we do know! We believe Scripture emphatically, and we listen respectfully and with discernment to the teachings and the stories of our spiritual predecessors who lived following the time of the first-century believers. The Bible is the basis for our faith—and we can draw so much encouragement and wisdom from the experiences of so many dynamic believers from centuries past.

The third and final section of the book deals with Present-Day Realities and Applications. As important as the biblical and historical aspects of this book are, if we don't receive spiritual and practical insights that we can put to practice in our lives and ministries, we may only walk away from this book with more head knowledge. As it was in the earliest days of the church, so it is today; there remains a great need for people *"of good reputation, full of the Holy Spirit and wisdom"* (Acts 6:3). Stephen was one of those meeting that criterion, and he was also *"full of faith"* (Acts 6:5,8). This is the need of the hour! We don't just need individuals who have information, but people who have been transformed, who are full of wisdom, and ready to take action with God's enablement and empowerment.

The purpose of this book is simple and is summed up in the title and subtitle—I want to introduce you to *Miracles and the Supernatural Throughout Church History*. I hope you stand in awe of the goodness and mercy of God as you consider the *Remarkable Manifestations of the Holy Spirit From the First Century Until Today.*

When I was young and first came into the things of the Spirit more than four decades ago, I was immature and unwise. I wanted to argue theology to prove I was right. Today, I am far more interested in partaking of the fullness of God's love, mercy, and power, so that I can express that to others. I want to be all that God wants me to be and do all that God wants me to do. That is also my prayer for you and for everyone who picks up this book.

The Biblical Basis for Supernatural Works

CHAPTER ONE

A SUPERNATURAL FAITH

The religion of the Bible is wholly supernatural.
—A. B. Simpson

THE idea of God's supernatural ability should hardly seem unusual to followers of Jesus Christ. If not for God's mighty power we would not exist, nor would our universe. The author of Hebrews tells us, "By faith we understand that the worlds were framed by the word of God, so that the things which are seen were not made of things which are visible" (Hebrews 11:3). Scripture teaches that Jesus, the eternal Son of God, was born of a virgin (Matthew 1:18-25) and was resurrected from the dead after He had died for our sins (1 Corinthians 15:3-4). Further, those trusting in the Lord Jesus Christ have been born again—God's Word and Spirit have caused them to become new creations (John 3:6-8; 2 Corinthians 5:17; 1 Peter 1:23). The reason we have a divinely inspired Bible is because "holy men of God spoke as they were moved by the Holy Spirit" (2 Peter 1:21). All of this is supernatural.

If you take the supernatural out of the Bible, there really isn't a Bible left. Reinhard Bonnke, the famed German evangelist whose ministry so powerfully impacted Africa, is absolutely correct when he states:

To be blunt, Christianity is either supernatural, or nothing at all. We had—and still have—a supernatural Jesus with a supernatural ministry, creating a supernatural church, with a supernatural gospel, and a supernatural Bible. Take the miraculous away, and you have taken Christianity's life away. The church becomes an ethical society, or a social club, when it is intended to be the grid system for transmitting the power of God into this powerless world. You and I are conductors of God's power to the world![1]

There are historic, factual, and informational elements of Christianity, and these are not to be dismissed or taken lightly, but Christianity should never be reduced to a mere intellectual or ethical proposition. While we are very appreciative of the instructional and moral implications of the gospel, following Jesus involves more than that. This is why Paul declares, *"My speech and my preaching were not with persuasive words of human wisdom, but in demonstration of the Spirit and of power."* He desired that their *"faith should not be in the wisdom of men but in the power of God"* (1 Corinthians 2:4-5).

The Holy Spirit is seen dynamically operating from the first page of the Bible to the last. In Genesis 1:2, the Holy Spirit is described as *"hovering over the face of the waters."* On the last page of the Bible, the Holy Spirit is heard issuing the invitation, *"Whoever desires, let him take the water of life freely"* (Revelation 22:17). It is important to remember that everything the Holy Spirit does is in perfect harmony with the Father and the Son. J. Oswald Sanders describes their seamless partnership this way:

The Persons of the Trinity cooperated for our redemption in perfect harmony and reciprocity. The Father planned. The Son made the plan possible of realization by yielding up His life to death on the cross. The Spirit bent His fiery energies to the implementation of the plan.[2]

Because of the cooperative working of the Father, Son, and Holy Spirit in accomplishing our redemption, it comes as no surprise that the Holy Spirit's presence and work are seen pervasively and powerfully throughout the Bible.

What the Holy Spirit Does

There are descriptions in the New Testament of how the Holy Spirit works in the lives of believers—a work that actually starts before we even come into faith. The following is a listing of some of what the Holy Spirit does:

- **He Brings Conviction:** *"Nevertheless I tell you the truth. It is to your advantage that I go away; for if I do not go away, the Helper will not come to you; but if I depart, I will send Him to you. And when He has come, He will convict the world of sin, and of righteousness, and of judgment: of sin, because they do not believe in Me; of righteousness, because I go to My Father and you see Me no more; of judgment, because the ruler of this world is judged"* (John 16:7-11).

- **He Brings the New Birth:** *"Most assuredly, I say to you, unless one is born of water and the Spirit, he cannot enter the kingdom of God. That which is born of the flesh is flesh, and that which is born of the Spirit is spirit"* (John 3:5-6).

- **He Provides Assurance:** *"The Spirit Himself bears witness with our spirit that we are children of God"* (Romans 8:16).

- *He Brings Illumination and Guides Us Into Truth*: "He will guide you into all truth" (John 16:13).

- *He Provides Sanctification (Cleansing, Separation)*: "God from the beginning chose you for salvation through sanctification by the Spirit and belief in the truth" (2 Thessalonians 2:13).

- *He Indwells and Abides With Us*: "And I will pray the Father, and He will give you another Helper, that He may abide with you forever—the Spirit of truth, whom the world cannot receive, because it neither sees Him nor knows Him; but you know Him, for He dwells with you and will be in you" (John 14:16-17).

- *He Teaches Us*: "But the Helper, the Holy Spirit, whom the Father will send in My name, He will teach you all things, and bring to your remembrance all things that I said to you" (John 14:26).

- *He Glorifies Jesus*: "He will glorify Me, for He will take of what is Mine and declare it to you" (John 16:14).

- *He Places Us in the Body of Christ*: "We have all been baptized into one body by one Spirit, and we all share the same Spirit" (1 Corinthians 12:13 NLT).

- *He Empowers Believers for Service*: "You shall receive power when the Holy Spirit has come upon you; and you shall be witnesses to Me..." (Acts 1:8).

- *He Fills Believers*: "And they were all filled with the Holy Spirit and began to speak with other tongues, as the Spirit gave them utterance" (Acts 2:4). "And the believers were filled with joy and with the Holy Spirit" (Acts 13:52 NLT).

When we welcome and allow the Holy Spirit to be involved in our lives, everything He does is in exact accordance with the will of God.

Nothing He does is weird or inconsistent with the normal Christian life, as God intended it. A believer's life is supposed to be a supernatural life, but keep in mind that half of the word *supernatural* is *natural*. His working may seem unusual to the carnal mind, but knowing and experiencing Him should become very normal to us; it should not seem strange or aberrant.

When it comes to what the Holy Spirit provides for the Church, the apostle Paul provides four main listings that can be broadly categorized as spiritual gifts. Some of what is in the following list refers to ministerial offices, but these are not all reserved exclusively for what we call "clergy." Several of these may operate in the life of any believer who is yielded to the Holy Spirit. These include:

- Romans 12:6-8: Prophecy, Ministry (Serving), Teaching, Exhortation, Giving, Leading, Mercy

- 1 Corinthians 12:8-10: Word of Wisdom, Word of Knowledge, Faith, Gifts of Healings, Working of Miracles, Prophecy, Discerning of Spirits, Different Kinds of Tongues, Interpretation of Tongues

- 1 Corinthians 12:28-30: Apostles, Prophets, Teachers, Miracles, Gifts of Healings, Helps, Administrations, Varieties of Tongues

- Ephesians 4:11: Apostles, Prophets, Evangelists, Pastors, Teachers

While these lists vary in terms of what Paul is addressing, Scripture indicates that these diverse gifts are distributed and operate under the direction and supervision of the Holy Spirit. For example, Paul states, *"In his grace, God has given us different gifts for doing certain things well"* (Romans 12:6 NLT). He also writes, *"It is the one and only Spirit who distributes all these gifts. He alone decides which gift each person should have*" (1 Corinthians 12:11 NLT). If God deems that all of these are necessary for the Church, who are we to say that they are not? Who are we to say that certain ones have been withdrawn when *"there is one body and one Spirit"* (Ephesians 4:4)?

The Holy Spirit gives these gifts for a very distinct purpose. For example, concerning what we often call the fivefold ministry gifts (apostle, prophet, evangelist, pastor, and teacher) listed in Ephesians 4, Paul states, *"Their responsibility is to equip God's people to do his work and build up the church, the body of Christ"* (Ephesians 4:12 NLT). Speaking to the Corinthians, Paul writes, *"But the manifestation of the Spirit is given to each one for the profit of all"* (1 Corinthians 12:7). It wasn't just the first-century church that recognized this. Later church leaders would talk about workings of the Holy Spirit that were active in their time as well. For example:

- Tertullian (AD 160-220) refers to "the powers of the Holy Spirit as an agency of the Church."[3]

- Origen (AD 184-253) states, "The name of Jesus can still remove distractions from the minds of men, expel demons, and also take away diseases."[4]

- Augustine (AD 354-430) writes, "I cannot record all the miracles I know."[5]

How desirous we should be for all that God has for us!

God's gracious initiative in these matters is reinforced in Hebrews 2:4 (NLT). Referencing the salvation that accompanies the preaching of the gospel, we read, *"And God confirmed the message by giving signs and wonders and various miracles and gifts of the Holy Spirit whenever he chose."* This correlates perfectly to the pattern and activity described in the Great Commission.

*And He said to them, "Go into all the world and preach the gospel to every creature. He who believes and is baptized will be saved; but he who does not believe will be condemned. And **these signs will follow those who believe**: In My name they will cast out demons; they will speak with new tongues; they will take up serpents; and if they drink anything deadly, it will by no means hurt them; they will lay hands on the sick, and they will recover." So then, after the Lord had spoken to them, He was received up into heaven, and sat down at the right hand of God. **And they went out and preached everywhere, the Lord working with them and confirming the word through the accompanying signs**. Amen* (Mark 16:15-20).

Notice that these signs were not designed to stand by themselves. Rather, they accompanied the preaching of the gospel and confirmed the word of God as it was proclaimed.

These gifts and confirmations were not restricted to the preaching of the original apostles, but also occurred as others ministered God's word. For example, we read that, *"Stephen, full of faith and power, did great wonders and signs among the people"* (Acts 6:8). We read of the ministry of another non-apostle who preached in Samaria, *"the multitudes with one accord heeded the things spoken by Philip, hearing and seeing the miracles which he did"* (Acts 8:6). Likewise, Ananias, a layman as best as we can tell, received divine direction through a vision and was used to impart healing and to pray for Saul of Tarsus (Paul) to be filled with the Holy Spirit (Acts 9:10-20).

It is very easy, reading the book of Acts, to get caught up in the more sensational operations of the Holy Spirit, such as healings, miracles, and spectacular forms of guidance—visions, dreams, angelic appearances, etc. However, it is important to remember and to appreciate all of the workings of the Holy Spirit, even when His workings are less dramatic in nature. Speaking of divine guidance, Kenneth E. Hagin writes, "The inward witness is just as supernatural as guidance through visions and so on; it is just not as spectacular. Many people are looking for the spectacular and missing the supernatural that is right there all the time."[6] Just like we should receive all that Scripture teaches, not just selected parts, it is also important for believers to appreciate and welcome all of what the Holy Spirit does.

Sometimes people wonder, *If God has all of this available for His people, and He desires His people to receive the benefits of His gifts and the blessings of His power, why don't we see more supernatural things happen?* What a great question!

As always, we look to Scripture for answers. In Galatians 3:5, Paul asks a question about the source and basis of God's blessings: *"He who supplies the Spirit to you and works miracles among you, does He do it by the works of the law, or by the hearing of faith?"* The Spirit is supplied and miracles are worked when faith is involved! It should not be a surprise, then, if we see little of the Spirit's working if no one actively believes God, trusts God, or expects Him to work powerfully.

God is the same today as He was in the book of Acts. However, believers today often have a different mindset from what we see in the first century. They had complete and total expectancy that God was going to do amazing things in their midst. As the early church prayed, their faith and sense of strong expectation is clearly seen and expressed:

> *And now, O Lord, hear their threats, and give us, your servants, great boldness in preaching your word. Stretch out your hand with healing power; may miraculous signs and wonders be done through the name of your holy servant Jesus* (Acts 4:29-30 NLT).

No one had told these early believers that God no longer did miracles. They knew better. No one had told them that the age of miracles had passed away. As a matter of fact, they had heard Jesus say that signs would accompany the preaching of the gospel (Mark 16:17). They had heard Jesus say, *"…he who believes in Me, the works that I do he will do also; and greater works than these he will do, because I go to My Father"* (John 14:12). They took God at His word; that's what faith is!

Endnotes

1. Reinhard Bonnke, *Daily Fire Devotional: 365 Days in God's Word* (New Kensington, PA: Whitaker House, 2015), June 14 entry, loc. 4591, Kindle.

2. J. Oswald Sanders, *The Incomparable Christ: The Person and Work of Jesus Christ* (Chicago: Moody Press, 1971), 10.

3. Tertullian, *The Passion of the Holy Martyrs Perpetua and Felicitas*, in *The Complete Works of Tertullian*, ed. Sir James Donaldson and Arthur Cleveland Coxe (Seattle, WA: Amazon Digital Services, 1885), loc. 45514, Kindle.

4. Origen, *Origen Against Celsus*, *The Works of Origen*, ed. Alexander Roberts, Sir James Donaldson, and Arthur Cleveland Coxe (Seattle, WA: Amazon Digital Services, 1885), loc 10133, Kindle.

5. Augustine, *The City of God*, trans. Marcus Dods (Peabody, MA: Hendrickson Publishers, www.hendrickson.com, 2009), loc. 19006, Kindle.

6. Kenneth E. Hagin, *How You Can Be Led by the Spirit of God* (Tulsa, OK: Faith Library Publications, www.rhema.org, 1989), 34.

CHAPTER TWO

THE BIBLICAL RECORD

The Bible is the Word of God: supernatural in origin, eternal in duration, inexpressible in valor, infinite in scope, regenerative in power, infallible in authority, universal in interest, personal in application, inspired in totality. Read it through, write it down, pray it in, work it out, and then pass it on. Truly it is the Word of God.

—Smith Wigglesworth

GOD is a supernatural God, and the Bible is a supernatural book. God created this natural world in which we live, and He remains involved in and continues to reach out to the people He loves. The Word of God contains multiple accounts of God expressing care and compassion toward humanity. Whether it is God visiting Adam and Eve in the cool of the day (Genesis 3:8), the Son of God coming to earth through the Incarnation (John 1:14), or the outpouring of the Holy Spirit on the Day of Pentecost (Acts 2:1-4), God comes to and reveals Himself to humanity. Two passages we can take great comfort in, one from each of the two testaments, are:

I am the Lord, and I do not change (Malachi 3:6 NLT).

Jesus Christ is the same yesterday, today, and forever (Hebrews 13:8).

The apostle James even describes God as *"the Father of lights, with whom there is no variation or the slightest hint of change"* (James 1:17 New English Translation). So, examining the works of God throughout Scripture can bring great insights about the nature of God and how He operates.

Supernatural Workings of God in the Old Testament

While the Bible contains an abundance of miraculous accounts, some people have an unrealistic perception as to how prevalent miracles were in the overall scope of things. One of the misconceptions that people have regarding the Old Testament is that extraordinary, spectacular miracles were happening constantly, on an everyday basis.

While numerous supernatural events are recorded in Scripture, there were times when God's people had only heard about miracles having happened in the past. For example, when the Midianites had been plundering the Israelites for seven years, the Angel of the Lord appeared to a doubting Gideon who promptly complained about the seeming absence of God's miraculous power.

> *Gideon said to Him, "O my lord, if the Lord is with us, why then has all this happened to us? And where are all His miracles which our fathers told us about, saying, 'Did not the Lord bring us up from Egypt?' But now the Lord has forsaken us and delivered us into the hands of the Midianites"* (Judges 6:13).

Up until this point in his life, Gideon had never seen a miracle, but he was about to! God had not changed, diminished in power, or lost interest in helping His people; Gideon had simply not personally witnessed God working this way before. Supernatural workings were not new to God, but they were to Gideon, at least on an experiential level.

There were other times when Old Testament figures looked back nostalgically to "the good old days" when God was doing powerful things. Consider these statements by the sons of Korah, Asaph, and Ethan respectively:

> *We have heard with our ears, O God, our fathers have told us, the deeds You did in their days, in days of old* (Psalm 44:1).
>
> *We no longer see your miraculous signs. All the prophets are gone, and no one can tell us when it will end* (Psalm 74:9 NLT).
>
> *Lord, where are Your former lovingkindnesses, which You swore to David in Your truth?* (Psalm 89:49)

Even the prophet Habakkuk cried out to God, "In this time of our deep need, help us again as you did in years gone by" (Habakkuk 3:2 NLT).

Does this discourage you in any way? I hope not. As a matter of fact, it actually encourages me. In some of these situations, the people may not have witnessed God's power because they had corporately turned away from God, but when they turned back to Him, He manifested His power.

For example, in Judges 6:1, leading up to the story of Gideon, we read: "Then the children of Israel did evil in the sight of the Lord. So the Lord delivered them into the hand of Midian for seven years." Deliverance was not sent until "the children of Israel cried out to the Lord because of the Midianites (Judges 6:7).

I have often wondered if we have experienced far less of God's presence than we should have. The psalmist writes:

I am the Lord your God, who brought you out of the land of Egypt; open your mouth wide, and I will fill it. But My people would not heed My voice, and Israel would have none of Me. So I gave them over to their own stubborn heart, to walk in their own counsels (Psalm 81:10-12).

There are times and seasons in life, and it has been noted that revivals and outpourings of God's Spirit tend to happen in cycles. The fact that some people today have not seen mighty works of God previously does not mean that they are not going to, and maybe that applies to you as well.

The children of Israel suffered Egyptian bondage for an extended time; none of them had seen miraculous works of God. But that was about to change.

God heard their cry, and they ended up witnessing the plagues that came upon the Egyptians, the splitting of the Red Sea, the healing of Marah's bitter waters, the cloud by day and the fire by night, water coming from the rock, and even the provision of manna that was provided from Heaven. The following generation of Israelites would see the parting of the Jordan River and the fall of mighty Jericho. Prior to God sending Moses, the people of Israel had not witnessed any miracles, but that changed! Just because someone has never seen a miracle before doesn't mean that he or she won't.

Another consideration is that not all miracles in the Old Testament involved large numbers of people. They were not necessarily "mass miracles" as when the children of Israel all passed through the Red Sea on dry ground. Elijah and Elisha both had several miracles happen during their respective ministries, and Jesus highlighted a miracle by each of them that involved individual recipients when He said:

Certainly there were many needy widows in Israel in Elijah's time, when the heavens were closed for three and a half years, and a severe famine devastated the land. Yet Elijah was not sent to any of them. He was sent instead to a foreigner—a widow of Zarephath in the land of Sidon. And there were many lepers in Israel in the time of the prophet Elisha, but the only one healed was Naaman, a Syrian (Luke 4:25-27 NLT).

Even with Jesus, some of His miracles were performed publicly, involved many beneficiaries, and were known by multitudes. But in other cases, Jesus ministered to individuals privately and even told them not to tell others about the miracle they experienced.

Attempting to Minimize Miracles

Some have stated that biblical miracles were primarily "clustered" around Moses, Elijah and Elisha, and Jesus and the apostles, and there were very few other miracles outside of those three time windows. The facts, though, do not support such a theory. While those were three high impact times for the supernatural, there are still a great abundance of additional miracles that occurred at various other times throughout the Old Testament.

For example:

- The creation of the universe, earth, and humankind (Genesis 1–2)
- Enoch's translation (Genesis 5:24)
- The Flood and the saving of Noah's family (Genesis 6–8)
- Lot's deliverance from Sodom and Gomorrah (Genesis 19:15-25)

- Sarah conceiving Isaac (Genesis 21:1-3)
- Joseph interprets dreams by God's ability (Genesis 40–41)
- Balaam's donkey speaks (Numbers 22:20-30)
- The conquest of Jericho (Joshua 6)
- The sun stands still (Joshua 10:12-15)
- Samson's supernatural strength (Judges 14–16)
- The reversal of Hannah's barrenness and the conception of Samuel (1 Samuel 1:8-20)
- Dagon falling before the Ark of the Covenant (1 Samuel 5:4-6)
- David defeating Goliath (1 Samuel 17)
- God's glory fills the temple (1 Kings 8:10-11)
- Jonah's deliverance from the great fish (Jonah 2:1-10)
- The healing of Hezekiah (Isaiah 38:1-6)
- The sun dial going backward ten degrees (2 Kings 20:9-11)
- The three Hebrews delivered from the fiery furnace (Daniel 3:19-27)
- Daniel delivered from the lion's den (Daniel 6:16-23)

This list is just a sample of the many miracles that are recorded in the Old Testament. There are many other supernatural workings of God in which God reveals Himself, inspires the utterances of the prophets, provides for and protects His people, etc. While miracles may not have been seen every day in the Old Testament, they were frequent enough that people could know that God was a supernatural, miracle-working God.

Supernatural Workings of God in the New Testament

While the Old Testament covers around 4,000 years of human history, the New Testament barely covers a single century. The Old Testament records a vast number of God's supernatural workings, but those in the New Testament—the much shorter time window— are more concentrated. This should not be surprising considering the matters of infinite importance that happened in that short time period: the coming of Jesus as the Savior of the world; the outpouring of the Holy Spirit at Pentecost; and the launching of the Church.

No one who believes the Bible to be the inspired, authoritative Word of God denies that supernatural expressions of God's power operated in and through the life of Jesus and the Church throughout the first century. John concludes his Gospel by stating that the recorded works and miracles of Jesus are not exhaustive. John writes:

> *This disciple is the one who testifies to these events and has recorded them here. And we know that his account of these things is accurate. Jesus also did many other things. If they were all written down, I suppose the whole world could not contain the books that would be written* (John 21:24-25 NLT).

Luke, who wrote both the Gospel bearing his name as well as the book of Acts, begins his sequel by stating, *"In my first book I told you, Theophilus, about everything Jesus **began to do** and teach until the day he was taken up to heaven..."* (Acts 1:1-2 NLT). It seems that Luke is implying that in the book of Acts, he is going to write about what Jesus continued to do through His church by the power of the Holy Spirit.

The book of Acts contains written accounts of mighty outpourings of the Holy Spirit, powerful preaching that brought thousands to repentance and regeneration, and healings and miracles that confirmed the Word that was preached. We also read of angelic interventions and of people receiving divine guidance from the Holy Spirit. When Stephen was martyred, he sees Jesus and proclaims, *"Look, I see the heavens opened and the Son of Man standing in the place of honor at God's right hand!"* (Acts 7:56 NLT). Jesus also appears to Saul of Tarsus and asks, *"Saul! Saul! Why are you persecuting me?"* (Acts 9:4 NLT). He later appears to Paul in prison, giving him great encouragement with these words, *"Be encouraged, Paul. Just as you have been a witness to me here in Jerusalem, you must preach the Good News in Rome as well"* (Acts 23:11 NLT). Jesus was clearly active and involved as the Head of the Church.

The Holy Spirit so permeates the content of Acts that several have suggested over the years that a better title for the book might be *The Acts of The Holy Spirit*, rather than *The Acts of the Apostles*. The following are just a few examples of the Holy Spirit's involvement in the church of the first century:

- The Holy Spirit is poured out on the Day of Pentecost. The disciples are *"all filled with the Holy Spirit and began to speak with other tongues, as the Spirit gave them utterance"* (Acts 2:4).

- The Holy Spirit speaks to Philip and gives him direction regarding his ministry (Acts 8:29). Afterward, the Holy Spirit catches Philip away, and he ends up in a different location (Acts 8:39-40).

- In Acts 11:12, the Holy Spirit speaks to Peter and tells him to go to the home of Cornelius. There, Peter preaches the very first gospel sermon to a Gentile audience.

- Agabus makes a prediction *"by the Spirit that a great famine was coming upon the entire Roman world"* (Acts 11:28 NLT). Agabus later prophesies to Paul by the Spirit (Acts 21:11).

- The Holy Spirit speaks in Antioch and says, *"Appoint Barnabas and Saul for the special work to which I have called them"* (Acts 13:2 NLT). The Holy Spirit then sends these two men out on their first missionary journey (Acts 13:4). Paul and Barnabas are later directed regarding their ministry by the Holy Spirit (Acts 16:6-7).

- Paul is *"compelled by the Spirit"* to travel to Macedonia, Achaia, Jerusalem, and Rome (Acts 19:21; 20:22).

- Paul tells the Ephesian elders that it was the Holy Spirit who appointed them to their ministerial positions (Acts 20:28).

- Paul tells the Corinthian church, *"My message and my preaching were very plain. Rather than using clever and persuasive speeches, I relied only on the power of the Holy Spirit"* (1 Corinthians 2:4 NLT).

Toward the very end of the first century, we see Jesus appearing to John in the first three chapters of the book of Revelation. Jesus is intimately aware of what is happening in the seven local congregations of Asia Minor (modern-day Turkey), and He is even described as the One who is walking in the midst of the seven churches (Revelation 2:1). To every single one of the local congregations, Jesus makes the statement, *"Anyone with ears to hear must listen to the Spirit and understand what he is saying to the churches"* (Revelation 2:7,11,17,29; 3:6,13,22 NLT). The Church was never meant to operate apart from the influence and presence of the Holy Spirit.

John was the last of the original band of apostles to die, and he was the only one to die of natural causes. I have visited his burial site several times among the ruins in ancient Ephesus. The other apostles, with the exception of Judas Iscariot, all gave their lives as martyrs for the cause of Christ. They chose death rather than to deny Jesus, the Savior who had been raised from the dead, and to whom they had pledged their lives.

Unfortunately, due to human traditions, this is where some confusion comes in. Some claim that "When the last apostle died," God somehow and for some reason withdrew at least certain gifts of the Spirit from the Church.

First, there is nothing in Scripture to indicate that certain gifts of the Spirit were only meant to be temporary. The only Scripture that I can see even remotely applying here has to be ripped out of its context and its simple, obvious meaning has to be ignored to arrive at such a conclusion. I am referring to Paul's phenomenal exposition on love:

> *Love never fails. But whether there are prophecies, they will fail; whether there are tongues, they will cease; whether there is knowledge, it will vanish away. For we know in part and we prophesy in part. But when that which is perfect has come, then that which is in part will be done away. When I was a child, I spoke as a child, I understood as a child, I thought as a child; but when I became a man, I put away childish things. For now we see in a mirror, dimly, but then face to face. Now I know in part, but then I shall know just as I also am known* (1 Corinthians 13:8-12).

We gather from this that prophecies, tongues, and knowledge are not eternal, but are temporal. It appears in context that the knowledge Paul speaks of pertains to "partial" bits of knowledge that are imparted or communicated as we mature in Christ. We certainly won't be ignorant in Heaven; we'll know far more then than we do now.

The question is not *whether* these gifts such as prophecy, tongues, and knowledge will pass away—Scripture clearly says they will—but *when* will they pass away. Some take the position that when the canon of Scripture—the establishing of the collection of the New Testament writings—came together, these particular gifts were withdrawn from the Church. After all, they reason, the Bible is perfect, so now we don't need these gifts.

However, there is a serious flaw with that line of thinking. Paul concludes that section by saying, *"Now I know in part, but then I shall know just as I also am known"* (1 Corinthians 13:12). As much as I thank God for the Bible, we still *"know in part"* even though we have the Bible. Paul wrote a large percentage of the New Testament, and yet he still knew in part. As much as I love, respect, and appreciate God's written Word, none of us yet know just as we are known.

> *Now we see things imperfectly, like puzzling reflections in a mirror, but then we will see everything with perfect clarity. All that I know now is partial and incomplete, but then I will know everything completely, just as God now knows me completely* (1 Corinthians 13:12 NLT).

As much as some seem to want to abolish tongues and prophecy for today based on Paul's words here, he cannot be referring to the New Testament Canon as *the perfect*. The only thing he could be referring to is when we reach perfection, and I assume that will be when we arrive in Heaven. It is in Heaven that *"I will know everything completely, just as God now knows me completely."* Thank God for the Bible and its awesome revelation, but we won't know everything until we get to Heaven. You won't need to speak in tongues there, prophesy there, or give someone a word of knowledge there. Heaven will be full of love, because love is eternal!

On a practical note, any modern "prophecy" or "knowledge" that comes to us is never superior to or even on par with what is revealed in Scripture; it is subordinate to and is to be judged by Scripture. If someone prophesies to you or claims to have a "word" for you and it disagrees with or contradicts the Bible, please do yourself a favor and disregard it!

When Paul lists the supernatural ministry gifts of apostle, prophet, evangelist, pastor, and teacher, he proceeds to tell us their exact purpose and the duration of their assignment:

> *Their responsibility is to equip God's people to do his work and build up the church, the body of Christ. This will continue until we all come to such unity in our faith and knowledge of God's Son that we will be mature in the Lord, measuring up to the full and complete standard of Christ* (Ephesians 4:12-13 NLT).

I have been preaching the gospel and working with churches and believers since 1980. I can assure you, the Church has not yet reached the kind of unity, knowledge, and maturity that Paul describes here, nor have we yet measured up *"to the full and complete standard of Christ."* Therefore, it seems clear and obvious that God has not withdrawn any of His gifts, including those of apostles and prophets. That does not mean that everyone who claims to be an apostle or prophet, or claims to be an evangelist, pastor, or teacher for that matter, is truly one—nor does it mean that they are infallible or always accurate—but God has not withdrawn these gifts from the Church.

So the Bible does not support the discontinuation of the supernatural gifts of God. We certainly need all the help that God has to offer, and we need His grace and the power of the Holy Spirit just as the earliest believers did.

But what is the witness of church history? Does history support the continuation or the cessation of the gifts of the Holy Spirit described in the New Testament? In the next chapter, I will begin introducing you to some of the individuals who ministered after the death of the apostle John.

The Book of Acts ends abruptly with Paul still in Rome around the year AD 62. He was released, traveled preaching, and was later martyred in Rome around the year AD 67. Several of the epistles were written prior to the conclusion of Acts, and some were written after. The book of Revelation was likely penned by John around the year AD 95.

If you are like many Christians, you have not heard much about the godly ministers who worked in the second century and beyond; and some Christians would be hard pressed to even name a Christian that ministered between the times of the apostle John and Martin Luther. I believe you are going to enjoy "meeting" some of God's great servants from this wide expanse of time and learning about their experiences with the Lord. I think you will be excited to learn about the continuing flow of God's Spirit throughout history.

Historical Accounts of Supernatural Works

CHAPTER THREE

THE FLOW CONTINUES

It is not possible to name the number of the gifts which the Church, scattered throughout the whole world, has received from God.
—**Irenaeus of Lyons**

THE work of God and the flow of the Holy Spirit did not stop when the book of Acts ended, nor when John—the longest living of the original apostles—passed off the scene toward the end of the first century. History records some amazingly vivid accounts of what happened in the lives and ministries of those John influenced and trained. Ignatius of Antioch and Polycarp of Smyrna were direct disciples of John, and Irenaeus of Lyons was a disciple of Polycarp. Their stories are amazing, and God was with them in very powerful ways.

Ignatius of Antioch (?-117)

In Acts 13, the apostles Paul and Barnabas launched out on their first missionary journey from Antioch, the city where believers were first called Christians (Acts 11:26). This happened around AD 47. Today, the modern city of Antakya (Antioch in Bible days) is in southern

Turkey, approximately thirteen miles from the Syrian border. After Paul and Barnabas left Antioch to undertake their apostolic work, the church there continued to thrive, and it would remain one of the greatest churches of the first few centuries. By the end of the fourth century, the bishop of Antioch, along with those of Rome, Constantinople, Alexandria, and Jerusalem were given special honor among all of the churches and bishops.[1]

In AD 83, a few decades after the inaugural mission of Paul and Barnabas, Ignatius, a disciple of the apostle John, became the bishop of the church in Antioch—this happened while John was still living. He was such fervent man that John Chrysostom, a later bishop from Constantinople, described him as "a soul boiling with passionate divine love." Ignatius even went by the nickname of Theophorus, which means Bearer of God.

After leading the congregation in Antioch for many years, Ignatius was condemned to death around AD 115 by the Roman Emperor Trajan. Ignatius wrote seven letters as he was escorted under guard from Antioch to Rome to face martyrdom. In his letter to the church of Smyrna, Ignatius describes them as a church that "has received mercy in every gracious gift, fulfilled in faith and love, not lacking in any gift."[2] Another letter of Ignatius was addressed to Polycarp, bishop of the church at Smyrna. Polycarp had also known and been a disciple of the apostle John. In that particular letter, Ignatius encourages Polycarp to "Linger constantly in prayers. Seek a greater understanding than you have."[3] He continues his exhortation:

> Be wise as a serpent in everything and always harmless as a dove. This is the reason you are physical and spiritual that you may handle gently the things as they appear to you. Ask

that the invisible things will be shown to you so that you will
not lack anything and abound in every [spiritual] gift."[4]

Notice that Ignatius acknowledges the church of Smyrna as "not
lacking in any gift," and he desires that their pastor, Polycarp, would
"not lack anything and abound in every spiritual gift." Without a doubt,
Ignatius was strongly implying the role of the Holy Spirit in these matters.
The words of Ignatius are reminiscent of Paul's acknowledgment to the
Corinthians, *"you are not lacking in any gift"* (1 Corinthians 1:7 English
Standard Version), and his admonition that they *"desire earnestly spiritual
gifts"* (1 Corinthians 14:1 New American Standard Bible).

Polycarp of Smyrna (AD 69-156)

Polycarp was a disciple of the apostle John, and had been ordained
by him to his leadership position in Smyrna. Some twenty years before
receiving Ignatius' letter, around AD 95, when Polycarp was around
twenty-seven years of age, another letter had come to the church of
Smyrna. This earlier letter was Jesus' message to the congregation of
Smyrna that is found in Revelation 2:8-11. Polycarp's decision many
years later to surrender his life as a martyr was possibly influenced by
Jesus' words to the church of Smyrna, *"Be faithful until death, and I will
give you the crown of life"* (Revelation 2:10).

In addition to his relationships with John and Ignatius, Polycarp also
held the apostle Paul in the highest regard. As a bishop, Polycarp wrote
the following gracious and insightful words to the church at Philippi, a
congregation that Paul himself established and nurtured:

Neither I nor anyone like me is able to emulate the wisdom
of the blessed and glorious Paul who, when he came among

you in person, taught the message of truth accurately and firmly. When absent, he wrote you letters by which, if you studied closely, you can be built up further in the faith given you. This faith is the mother of us all as hope accompanies it with love leading the way to God, Christ, and neighbor. If any one is centered on these, he has fulfilled the command of righteousness. For the one who has love is far from all sin.[5]

Profoundly affected by the ministries of Paul and John, Polycarp's life reveals him as an intensely dedicated follower of Christ, full of faith, and highly consecrated to God.

Ignatius had admonished Polycarp to ask for invisible things so that he would lack nothing and would abound in every spiritual gift. It is common for people to think only of healing or a few other selected "gifts" along these lines. While Polycarp likely experienced many of these in his lifetime, we know for a fact that he experienced, by the Holy Spirit, foreknowledge and a supernatural grace to endure suffering in his latter days.

In AD 156, when Polycarp was eighty-six years old and revered as the Bishop of Smyrna (modern-day Izmir in the nation of Turkey), orders were given for his arrest. At first, Polycarp had no intention of fleeing, but was persuaded by friends to take refuge in a house not far from the city. While he was praying there, Polycarp had a vision of a burning pillow under his head, and he told those with him that he was to be burnt alive. When the authorities came to arrest him, Polycarp demonstrated hospitality and kindness, requesting that they be given a meal, and that he be allowed to pray a bit more. In order to secure his release, Polycarp was advised to simply make the declaration, "Caesar is Lord," and offer sacrifice to the Roman gods, but Polycarp was firm and unwavering in his faith.

As he entered the stadium, a voice was heard from Heaven encouraging Polycarp to be strong and to "play the man." He refused continued offers to be set free by offering sacrifice to Caesar, and when they threatened him with fire, he responded, "Your fire burns for an hour and goes out, but the fire of the coming judgment is eternal." Ultimately, Polycarp demonstrated his absolute resolve with the words, "Eighty-six years I have served Him, and He has done me no wrong. How then can I blaspheme my King who has saved me?"

Long before this event, Jesus spoke to Peter about the kind of death by which Peter would glorify God (John 21:19), and Polycarp walked the same type of path. Clearly, Polycarp received much grace and supernatural help as he offered up his life for the Lord Jesus Christ. Unbelievers were profoundly moved by the grace with which he faced death, and believers were tremendously encouraged as well.

Polycarp fits the description of an honored class of believers in Hebrews 11:35 (NLT) who by faith, "were tortured, refusing to turn from God in order to be set free. They placed their hope in a better life after the resurrection." Polycarp did in fact see invisible things, and he abounded mightily in the power of the Holy Spirit.

Irenaeus of Lyons (AD 125-202)

Approximately six years before his death in AD 150, Polycarp sent one of his disciples named Irenaeus to the city of Lyons, located in Gaul, the modern nation of France. At that time, false doctrines were assaulting the church from within, and severe persecutions were threatening the church from without. Author Bryan M. Liftin notes, "Irenaeus was the first to use the term 'New Testament' in connection with a body of writings."[6]

While Irenaeus is primarily remembered for his theological writings against Gnosticism, he clearly affirms the continuation and the active manifestations of a variety of spiritual gifts that were operating in the Church at the end of the second century:

> His disciples, receiving grace from Him, do in His name perform [miracles], so as to promote the welfare of other men, according to the gift which each one has received from Him. For some do certainly and truly drive out devils, so that those who have thus been cleansed from evil spirits frequently both believe [in Christ], and join themselves to the Church. Others have foreknowledge of things to come: they see visions, and utter prophetic expressions. Others still, heal the sick by laying their hands upon them, and they are made whole. Yea, moreover, as I have said, the dead even have been raised up, and remained among us for many years. And what shall I more say? It is not possible to name the number of the gifts which the Church, [scattered] throughout the whole world, has received from God, in the name of Jesus Christ, who was crucified under Pontius Pilate, and which she exerts day by day for the benefit of the Gentiles, neither practicing deception upon any, nor taking any reward from them [on account of such miraculous interpositions]. For as she has received freely from God, freely also does she minister [to others].[7]

Having made such a powerful statement about the charismatic nature of the Church, Irenaeus proceeds to delineate the supernatural work of God from pagan or magical practices. Believers in Jesus Christ, he declares, operate totally different from counterfeit workers:

But, directing her prayers to the Lord, who made all things, in a pure, sincere, and straightforward spirit, and calling upon the name of our Lord Jesus Christ, she has been accustomed to work miracles for the advantage of mankind, and not to lead them into error. If, therefore, the name of our Lord Jesus Christ even now confers benefits [upon men], and cures thoroughly and effectively all who anywhere believe on Him.[8]

In addition to these dynamic statements, Irenaeus also communicates the prevalence of speaking in tongues that was still occurring at the end of the second century.

For this reason does the apostle declare, "We speak wisdom among them that are perfect," terming those persons "perfect" who have received the Spirit of God, and who through the Spirit of God do speak in all languages, as he used Himself also to speak. In like manner we do also hear many brethren in the Church, who possess prophetic gifts, and who through the Spirit speak all kinds of languages, and bring to light for the general benefit the hidden things of men, and declare the mysteries of God....[9]

Clearly, Irenaeus considers the supernatural workings of God normative for the Church. He recognizes, affirms, and appreciates the gifts of the Holy Spirit.

In examining these three leaders, the involvement of the Holy Spirit in their lives and ministries is pronounced. Ignatius encouraged Polycarp to ask for invisible things, things of the Spirit, so he would abound in spiritual gifts. Polycarp received supernatural foreknowledge from the

Holy Spirit that helped prepare him for what he was about to face and also received supernatural grace and strength to endure his suffering.

Polycarp's disciple, Irenaeus, described prolific expressions of the Spirit's gifts, including miracles, exorcisms, foreknowledge, visions, prophecies, healing through the laying on of hands, the raising of the dead, and tongues.

History clearly demonstrates that the gifts of the Spirit described in the New Testament flowed freely after the death of John, the last of the original apostles.

Endnotes

1. Robert C. Walton, *Chronological and Background Charts of Church History* (Grand Rapids, MI: Zondervan, 2005), Chart 22. Used by permission of Zondervan. www.zondervan.com

2. Kenneth J. Howell, *Ignatius of Antioch & Polycarp of Smyrna* (Zanesville, OH: CHResources, 2009), loc. 2289, Kindle.

3. Ibid., loc. 2448, Kindle.

4. Ibid., loc. 2458, Kindle.

5. Ibid., loc. 2600, Kindle.

6. Bryan M. Liftin, *Getting to Know the Church Fathers: An Evangelical Introduction* (Grand Rapids, MI: Brazos Press, 2007), loc. 1634, Kindle.

7. Irenaeus of Lyons, *Against Heresies & Fragments*, vol. 1 of *Ante-Nicene Fathers*, trans. A. Roberts & J. Donaldson with A. Cleveland Coxe (Grand Rapids, MI: CCEL, 2012), loc. 3669, Kindle.

8. Ibid., loc. 3678, Kindle.

9. Ibid., loc. 8309, Kindle.

CHAPTER FOUR

SUPERNATURAL WORKS IN ROME

We hold to doctrines that are filled with the Spirit of God. They gush forth with power and are teeming with grace.

—**Justin Martyr**

IN New Testament times, Rome was the capital of the Gentile world, and yet it was home to many Jews. On the day of Pentecost in Acts 2, approximately AD 30, Jewish pilgrims from many nations were visiting Jerusalem to celebrate that special holiday. Luke lists the home countries of several who were visiting the city and states that there were *"visitors from Rome, both Jews and proselytes"* (Acts 2:10). It is very likely that some of those Roman Jews were among the 3,000 who were saved listening to Peter's preaching on that day after the Holy Spirit was poured out; and it is possible that some of them returned to Rome after Pentecost and formed an early Christian community.

In AD 49, the Roman Emperor Claudius expelled all Jews from Rome—this would have included Jewish Christians—and one of the couples that faced eviction was Aquila and Priscilla (Acts 18:2). Paul met them when he came to Corinth. He lived and worked with them, and they became his faithful partners in ministry. It was during a later visit to Corinth that Paul wrote his epistle to the church in Rome in AD 56 or 57. By that time, the edict of Claudius had been lifted, and Aquila and Priscilla were back in Rome. Paul not only greeted his old friends and coworkers but also expressed regards to *the church that is in their house*" (Romans 16:4-5).

The book of Acts ends with Paul under house arrest in Rome for two years (Acts 28). He was released approximately AD 62, continued traveling for a few years, and returned to Rome. Paul was rearrested, wrote his second epistle to Timothy from the Mamertine Prison in Rome, and was martyred under Nero's persecution against the Church in AD 67. It is believed that Peter was also martyred in Rome around the same time.

Clement of Rome (AD 35-99)

After the turbulence of the Neronian persecution, Clement provided stability and guidance to the Roman Christians, possibly the same Clement that Paul mentions in Philippians 4:3. Irenaeus of Lyons describes Clement as one who "had seen the blessed apostles, and had been conversant with them, might be said to have the preaching of the apostles still echoing [in his ears] and their traditions before his eyes."[1] In a letter Clement wrote to the Corinthian church, he encouraged them to eradicate strife from the congregation, something Paul had encouraged them to do much earlier.

In the fifth chapter of his letter, Clement refers to Peter and Paul as "the athletes, the noble examples, the greatest and most righteous pillars, and the good apostles."[2] He spoke of their endurance through hardships, and said of Peter, "Once he gave his testimony, he went to the place of glory owed him."[3] Of Paul, Clement was even more effusive:

Paul showed forth a prize of endurance. Being imprisoned seven times, banished and stoned, he became a herald in the East and the West and received the noble renown of his faith. Having taught the whole world righteousness and arrived at the farthest boundary of the West, he gave his testimony before rulers; so he exchanged this world and arrived at the holy place, after he became a great example of endurance.[4]

Clement passed off the scene around AD 100, but others would come and minister powerfully in Rome. One of these was a man who would be known after his death as Justin Martyr.

Justin Martyr (AD 100-165)

Justin was born in Samaria around AD 100, close to the time when Clement died. Justin had a great interest in philosophy, and studied it fervently in Ephesus. While there, he had a salvation experience and he developed a tremendous desire to present the gospel to those whose minds had been shaped by Greek thought. Justin describes his salvation experience:

Straightway a flame was kindled in my soul; and a love of the prophets, and of those men who are friends of Christ, possessed me; and while revolving his words in my mind, I found this [Christian] philosophy alone to be safe and profitable. Thus, and for this reason, I am a philosopher. Moreover, I wish that everyone making a resolution similar to my own, would not keep themselves away from the words of the Savior.[5]

Perhaps we can best understand Justin's mindset through a modern analogy. A banker who gets saved might have a great burden to see other bankers saved, and because they all come from the world of banking, he or she might know how best to communicate with other bankers. The same could be said of athletes or musicians. Sharing similar backgrounds and experiences can help establish common ground in understanding and communication.

While Justin is primarily known for his groundbreaking work as a Christian thinker, philosopher, and apologist, he also makes references to supernatural workings of God in his writings. In Justin's *Dialogue with Trypho*, he states:

> Knowing that daily some [of you] are becoming disciples in the name of Christ, and quitting the path of error; who are also receiving gifts, each as he is worthy, illumined through the name of this Christ. For one receives the spirit of understanding, another of counsel, another of strength, another of healing, another of foreknowledge, another of teaching, and another of the fear of God.[6]

Later, in the same communication, he asserts that "the prophetical gifts remain with us, even to the present time,"[7] and that "Now, it is possible to see amongst us women and men who possess gifts of the Spirit of God."[8]

Justin also provides insight into the prevalence of supernatural ministry in the second century church in his *Second Apology*. This is not an apology in the modern usage of the term as, "I'm sorry," but rather is a reasoned defense and persuasive commendation of the Christian faith. Justin describes the exploits and effectiveness of Christians who ministered to the needs of people:

> Numberless demoniacs throughout the whole world, and in your city, many of our Christian men exorcising them in the name of Jesus Christ, who was crucified under Pontius

Pilate, have healed and do heal, rendering helpless and driving the possessing devils out of the men, though they could not be cured by all the other exorcists, and those who used incantations and drugs.[9]

These descriptions by Justin give clear indication that the gifts of the Holy Spirit were operating to a notable degree in the church at Rome in the mid-second century.

Justin eventually was put to death for his faith, and was thereafter known as Justin Martyr. Others would come, though, and would also reference the supernatural work of God in Rome. One of these is an elder in the church at Rome by the name of Novatian.

Novatian (AD 200-258)

Novatian, an elder in the church at Rome, wrote a piece titled *Concerning the Trinity*. The majority of his treatise deals with the nature of God and the deity of Christ, but he also shares powerful insights about the role and work of the Holy Spirit in the life of the church.

This is He who places prophets in the Church, instructs teachers, directs tongues, gives powers and healings, does wonderful works, offers discrimination of spirits, affords powers of government, suggests counsels, and orders and arranges whatever other gifts there are of charismata; and thus make the Lord's Church everywhere, and in all, perfected and completed.[10]

Novatian also said that followers of Christ were "armed and strengthened by the same Spirit, having in themselves the gifts which this same Spirit distributes, and appropriates to the Church."[11]

In addition to recognizing the role of the Holy Spirit relative to his gifts, Novatian also remarks on the sanctifying influence of the Holy Spirit in the lives of believers and of the church:

> This is He who restrains insatiable desires, controls immoderate lusts, quenches unlawful fires, conquers reckless impulses, repels drunkenness, checks avarice, drives away luxurious revellings, links love, binds together affections, keeps down sects, orders the rule of truth, overcomes heretics, turns out the wicked, guards the Gospel....[12]

Gregory the Great (AD 540-604)

A few hundred years after Novatian, Rome had undergone unimaginable changes. The Emperor Constantine had moved the headquarters of the Empire to Byzantium—Constantinople, now called Istanbul—in 330, leaving a significant power vacuum in Rome that the church and its leaders eventually filled. Rome had experienced many setbacks and numerous invasions from European tribes, resulting in its demise and ultimate fall in 476.

Historian John Moorhead writes, "There was now no senate in Rome and its people were perishing; the few people who were left had to endure greater sufferings."[13] Speaking of this same time period, author Bruce L. Shelley explains, "Rome was in agony. The city suffered through the tragedies of floods and the atrocities of war only to be smitten by the relentless spread of the plague."[14] It was into this dismal scenario in the year 590 that a monk named Gregory, the former mayor of Rome, was elected the bishop of Rome—its new pope.

Reluctant to step into a role of authority, Gregory exemplified great humility. Rejecting lofty titles, Gregory referred to himself only as the "servant of the servants of God." Protestant Reformer John Calvin, who had many harsh criticisms of both the doctrine and the hierarchy of the Roman church, respected Gregory's humility, and referenced "Gregory, whom you can rightly call the last bishop of Rome."[15] Calvin's affirmation of Gregory and his stinging indictment of the church was made, according to Calvin's perspective, "while one drop of integrity remained in the church" as opposed to "four hundred years after his death, when all things had already degenerated."[16]

When Gregory led the church at Rome, it was a very different city than it was in the book of Acts, or even during the times of Clement, Justin, or Novatian, and yet Gregory gives indications of miracles and workings of the Holy Spirit in his day. Moorhead states that Gregory's book, *Dialogues*, "overflows with stories of holy men working miracles, some 200 in number. Its content gives the work a popular, folksy feeling."[17] In one case, Gregory writes, "I, your unworthy servant, know how many soldiers who have become monks in my own days have done miracles, have wrought signs and mighty deeds."[18]

In his *Homilies on Ezekiel*, Gregory writes:

> Now, generally, we see holy men do wonderful things, perform many miracles, cleanse lepers, cast out demons, dispel bodily sicknesses by touch, [and] predict things to come by the spirit of prophecy.[19]

Gregory was especially prolific in writing to Augustine of Canterbury, the leader of a missionary team Gregory had sent to evangelize England. Commending the work of the missionaries, Gregory speaks of the "mighty works in the nation of the Angli," and "that Almighty God has displayed great miracles" through the love of Augustine and his fellow workers. He further notes, "the souls of the Angli are drawn by outward miracles to inward grace."[20]

Then, acknowledging that Augustine had received "the gift of doing signs," Gregory encouraged him to stay humble and to not be lifted up in pride because of the miracles that had occurred. Gregory expresses great wisdom in reminding Augustine (my paraphrase), "Whatever gifts you have received relative to doing signs, remember that these powers were not granted for your benefit, but so that others may receive salvation."[21]

Benedict (AD 480-547)

In addition to his other writings, Gregory also recorded various details about the life and ministry of Benedict. Born in Nursia, but educated in Rome, Benedict is often referred to as the father of Western monasticism. Disappointed with his experience in Rome, Benedict lived as a hermit for a season before establishing several monasteries, the most famous one being Monte Cassino, more than eighty-five miles from Rome. The stories written by Gregory reveal certain supernatural events that happened through Benedict's life.

One of these involves Benedict receiving what might be considered a word of knowledge. One of the young men named Placidus had gone to the lake to obtain water, and in doing so, fell in. Being some distance away, Benedict perceives this and tells one of the other young men, Maurus, what had been revealed to him. He instructs Maurus to run as fast as he could to help Placidus. Obeying Benedict's instructions, Maurus runs to the lake and sees Placidus away from the shore, struggling. Without fully realizing what is happening, Maurus rescues Placidus, but then realizes he had run on top of the water in doing so. Benedict writes of the young man's experience:

...taking fast hold of him by the hair of his head, in all haste he returned back again: and so soon was he at land, coming to himself he looked behind him, and then knew very well that he had before run on the water...he both marveled, and was afraid at that which he had done.[22]

When they returned safely and shared the story of the miraculous rescue, both Benedict and Maurus refused to take any credit for what had happened.

In another situation, some of the monks were building a wall when it collapsed, killing a young boy. Benedict commanded that the lifeless body of the child be brought to him, and after a time of prayer, the boy was raised up and made completely whole. Gregory records other supernatural events in Benedict's life, including healings, prophecies, and discerning of spirits.

Endnotes

1. Irenaeus, *Against Heresies*, loc. 3882, Kindle.

2. Clement of Rome, *Letter to the Corinthians*, *Clement of Rome and the Didache*, trans. Kenneth J. Howell (Zanesville, OH: CHResources, 2012), loc. 1416, Kindle.

3. Ibid.

4. Ibid.

5. Litfin, *Getting to Know the Church Fathers*, 58.

6. Justin Martyr, *Saint Justin Martyr: Collection, Dialogue of Justin with a Jew*, trans. A. Roberts and J. Donaldson with A. Cleveland Coxe (Seattle, WA: Aeterna Press, 2016), loc. 1067, Kindle

7. Ibid., loc. 1993, Kindle.

8. Ibid., loc. 2117, Kindle.

9. Justin Martyr, *Saint Justin Martyr: Collection, The Second Apology of Justin*, trans. A. Roberts and J. Donaldson with A. Cleveland Coxe (Seattle, WA: Aeterna Press, 2016), loc. 1331, Kindle.

10. Novatian, *Concerning the Trinity*, in *The Complete Works of the Church Fathers*, ed. Phillip Schaff (Seattle, WA: Amazon Digital Services, 2016), loc. 442326, Kindle.

11. Ibid.

12. Ibid., loc. 492423, Kindle.

13. John Moorhead, *Gregory the Great*, in *The Early Church Fathers* (New York: Routledge, 2005), 6, Kindle.

14. Bruce L. Shelley, *Church History in Plain Language* (Nashville, TN: Thomas Nelson, www.thomasnelson.com, 2008), 163, Kindle. Used by permission of Thomas Nelson.

15. John Calvin, *The Institutes of the Christian Religion*, vol. 2, trans. Ford Lewis Battles, ed. John T. McNeill (Philadelphia, PA: Westminster Press, 1960), 1427.

16. Ibid.

17. Moorhead, *Gregory the Great*, 14, Kindle.

18. Gregory the Great, *The Book of Pastoral Rule and Selected Epistles*, Book III, Epistle LXV, trans. James Barmby (Veritatis Splendor Publications, 2012), 239, Kindle.

19. Gregory the Great, *Homilies on Ezekiel*, cited by Stanley M. Burgess, *The Holy Spirit: Medieval Roman Catholic and Reformation* (Peabody, MA: Hendrickson Publishers, www.hendrickson.com, 1984), loc. 418, Kindle.

20. Gregory the Great, *The Book of Pastoral Rule and Selected Epistles*, Book X, Epistle XXVIII, trans. James Barmby, ed. Paul A. Boer Sr. (Veritas Splendor Publications, 2012), 515-516, Kindle.

21. Ibid., 516.

22. Gregory the Great, *Dialogues* (Seattle, WA: Amazon Digital Services, 593), loc. 1073, Kindle.

CHAPTER FIVE

THE HOLY SPIRIT AT WORK IN NORTHERN AFRICA

I cannot record all the miracles I know.

—Augustine

W HEN the Holy Spirit was poured out in Jerusalem on the day of Pentecost, Christianity was poised to spread quickly throughout the Mediterranean world. Jewish pilgrims from three continents—Asia, Africa, and Europe—were in the Jewish capital when Peter preached and 3,000 came to the Lord.

Luke tells us that among those present were Jews from *"Egypt and the areas of Libya around Cyrene"* (Acts 2:10 NLT). Cyrene was an ancient city in modern-day Libya and is located close to modern Benghazi. It is very likely that a good number of those responding to Peter's message that day were Africans.

Consider these other New Testament references to Africa:

- Egypt was the nation of refuge for Joseph, Mary, and Jesus when King Herod was seeking to kill the Christ child (Matthew 2:13-20).

- As Jesus was led to Golgotha for crucifixion, it was an African—Simon of Cyrene—who was compelled to carry the Savior's cross (Mark 15:21). Interestingly, Mark notes that one of Simon's sons was Rufus, and Paul greets a Rufus in Romans 16:13. Paul even says that Rufus' mother was like a mother to him also. It is likely that the Simon, who carried Christ's cross, became part of the early Christian community, and that his entire family became very dear to Paul and other early believers.

- Philip the evangelist received divine direction to share the gospel with a high-ranking government official that served in the administration of Candace, the queen of the Ethiopians (Acts 8:26-39). He received Jesus, was baptized, and returned to Ethiopia.

- Antioch, in modern-day Turkey, became a very important center of Christianity in the first century and beyond, and Acts 11:20 tells us that believers from Cyrene (modern Libya) were among the very first people to take the gospel to that strategic city.

- Bible students know that Paul and Barnabas were among the five "prophets and teachers" listed as laborers in the church at Antioch, but many forget that two of the others were *Simeon (called 'the black man'), Lucius (from Cyrene)"* (Acts 13:1 NLT).

Eusebius, the church historian, writes that Mark "is said to have been the first sent to Egypt to preach the Gospel that he had also written down and the first to found churches in Alexandria itself."[1] While he was not one of Jesus' original disciples, Mark was a trusted aid to both Paul and Peter. Paul said that Mark was helpful to him in the ministry

(2 Timothy 4:11 NLT), and Peter referred to Mark as his son (1 Peter 5:13). Alexandria was the second largest city in the empire behind Rome, and the church of Alexandria became one of the most influential churches in the first few centuries.

Tertullian (AD 160-220)

This great church father ministered in ancient Carthage, near modern-day Tunis in Tunisia, located between Libya and Algeria. A powerful proponent and defender of the faith, Tertullian was the first person to use the term "Trinity" to describe the One God who exists in three persons: Father, Son, and Holy Spirit. He also famously declared, in a time of significant persecution against Christians, that the blood of the martyrs is the seed of the Church. His specific statement was, "The oftener we are mown down by persecutors, the more in number we grow; the blood of Christians is seed."[2]

While much of Tertullian's writing focused on promoting orthodox biblical doctrine and opposing heretical teachers, such as Marcion, Tertullian also spoke forcefully and clearly in favor of the supernatural workings of the Holy Spirit. Tertullian asserts, "many men of rank (to say nothing of common people) have been delivered from devils and healed of diseases"[3] and states that droughts had "been put away by our kneelings and our fastings."[4] He also writes that, "we acknowledge spiritual charismata, or gifts," referred specifically to prophecy, and then spoke of a lady in his congregation, "favored with sundry gifts of revelation, which she experiences in the Spirit." Tertullian also said that this lady would sometimes have spiritual insight into the hearts and lives of people in need, and as she did, "she distributes remedies."[5]

In addition to these statements, Tertullian also wrote:

And thus we—who both acknowledge and reverence, even as we do the prophecies, modern visions as equally promised to us, and consider the other powers of the Holy Spirit as an agency of the Church for which also He was sent, administering all gifts in all, even as the Lord distributed to every one.[6]

What is nobler than to tread under foot the gods of the nations, to exorcise evil spirits, to perform cures, to seek divine revelations, and to live to God? These are the pleasures—these are the spectacles—that befit Christian men—holy, everlasting, free.[7]

Tertullian gave instructions to new believers, having been baptized, to desire and request the gifts of the Spirit. He writes:

When you ascend from that most sacred font [bath] of your new birth, and spread your hands for the first time in the house of your mother [the church], together with your brethren, ask from the Father, ask from the Lord, that His own specialties of grace and distributions of gifts may be supplied to you.[8]

Tertullian saw the prevalence of spiritual gifts among believers as evidence of the Spirit's presence. In writing against his theological antagonist, he indicates that Marcion, with his gnostic doctrines, had no manifestations of God's Spirit because his life and ministry were void of truth. In contrast, Tertullian asserts that the prevalence of gifts of the Spirit among believers reflected the truth of their own beliefs:

Now all these signs (of spiritual gifts) are forthcoming from my side without any difficulty, and they agree, too, with the rules, and the dispensations, and the instructions of the Creator; therefore without doubt the Christ, and the Spirit, and the apostle, belong severally to my God.[9]

In addition, Tertullian speaks of the power of the Holy Spirit relative to our entire being.

He writes:

Our birth He reforms from death by a second birth from heaven; our flesh he restores from every harassing malady; when leprous, He cleanses it of the stain; when blind, He rekindles its light; when palsied, He renews its strength; when possessed with devils, He exorcises it; when dead, He reanimates it.[10]

Origen (AD 184-253)

Raised in Alexandria, Egypt, Origen exerted tremendous influence in the church through his writings and his ministry. His father, Leonidas, was martyred for his faith when Origen was sixteen or seventeen, and this teenager, sharing his father's faith, was resolved to turn himself in and be put to death along with his father. His mother, however, hid his clothes and kept him from leaving the house, thereby sparing his life.

Two years later, Origen was appointed the leader of a school that taught Christian doctrine, a school that had previously been headed by Clement of Alexandria. One author describes Origen as "the most prolific scholar of his age (with hundreds of works to his credit), a first-rate Christian philosopher, and a profound student of the Bible."[11] Later, Origen traveled to and based his ministry in Caesarea in Palestine. He would also suffer imprisonment and torture under the Roman Emperor

Decius. His tenacity earned him the nickname *Adamanatius,* meaning Unbreakable or Man of Steel.

Having witnessed miracles personally, Origen made several profound statements about supernatural workings of God. For example, he states, "The name of Jesus can still remove distractions from the minds of men, and expel demons, and also take away diseases; and produce a marvelous meekness of spirit and a complete change of character."[12] Origen also notes the tremendous growth of Christianity and writes, "Not a few cures are wrought in the name of Jesus, and certain other manifestations of no small moment [significance] have taken place."[13]

Noting significant conversions to the Christian faith, Origen writes that he can present:

> a countless multitude of Greeks and barbarians who acknowledge the existence of Jesus. And some give evidence of their having received through this faith a marvelous power by the cures which they perform, invoking no other name over those who need their help than that of the God of all things, and of Jesus, along with a mention of His history. For by these means we too have seen many persons freed from grievous calamities, and from distractions of mind, and madness, and countless other ills, which could be cured neither by men or devils.[14]

Origen not only witnessed and reported these supernatural workings of the Holy Spirit, but he had also clearly thought out the theological basis for them. He writes:

> I consider that the Holy Spirit supplies to those who, through Him and through participation in Him, are called saints, the material of the gifts, which come from God; so that the said

material of the gifts is made powerful by God, is ministered by Christ, and owes its actual existence in men to the Holy Spirit. I am led to this view of the charisms by the word of Paul which he writes somewhere, "There are diversities of gifts but the same Spirit, and diversities of ministrations, and the same Lord. And there are diversities of workings, but it is the same God that worketh all in all."[15]

Athanasius (AD 296-373) and Antony (AD 251-356)

As the unrelenting defender of the doctrines of the Deity of Jesus and the Trinity at the Council of Nicaea (AD 325), Athanasius is one of the most important figures in church history. He fearlessly stood against the false teaching of Arius, which presented Jesus as less than divine. The enemies of Athanasius called him the "Black Dwarf," but this Egyptian bishop withstood all opposition and held fast to the truth in spite of being exiled from his native Alexandria five times for a total of seventeen years.

In addition to being a theological and intellectual giant, Athanasius also recognized the importance of the power of the Holy Spirit. This is seen especially in his written account of the famed monk, Antony. Around the age of eighteen, Antony's parents, well-to-do Egyptians, died. The young man gave his substantial inheritance to the poor and embraced a monastic lifestyle. Athanasius makes it clear that his knowledge of Antony is not second-hand or hearsay type of information. Rather, his account is based upon, "What I myself know, having seen him many times, and what I was able to learn from him, for I was his attendant for a long time, and poured water on his hands."[16]

Athanasius was not only impressed with the spiritual gifts that flowed through Antony, but was equally admiring of his godly character, describing him as a person of humility, tolerance, serenity, purity, joy, and possessing a cheerful countenance. He further described Antony as a man whose "soul was free from disturbances"[17] and who was "initiated in the mysteries and filled with the Spirit of God."[18] Antony's reputation for healing was profound, and many sought him out for help. Athanasius provides some of the following vivid descriptions of healings and miracles that took place through Antony's ministry:

- Through him [Antony] the Lord healed the bodily ailments of many present, and cleansed others from evil spirits. And He gave grace to Antony in speaking, so that he consoled many that were sorrowful, and set those at variance at one, exhorting all to prefer the love of Christ before all that is in the world.[19]

- And with those who suffered he [Antony] sympathized and prayed. And oft-times the Lord heard him on behalf of many: yet he boasted not because he was heard, nor did he murmur if he were not. But always he gave the Lord thanks and besought the sufferer to be patient, and to know that healing belonged neither to him nor to man at all, but only to the Lord, who does good when and to whom He will. The sufferers therefore used to receive the words of the old man as though they were a cure, learning not to be downhearted but rather to be long-suffering. And those who were healed were taught not to give thanks to Antony but to God alone.[20]

- For in that place also the Lord cleansed many of demons, and healed those who were mad. And many Greeks asked that they might even but touch the old man, believing that they should be profited. Assuredly as many became Christians in those few days as one would have seen made in a year.[21]

- Antony, at any rate, healed not by commanding, but by prayer and speaking the name of Christ. So that it was clear to all that it was not he himself who worked, but the Lord who showed mercy by his means and healed the sufferers.[22]

One of Antony's most admirable traits was his insistence on giving God all glory and credit for whatever His mercy and power produced. Every child of God should realize that whatever ministerial gifts he or she has received have been given for the benefit of others, not for the exaltation of the one who stewards that gift. As Paul states, *"What do you have that God hasn't given you? And if everything you have is from God, why boast as though it were not a gift?"* (1 Corinthians 4:7 NLT).

Expressing this same line of thinking, Antony gives this admonition:

And it is not fitting to boast at the casting forth of the demons, nor to be uplifted by the healing of diseases: nor is it fitting that he who casts out devils should alone be highly esteemed, while he who casts them not out should be considered nought.... For the working of signs is not ours but the Savior's work: and so He said to His disciples: Rejoice not that the demons are subject to you, but that your names are written in the heavens (Luke 10:20).[23]

In addition to recording accounts from Antony's life, Athanasius also addresses certain stereotypes that existed in his time. Based on what he writes, it appears that people generally believed that monks, with their ascetic lifestyles, were more spiritual and disciplined than were the bishops. Athanasius counters this presupposition.

For we know both bishops who fast, and monks who eat. We know bishops who drink no wine, as well as monks who do. We know bishops who work wonders, as well as monks who do not. Many also of the bishops have not even married, while monks have been fathers of children; just as conversely we know bishops who are fathers of children and monks of the completest kind.[24]

In making this contrast, Athanasius points out that it was not just Antony, or monks like him, who saw miracles and healings. Others did as well, including pastors of local congregations. Recognizing that different people have different types of gifts, Athanasius concludes with a wise and insightful statement: "But let a man, wherever he is, strive earnestly; for the crown is given not according to position, but according to action."[25]

Augustine of Hippo (AD 354-430)

Born in the ancient North African city of Tagaste in modern-day Algeria, Augustine was educated in Carthage, the same city where Tertullian had ministered nearly 200 years before. As a professor in Milan, Augustine, who was not yet a Christian, began attending the cathedral in Milan under the famous bishop, Ambrose. Having lived a sensual life, Augustine experienced a transformational moment from the Holy Spirit upon reading, *"Let us walk properly, as in the day, not in revelry and drunkenness, not in lewdness and lust, not in strife and envy. But put on the Lord Jesus Christ, and make no provision for the flesh, to fulfill its lusts"* (Romans 13:13-14). Augustine's description of what happened in his heart at that moment is powerful. He writes, "For instantly, as the sentence ended, there was infused in my heart something like the light of full certainty and all the gloom of doubt vanished away."[26]

Augustine eventually returned to his home in northern Africa as a monk, and ended up settling in the coastal town of Hippo (modern-day Annaba, the fourth largest city in Algeria today) where he served as a priest and eventually as the bishop. Theological controversies abounded in Augustine's time, and he was at the forefront of confronting and addressing vital doctrinal issues. Augustine was a prolific writer, a great thinker, and an articulate and outspoken theologian. While primarily known for his intellectual and doctrinal prowess, Augustine also speaks freely of miracles and supernatural works of God.

In his classic work *City of God*, Augustine writes, "Even now, therefore, many miracles are worked, the same God who worked those we read of still performing them, by whom He will and as He will."[27] He further elaborates:

> I cannot record all the miracles I know; and doubtless several of our adherents, when they read what I have narrated, will regret that I have omitted so many which they, as well as I, certainly know. Even now I beg these persons to excuse me, and to consider how long it would take me to relate all those miracles, which the necessity of finishing the work I have undertaken forces me to omit.[28]

Augustine also notes that the miracles in his day did not seem to be as "famous" as those described in the Bible. He states:

> These modern miracles are scarcely known even to the whole population in the midst of which they are worked, and at the best are confined to one spot. For frequently they are known only to a very few persons, while all the rest are ignorant of them, especially if the state is a large one; and when they are reported to other persons in other localities, there is no

sufficient authority to give them prompt and unwavering credence, although they are reported to the faithful by the faithful.[29]

Even if the miracles Augustine knew of around Hippo were less pronounced or publicized than those around the Sea of Galilee, Augustine certainly believed in their validity. He also affirmed the efficacy of integrating faith and medicine: "The Holy Spirit, too, works within, that the medicine externally applied may have some good result."[30]

Endnotes

1. Taken from *The Church History* © Copyright 2007 by Eusebius, trans. Paul L. Meier. Published by Kregel Publications, Grand Rapids, MI. Used by permission of the publisher. All rights reserved.

2. Tertullian, *The Apology*, ed. Alexander Roberts, trans. Sir James Donaldson and Arthur Cleveland Coxe (Seattle, WA: Amazon Digital Services, 1885), loc. 83, Kindle.

3. Tertullian, *To Scapula*, in *The Complete Works of Tertullian*, ed. Alexander Roberts, trans. Sir James Donaldson and Arthur Cleveland Coxe (Seattle, WA: Amazon Digital Services, 1885), loc. 49417, Kindle.

4. Ibid.

5. Tertullian, *On the Soul*, in *The Complete Works of Tertullian*, ed. Alexander Roberts, trans. Sir James Donaldson and Arthur Cleveland Coxe (Seattle, WA: Amazon Digital Services, 1885), loc. 25610, Kindle.

6. Tertullian, *The Passion of the Holy Martyrs Perpetua and Felicitas*, in *The Complete Works of Tertullian*, ed. Alexander Roberts, trans. Sir James Donaldson and Arthur Cleveland Coxe (Seattle, WA: Amazon Digital Services, 1885), loc. 45514, Kindle.

7. Tertullian, *The Shows*, in *The Complete Works of Tertullian*, ed. Alexander Roberts, trans. Sir James Donaldson and Arthur Cleveland Coxe (Seattle, WA: Amazon

Digital Services, 1885), loc. 48234, Kindle.

8. Tertullian, *On Baptism*, in *The Complete Works of Tertullian*, ed. Alexander Roberts, trans. Sir James Donaldson and Arthur Cleveland Coxe (Seattle, WA: Amazon Digital Services, 1885), loc. 48234, Kindle.

9. Tertullian, *The Five Books Against Marcion*, in *The Complete Works of Tertullian*, ed. Alexander Roberts, trans. by Sir James Donaldson and Arthur Cleveland Coxe (Seattle, WA: Amazon Digital Services, 1885), loc. 43531, Kindle.

10. Tertullian, *On the Flesh of Christ*, in *The Complete Works of Tertullian*, ed. Alexander Roberts, trans. Sir James Donaldson and Arthur Cleveland Coxe (Seattle, WA: Amazon Digital Services, 1885), loc. 20637, Kindle.

11. Mark Galli and Ted Olsen, ed., *131 Christians Everyone Should Know* (Nashville, TN: Christianity Today, 2000), loc. 6756, Kindle.

12. Origen, *Origen Against Celsus*, *The Works of Origen*, ed. Alexander Roberts, Sir James Donaldson, and Arthur Cleveland Coxe (Seattle, WA: Amazon Digital Services, 1885), loc. 10133, Kindle.

13. Ibid., loc. 13020, Kindle.

14. Ibid., loc. 12910, Kindle.

15. Origen, *Commentary on John* (Pickerington, OH: Beloved Publishing, 2014), 58.

16. Athanasius, *Life of St. Antony*, in *The Complete Works of Saint Athanasius*, trans. Philip Schaff (Seattle, WA: Amazon Digital Services, 2016), loc. 4984, Kindle.

17. Ibid., loc. 5664, Kindle.

18. Ibid., loc. 5140, Kindle.

19. Ibid., loc. 5145, Kindle.

20. Ibid., loc. 5560, Kindle.

21. Ibid., loc. 5588, Kindle.

22. Ibid., loc. 5808, Kindle.

23. Ibid., loc. 5373, Kindle.

24. Athanasius, *Life of St. Antony*, Letter 49, loc. 15421, Kindle.

25. Ibid., loc. 15426, Kindle.

26. Augustine, *The City of God*, trans. Marcus Dods (Peabody, MA: Hendrickson Publishers, www.hendrickson.com, 2009), loc. 82, Kindle.

27. Ibid., loc. 19032, Kindle.

28. Ibid., loc. 19006, Kindle.

29. Ibid., loc. 18851, Kindle.

30. Ibid., loc. 11046, Kindle.

OUTPOURINGS IN THE EAST (ASIA MINOR)

And when the stream of doctrine is gushing forth in the Church and a devout heart is welling up with the gifts of the Holy Spirit, do you not gladly give your attention? Do you not receive this favor with thanksgiving?

—Basil of Caesarea

PETER'S first epistle was addressed to believers who lived in what is modern-day Turkey. In New Testament times, the overall area was referred to as Asia Minor. He greets the Christians who had fled persecution with these words: *"This letter is from Peter, an apostle of Jesus Christ. I am writing to God's chosen people who are living as foreigners in the provinces of Pontus, Galatia, Cappadocia, Asia, and Bithynia"* (1 Peter 1:1 NLT).

One of Paul's friends, Aquila, was born in Pontus—he labored with Paul in both Corinth and Ephesus, and Paul greeted him in his epistle to the Romans. Galatia, near modern Ankara, Turkey's capital, is the region where Paul and Barnabas traveled on their first missionary journey, and they established churches in the cities of Lystra, Derbe, Iconium, and Antioch Pisidia. Asia is the most frequently mentioned of these provinces—

eighteen times in the New Testament—and is most often associated with Ephesus, its leading city, along with the other churches mentioned in John's vision of Jesus on the island of Patmos (Revelation 2-3).

In Chapter Three, The Flow Continues, we examined two of the early leaders who lived in this region: Polycarp of Smyrna and Ignatius of Antioch. In this chapter, we will explore some of the later individuals who impacted this region and beyond.

The Montanists (Late 2nd Century)

One of the major lessons from history is that people tend to repeat the same patterns over and over, even when it comes to making mistakes. Relative to revival and spiritual outpourings, it is not uncommon for a movement to emerge from the influence of a vibrant, gifted, and dynamic leader. An organizational framework then forms; and even though the spiritual impetus may diminish greatly over time, the structure and the institution often remain.

Organization is not a bad thing, but when the initial power and fervor of a movement is lost, it is often replaced with formalism, intellectualism, and ritualism. Sometimes the core values and practices that were present at the beginning erode and are compromised. This is likely the scenario that was occurring when Montanus launched his ministry around the year 156 in Phrygia—an area located today in east-central Turkey. Montanus and his followers, known as Montanists, placed a strong emphasis on the prophetic elements of Christianity. This was in contrast to a growing emphasis on hierarchy that was taking place elsewhere in much of Christendom.

Depending on which historical account one reads, it is not unusual to see Montanism described as heretical. However, there are questions as to the possibility that some of the charges were at least exaggerated, if not viciously and slanderously made. There are several respected church historians who are reluctant to affix the "heretic" label to the Montanists.

Noted scholar F. F. Bruce states that while they concentrated excessively on the inspirational side of Christianity, "the Montanists for the most part did not depart from the apostolic foundation of the Church."[1] Similarly, Philip Schaff writes that "In doctrine, Montanism agreed in all essential points with the Catholic Church, and held very firmly to the traditional rule of faith."[2] Bruce also recognizes a recurring pattern over many centuries when he notes "manifestations which have recurred time and again in the history of Christianity when the new wine of a spiritual movement has proved too potent to be restrained within the old wineskins of a too rigid organization."[3]

In addition to emphasizing the gift of prophecy, Montanus and his followers promoted a high standard of holiness, proclaimed the imminent return of the Lord, and challenged the sense of worldliness that was infecting many churches. Church historian Bruce L. Shelley describes the prevailing atmosphere in the church world when Montanism blossomed:

> In the second half of the second century a change was coming over the church. The days of enthusiasm were passing and the days of ecclesiasticism were arriving. The church was no longer a place where the Spirit of prophecy could be heard. More and more people were joining the churches, but the distinction between church and world was fading. The church was becoming secularized.[4]

It is entirely possible that the Montanists were extreme on some issues. But it is also possible that certain criticisms were highly prejudicial, unwarranted, and based on false information. For example, some accused Montanus of claiming that he was actually the Holy Spirit. However, distinguished church historian Philip Schaff refutes this. He states, "His adversaries wrongly inferred from the use of the first person for the Holy Spirit in his oracles, that he made himself directly the Paraclete, or, according to Epiphanius, even God the Father."[5]

An allegation reported by the early church historian Eusebius is that "Some of these sectarians slithered like poisonous reptiles over Asia and Phrygia, boasting that Montanus was the Paraclete and that his female followers Priscilla and Maximilla were his prophetesses."[6] It was also reported that Montanus engaged in bizarre behavior when he ministered, that he "became obsessed and, in his frenzy, fell into a trance. He began raving, chattering, and speaking nonsense, prophesying contrary to church tradition and custom from the beginning."[7]

Honestly, I wasn't there, so I don't know if this is a fair assessment or not. What I do know is that similar accusations have been made against wonderful believers throughout many revivals and outpourings throughout history, including the earliest disciples at Pentecost (Acts 2:13), at the Cane Ridge revival in Kentucky in 1801, and during the Azusa Street outpouring in Los Angeles in the early twentieth century.

I am reminded of when I first came into the Charismatic movement in 1977. Several young people who had all experienced the infilling of the Holy Spirit gathered for fellowship, teaching, and worship. We met in different homes, church basements, and even in a garage. We were full of zeal and enthusiasm, but we lacked experience, wisdom, and maturity. Some of what was said and done in those early meetings would have been considered extreme or imbalanced, and yet God still blessed us mightily. We were sincere, and our hearts were right, even if we acted or spoke unwisely at times.

When I read Montanus allegedly claimed to be the Holy Spirit or even God the Father, it reminded me of prophecies that were given in some of our early meetings. Many of the young people in our groups were genuinely inspired by the Holy Spirit to give words of encouragement and exhortation. Because the young people sensed an inspiration and leading, they would frequently attach, "Thus saith the Lord…" to their message, and would speak in the first person singular, as though God was speaking to the group. If someone were to come into a meeting and was unfamiliar with this, they might think that the person was claiming to be God, but nothing could be further from the truth.

Everyone who was part of the group understood that the person was conveying a fresh word he or she believed God was expressing to the group through the prophecy. No one believed the person giving the message was God or claiming to be God; no one believed the message or the messenger was infallible; and no one believed the prophecy was on par with the authority of Scripture. This is why Paul said, *"Do not stifle the Holy Spirit. Do not scoff at prophecies, but test everything that is said. Hold on to what is good"* (1 Thessalonians 5:19-21 NLT).

What the Holy Spirit expresses today is perfect at its source, but it is expressed through imperfect, fallible people. If prophecies in church services were infallible or carried the same authority of Scripture, they would need to be received without question, but that is not what the New Testament teaches. This is why Paul instructs the Corinthians—who tended to be unruly in their meetings and excessive in their practice of spiritual gifts—to have prophecies judged or evaluated by leaders in the congregation (1 Corinthians 14:29).

It is very important to recognize that even though the Corinthians misused and mismanaged spiritual gifts, Paul did not try to eradicate all such gifts; rather, he taught them how to use the gifts properly so that all could be edified. Paul did not believe that immature expressions of spiritual gifts invalidated the reality or benefit of spiritual gifts. The gifts needed to be used wisely and properly, not purged from the church.

If I say, "I am inspired to say something," I do not equate that to my belief regarding the Bible being inspired; the inspiration of Scripture is on a totally different level. Paul communicates, *"All Scripture is given by inspiration of God"* (2 Timothy 3:16). I appreciate Paul Enns' definition of this beautiful word:

> Inspiration may be defined as the Holy Spirit's superintending over the writers so that while writing according to their own styles and personalities, the result was God's Word written—authoritative, trustworthy, and free from error in the original autographs.[8]

With this in mind, whatever anyone may say, whether it be through teaching, preaching, exhortation, or prophecy, it is to be evaluated in the light of God's written Word—the Bible. If anyone's statements contradict Scripture, especially the teaching of the New Testament, they should be rejected.

Another charge against the Montanists is that they gave their prophecies while in an ecstatic or frenzied state. It is hard to tell exactly what this charge entailed, but a potentially rich source of insight on this issue has been lost to us. In defending the Montanists, Tertullian wrote seven books titled *Ecstasy*, but unfortunately, these were either lost or destroyed by theological opponents. It should be noted, though, that charging someone with giving ecstatic utterances could be a very subjective allegation.

In addition, people's personalities can vary significantly. What is mere excitement to one person might be considered frenzied to another. Even if some of the Montanists were overly emotionally charged at times, is that really reason to reject an entire movement? Too often people have "thrown out the baby with the bathwater," and in doing so, have missed great blessing.

What may have been a major source of conflict between the Montanists and the established, institutional church was the strong emphasis the Montanists placed on being led by the Holy Spirit as opposed to rigid church hierarchy. Philip Schaff writes:

> The Montanists found the true qualification and appointment for the office of teacher in direct endowment by the Spirit of God, in distinction from outward ordination and episcopal succession. They everywhere proposed the supernatural element and the free motion of the Spirit against the mechanism of a fixed ecclesiastical order.[9]

Two Great Church Leaders Weigh In

One of the reasons I am inclined to believe some of the allegations against the Montanists were exaggerated is because Tertullian, the great church father referenced in Chapter Five, threw his support behind the Montanists. He believed their spiritual experiences and expressions had value and merit. The brilliant theologian Tertullian points out that Montanus, Priscilla, and Maximilla were not rejected because of essential doctrinal points, saying that they did not "preach another God, nor that they disjoin Jesus Christ (from God), nor that they overturn any particular rule of faith or hope."[10] Rather, Tertullian insists they were rejected, at least by some, on issues of lesser importance, such as their views on fasting and marriage.

Likewise, John Wesley, a great student of history, wrote that he had become fully convinced:

That the Montanists, in the second and third centuries, were real, scriptural Christians; and, that the grand reason why the miraculous gifts were so soon withdrawn, was not only that faith and holiness were well-nigh lost; but that dry, formal, orthodox men began even then to ridicule whatever gifts they had not themselves, and to decry them all as either madness or imposture.[11]

Wesley faced some of the same types of criticisms that Montanus and his followers faced, and his work will be examined in Chapter Ten. Other supernaturally empowered ministries were to follow those of the Montanists.

Gregory Thaumaturgus (AD 213-270)

Gregory was born into a well-to-do family in Neocaesarea in the province of Pontus (modern Niksar in the nation of Turkey). Leaving his home country for additional education, Gregory studied under and was led to saving faith in Christ by Origen, whom we studied in Chapter Five. Distinguished New Testament scholar F. F. Bruce called Gregory "one of Origen's most illustrious and devoted pupils."[12] In vivid and dramatic language, Gregory gives testimony of his own conversion experience:

And thus, like some spark lighting upon our inmost soul, love was kindled and burst into flame within us—a love at once to the Holy Word, the most lovely object of all, who attracts all irresistibly toward Himself by His unutterable beauty...And being most mightily smitten by this love, I was persuaded to give up all those objects or pursuits which seem to us befitting....[13]

Church historian Justo Gonzalez notes that Gregory's "great evangelistic success was due, not to his theological arguments, but to the miracles he was said to perform." Gonzalez also remarks that Gregory was innovative in introducing a method that would be repeated by many others in later times, "he substituted Christian festivals for the old pagan ones, and made sure that the Christian celebrations outdid the others."[14]

Also called Gregory the Wonderworker, his impact and influence in Neocaesarea was nothing short of remarkable. Basil, whom we will look at later in this chapter, writes of Gregory:

> But where shall I rank the great Gregory, and the words uttered by him? Shall we not place among Apostles and Prophets a man who walked by the same Spirit as they; [2 Corinthians 12:18] who never through all his days diverged from the footprints of the saints; who maintained, as long as he lived, the exact principles of evangelical citizenship? I am sure that we shall do the truth a wrong if we refuse to number that soul with the people of God, shining as it did like a beacon in the Church of God; for by the fellow-working of the Spirit the power which he had over demons was tremendous, and so gifted was he with the grace of the word for obedience to the faith among...the nations, [Romans 1:5] that, although only seventeen Christians were handed over to him, he brought the whole people alike in town and country through knowledge to God.... Moreover his predictions of things to come were such as in no wise to fall short of those of the great prophets. To recount all his wonderful works in detail would be too long a task. By the superabundance of gifts, wrought in him by the Spirit in all power and in signs and in marvels, he was styled a second

Moses by the very enemies of the Church. Thus in all that he through grace accomplished, alike by word and deed, a light seemed ever to be shining, token of the heavenly power from the unseen which followed him.[15]

Basil's brother, Gregory of Nyssa, also speaks admirably of Gregory Thaumaturgus, acknowledging the significant impact of his ministry:

In the morning the common people were again at the doors, the same people plus women and children and those old in years and some of those whose body was plagued by demons or some other affliction; and he was in their midst sharing by the power of the Spirit in accord with the need of each in the crowd; proclaiming, discerning, directing, teaching, healing. For most of all he won the multitude over by proclamation, because vision coincided with hearing and the tokens of divine power illumined it through both. For his word amazed the hearing as his mighty deeds with the sick amazed the eyes.[16]

Gregory of Nyssa further remarked that Gregory "accomplished the healing types of miracles without any special fuss" and noted the number of miracles by saying, "To go through in order all the marvels worked by him would require a long book and a discourse exceeding the time we have now."[17]

Jerome referred to Gregory as "a man endowed with apostolic miracles as well as with apostolic virtues."[18]

Basil of Caesarea (AD 329-379)

Church historian Stanley Burgess states that Basil's "grasp of the full range of the Holy Spirit's work in the life of the believer is perhaps the most exceptional in the ancient world."[19] The modern city of Kayseri in central Turkey was once known as Caesarea in Cappadocia; it was the birthplace of Basil. Often called "Basil the Great," this church father is known for writing guidelines for monastic communal living, combatting Arianism (the teaching that Jesus is less than divine), and was also a powerful advocate for the divinity of the Holy Spirit.

In his writings, Basil presents a very balanced view of good doctrine, the operations of the Holy Spirit, and the need for the corporate benefit of all believers in the local congregation. For example, he states, "And when the stream of doctrine is gushing forth in the Church and a devout heart is welling up with the gifts of the Holy Spirit, do you not gladly give your attention? Do you not receive this favor with thanksgiving?"[20]

In another place, Basil refers to many of the spiritual gifts to which Paul refers—word of wisdom, word of knowledge, faith, prophecy, and "the grace of healing"—and remarks, "He who receives any of these gifts does not possess it for his own sake but rather for the sake of others, so that, in the life passed in community, the operation of the Holy Spirit in the individual is at the same time necessarily transmitted to all."[21]

Basil was very clear in recognizing the gifts of the Holy Spirit that were operating in the church in his day. He asserts that the "working of miracles, and gifts of healing are through the Holy Spirit."[22] His keen insight into the presence and operation of the Holy Spirit is also seen in this statement:

> And as the art in him who has acquired it, so is the grace of the Spirit in the recipient ever present, though not continuously in operation. For as the art is potentially in the artist, but only in operation when he is working in accordance with it, so also the Spirit is ever present with those that are worthy, but works, as need requires, in prophecies, or in healings, or in some other actual carrying into effect of His potential action.[23]

Basil also embraced Jesus' principle of "freely you have received, freely give" (Matthew 10:8) as it related to operating in the gifts of the Holy Spirit. After referring to the different manifestations listed in 1 Corinthians 12:7-10, Basil writes, "Since the gift of God is received as a free gift, it is our duty to share it freely and not make it a means of profit for self-gratification."[24] None of these statements by Basil would make sense unless the gifts of the Holy Spirit were in operation in his day.

While Basil spoke frequently of the Holy Spirit, he did not do so to the exclusion of the Father and the Son; he also spoke beautifully of the cooperative working of the Trinity. In this statement, he speaks eloquently of the work of the Son:

> Those that have lapsed from the lofty height of life into sin, He raises from their fall: for this reason He is Resurrection (John 11:25). Effectually working by the touch of His power and the will of His goodness, He does all things. He shepherds; He enlightens; He nourishes; He heals; He guides; He raises up; He calls into being things that were not; He upholds what has been created. Thus the good things that come from God reach us through the Son, who works in each case with greater speed than speech can utter.[25]

These types of assertions by Basil indicate his profound appreciation for the personal and present supernatural workings of God in the lives of individuals and in the life of the church.

John Chrysostom (AD 349-407)

John Chrysostom was born, raised, and educated in Antioch, where believers were first called Christians (Acts 11:26). He served as both a deacon and as a preacher in the church of Antioch, and developed a reputation as a gifted orator who boldly and fearlessly confronted sin both in society and in the church, sometimes to his own peril. "Chrysostom" was not his last name, but rather a nickname meaning "golden mouth" in Greek. In AD 398, the Emperor Arcadius appointed Chrysostom as the Bishop of Constantinople, a position he did not desire, but accepted the position believing it to be God's will.

The timing involved of Chrysostom becoming the Bishop of Constantinople is very significant in the light of three major events in the history of the Roman Empire:

- In 313, the Emperor Constantine signed the Edict of Milan that provided for the toleration of all religions and outlawing persecution based on one's faith, especially for Christians.

- In 330, Constantine moved the capital away from Rome and relocated it to Byzantium. It was later named Constantinople. This is the city of Istanbul in Turkey today.

- In 380, the Emperor Theodosius decreed that Orthodox Christianity was to be the official religion of the Roman Empire. This elevated Christianity above all other faiths, and had negative ramifications for those of other faiths.

Many noted that with the "success" of Christianity came a significant decline in the overall spirituality of the church. Jerome (AD 347-420), best known for translating the Scripture into Latin, contrasts the church under persecution with the church that gained favored social status and recognition. In its early days, "[The church] as it gained strength, grew by persecution and was crowned with martyrdom," Jerome continues, "then, after reaching the Christian emperors, how it increased in influence and wealth but decreased in Christian virtues."[26]

More recently, author and church historian Eddie Hyatt describes the chilling effect that came about when the government made Christianity the official religion of the empire:

> As a result, hordes of unconverted pagans filled the churches, bringing with them heathen ideas and practices. Moral laxity, already having fractured the pristine nature of the church, now dominated much of her life.[27]

It was into this type of scenario, in the Imperial City itself, that the "golden mouthed" preacher found himself, and he was not one who would compromise with evil and unrighteousness.

Chrysostom wasted no time in seeking to bring reform and godliness into the church and the city. He was a strong advocate of righteousness, and even preached against sin among the clergy, including the decadent practice of unmarried priests cohabiting with "spiritual sisters." While some were pleased with his bold preaching, many among the elite resented him, including Eudoxia, the emperor's ambitious and self-indulgent wife. Existing tensions erupted when the empress had a statue of herself placed next to the Hagia Sophia, the elegant cathedral where Chrysostom preached. He responded by likening her to Herodias in a sermon. Chrysostom was then banished from Constantinople and later died in exile.

Chrysostom did speak of many who "have put away diseases by anointing themselves with oil in faith and in due season."[28] However, unlike most referred to in this book, Chrysostom made certain statements that seem to imply his belief that miracles and the gifts of the Spirit had ceased. For example, in teaching on 1 Corinthians 12:1, he states:

> Now concerning spiritual gifts, brethren, I would not have you ignorant.... This whole place is very obscure: but the

obscurity is produced by our ignorance of the facts referred to and by their cessation, being such as then used to occur but now no longer take place.[29]

Understandably, those who believe that the Holy Spirit withdrew His miraculous and extraordinary gifts at some point in the early years of the church will cite this and a few other statements by Chrysostom to support their view.

It is important to ask a clarifying question here. Did the cessation of spiritual gifts that Chrysostom speaks of happen because God sovereignly withdrew the gifts of the Spirit from the church-at-large, or did this cessation happen because the Christians in Constantinople, perhaps some in name only, had badly neglected the Holy Spirit and His work? In other words, was Chrysostom making an absolute doctrinal statement regarding a sovereign decree of God, or was he grieving over a church that had persistently ignored the Holy Spirit and had consistently refused to allow the Spirit to work as he desired?

Based on the fact that other ministers throughout the Mediterranean world, such as Basil of Caesarea, Martin of Tours, and Augustine of Hippo, were reporting miracles and supernatural workings of God around the same time, I am strongly inclined to go with the latter explanation—that those in the church were so distant in their fellowship from God that they no longer welcomed the Holy Spirit, thus the basis for Chrysostom's statements.

Consider Chrysostom's descriptions of the spiritual condition in Constantinople and consider if this was the kind of environment where the Holy Spirit was welcome to move, or if this was a place where the Spirit would have been quenched, resisted, and grieved. He speaks of his ministry, "My work is like that of a man who is trying to clean a piece of ground into which a muddy stream is constantly flowing."[30]

Chrysostom reflects back on the unity of the church in previous times, when there was "one soul and one heart," but then highlights the stark contrast, saying "now not in one single soul can one see that unanimity, rather great is the warfare every where."[31] He also speaks of the disrespectful and irreverent attitude in the church saying, "Here great is the tumult, great the confusion, and our assemblies differ in nothing from a vintner's [wine maker's] shop, so loud is the laughter, so great the disturbance; as in baths, as in markets, the cry and tumult is universal."[32]

In contrast to this grim description of the way the church was, Chrysostom also paints of picture of what the church was intended to be: "For the church is no barber's or perfumer's shop, nor any other merchant's warehouse in the marketplace, but a place of angels, a place of archangels, a palace of God, heaven itself." Chrysostom also describes the disdain people had for the word of God that was preached: "When God is speaking from heaven…we behave ourselves more impudently than dogs, and even to the harlot women we pay greater respect than to God."[33]

In yet another place, after describing the provocative dress of women in the church and those who were thereby seduced, Chrysostom decries the worldliness, carnality corrupting influence that was prevalent in the church:

> If any one is trying or intending to corrupt a woman, there is no place, I suppose, that seems to him more suitable than the church. And if anything be to be sold or bought, the church appears more convenient than the market. For on such subjects also there is more talk here than in the shops themselves. Or if any wish to say or to hear any scandal, you will find that this too is to be had here more than in the forum [marketplace] without. And if you wish to hear any

thing of political matters, or the affairs of private families, or the camp, go not to the judgment-hall, nor sit in the apothecary's shop; for here, here I say are those who report all these things more accurately; and our assemblies are any thing rather than a church.[34]

What an indictment! Chrysostom even used the analogy of the destruction from horrible storms at sea to describe what was happening in the church of his day: "so also when the Church has admitted corrupt men, its once tranquil surface is covered with rough surf and strewn with shipwrecks."[35]

Perhaps the most telling statement Chrysostom makes is in his commentary on 1 Corinthians 14, a chapter that deals extensively with the vocal gifts of the Spirit—prophecy, tongues, and interpretation. While the context of his remarks pertain to the gifts of the Spirit, he makes it clear that he is also referencing the life and the virtue of the church, and he contrasts the way the church used to be compared to how it had declined in his days:

> What now can be more awful than these things? For in truth the Church was a heaven then, the Spirit governing all things, and moving each one of the rulers and making him inspired. But now we retain only the symbols of those gifts.... But the present Church is like a woman who hath fallen from her former prosperous days, and in many respects retains the symbols only of that ancient prosperity...but bereft of her wealth: such an one doth the present Church resemble...now she is made desolate and void, and the tokens only remain.[36]

More than anything, it seems that Chrysostom was bemoaning how far the church in his day was from God's plan, how distant it was from its own potential. Recognizing that so many had not yielded and aligned their lives to God's will, he writes, "Were we all partakers of the Spirit, as we ought to be partakers, then should we behold heaven, and the order of things that is there."[37]

More than thirteen centuries later, John Wesley would express his opinion on why the extraordinary gifts of the Spirit had diminished. Speaking of the diminishing of the gifts of the Spirit in the church at large, Wesley writes of the significant decline that occurred:

> ...after that fatal period when the Emperor Constantine called himself a Christian; and, from a vain imagination of promoting the Christian cause thereby, heaped riches and power and honor upon the Christians in general, but in particular upon the Christian Clergy. From this time they almost totally ceased; very few instances of the kind were found. The cause of this was not, (as has been vulgarly supposed,) "because there was no more occasion for them," because all the world was become Christians. This is a miserable mistake; not a twentieth part of it was then nominally Christian. The real cause was, "the love of many," almost of all Christians, so called, was "waxed cold." The Christians had no more of the Spirit of Christ than the other heathens the Son of Man, when he came to examine his Church, could hardly "find faith upon earth." This was the real cause why the extraordinary gifts of the Holy Ghost were no longer to be found in the Christian Church; because the Christians were turned Heathens again, and had only a dead form left.[38]

Wesley saw the power and supernatural works of God in his life and ministry, and these events will be explored later in Chapter Ten.

In Chrysostom's case, he clearly made various statements about the absence of the gifts of the Spirit in his day. However, the condition of the church that he vividly and painfully describes is one that was highly resistant to both the Holy Spirit and His works. Fortunately, in many other locations around the world, people would welcome the Holy Spirit and His gifts. In those places we do see mighty signs and wonders accompanying the preaching of the glorious gospel—before, during, and after the time of John Chrysostom.

Endnotes

1. F. F. Bruce, *The Spreading Flame: The Rise and Progress of Christianity From its First Beginnings to Eighth-Century England* (Nashville, TN: Kingsley Books, 1981), loc. 4949, Kindle.

2. Philip Schaff, *The History of the Christian Church*, vol. II (Grand Rapids, MI: Eerdmans, 1910), 421.

3. Bruce, *The Spreading Flame*, loc. 5049, Kindle.

4. Bruce L. Shelley, *Church History in Plain Language* (Nashville, TN: Thomas Nelson Publishers, www.thomasnelson.com, 2008), 64, Kindle. Used by permission of Thomas Nelson.

5. Schaff, *The History of the Christian Church*, vol. II, 418.

6. Eusebius, *The Church History*, 169.

7. Ibid., 170.

8. Paul Enns, *The Moody Handbook of Theology* (Chicago: Moody Publishers, 2014), 163, Kindle.

9. Schaff, *The History of the Christian Church*, vol. II, 424.

10. Tertullian, *On Fasting, In Opposition to the Psychics*, in *The Works of Tertullian*, ed. Alexander Roberts, trans. Sir James Donaldson and Arthur Cleveland Coxe (Seattle, WA: Amazon Digital Services, 1885), loc. 13622.

11. John Wesley, *Journal*, August 15, 1750, *The Works of John Wesley*, vol. II (Grand Rapids, MI: Baker Book House, 1986), 204.

12. Bruce, *The Spreading Flame*, loc. 7234, Kindle.

13. Gregory Thaumaturgus, *Oration and Panegyric Addressed to Origen*, Argument 6, in *The Complete Works of Gregory Thaumaturgus* (Seattle, WA: Amazon Digital Services, 2016), loc 727, Kindle.

14. Justo L. Gonzalez, *The Story of Christianity*, vol. I (New York: HarperCollins e-books, 2014), 115-116.

15. Basil, De Spiritu Sancto, Chapter 29, in *The Complete Works of Saint Basil* (Seattle, WA: Amazon Digital Services, 2016), loc. 3453, Kindle.

16. Gregory of Nyssa, *On the Life and Wonders of Our Father Among the Saints, Gregory the Wonderworker*, in *St. Gregory Thaumaturgus: Life and Works*, trans. Michael Slusser (Washington, DC: The Catholic University of America Press, 1998), 61.

17. Ibid., 75.

18. Jerome, *The Complete Works of Saint Jerome*, Letter 70 (Seattle, WA: Amazon Digital Services, 2016), Loc. 5819, Kindle.

19. Stanley Burgess, ed. *Christian Peoples of the Spirit: A Documentary History of Pentecostal Spirituality from the Early Church to the Present* (New York: New York University Press, 2011), 63.

20. Basil, *Ascetical Works, Homily 11, Concerning Envy*, in *The Complete Works of Saint Basil* (Seattle, WA: Amazon Digital Services, 2016), loc. 17693, Kindle.

21. Basil, *Ascetical Works, The Long Rules*, in *The Complete Works of Saint Basil* (Seattle, WA: Amazon Digital Services, 2016), loc. 14787, Kindle.

22. Basil, De Spiritu Sancto, in *The Complete Works of Saint Basil* (Seattle, WA: Amazon Digital Services, 2016), loc. 2960, Kindle.

23. Basil, De Spiritu Sancto, in *The Complete Works of Saint Basil* (Seattle, WA: Amazon Digital Services, 2016), loc. 3206, Kindle.

24. Basil, *Ascetical Works, The Morals*, in *The Complete Works of Saint Basil* (Seattle, WA: Amazon Digital Services, 2016), loc. 13428, Kindle.

25. Basil, De Spiritu Sancto, in *The Complete Works of Saint Basil* (Seattle, WA: Amazon Digital Services, 2016), loc. 2377, Kindle.

26. Jerome, *Life of Malchus*, in *The Complete Works of Saint Jerome* (Seattle, WA: Amazon Digital Services, 2016), Loc. 14817, Kindle.

27. Eddie L. Hyatt, *2000 Years of Charismatic Church History: A 21st Century Look at Church History From a Pentecostal/Charismatic Perspective* (Lake Mary, FL: Charisma House, 2002), 34, Kindle.

28. John Chrysostom, *Homily XXXII, Matthew 9:27-30*, in *The Complete Works of Saint John Chrysostom*, trans. Philip Schaff (Seattle, WA: Amazon Digital Services, 2011), loc. 33650, Kindle.

29. John Chrysostom, *Homily XXIX, 1 Corinthians 12:1-2*, in *The Complete Works of Saint John Chrysostom*, trans. Philip Schaff (Seattle, WA: Amazon Digital Services, 2011), loc. 68597, Kindle.

30. Kevin Dale Miller, *Did You Know? Little Known and Remarkable Facts About John Chrysostom*, Christian History, Issue 44 (1994), 2.

31. John Chrysostom, *Homily XXXVI, 1 Corinthians 14:20*, in *The Complete Works of Saint John Chrysostom*, trans. Philip Schaff (Seattle, WA: Amazon Digital Services, 2011), loc. 71285, Kindle.

32. Ibid., loc. 71292, Kindle.

33. Ibid., loc. 71295, Kindle.

34. Ibid., loc. 71325, Kindle.

35. John Chrysostom, *Treatise on the Priesthood*, in *The Complete Works of Saint John Chrysostom*, trans. Philip Schaff in1886 (Seattle, WA: Amazon Digital Services, 2011), loc. 154064, Kindle.

36. Chrysostom, *Homily XXXVI*, loc. 71254, Kindle.

37. John Chrysostom, *Homily II, Ephesians 1:11-14*, in *The Complete Works of Saint John Chrysostom*, trans. Philip Schaff (Seattle, WA: Amazon Digital Services, 2011), loc. 115746, Kindle.

38. John Wesley, *The More Excellent Way*, Sermon 89, in *The Works of John Wesley*, vol. 7, (Grand Rapids, MI: Baker Book House, 1986), 26-27.

CHAPTER SEVEN

GOD IN GAUL (FRANCE)

> *How truly is the manifestation of the Spirit seen in the bestowal of such useful gifts!*
>
> —**Hilary of Poitiers**

WE discussed in Chapter Three a great spiritual leader, Irenaeus of Lyons, who ministered powerfully in Gaul, which is modern-day France. Polycarp of Smyrna, a disciple of the apostle John, sent Irenaeus to assume spiritual leadership in Lyons. But this land was to know other great ministers as well who would carry and minister the power of God's Spirit.

Hilary of Poitiers (AD 310-367)

The city of Poitiers, located in west-central France, was the home of an influential bishop named Hilary in the fourth century. This church leader was most well known as defender of Nicene orthodoxy, which means he stood in favor of the deity of Christ in contrast to the Arians who believed Jesus was not equal to or of the same substance as the

Father. So strong was his defense of truth that he was often referred to as the "Athanasius of the West."

His unyielding defense of the faith resulted in him being exiled to Phrygia (modern-day Turkey) for nearly four years, and yet he remained a powerful influence through his writings. Even though Hilary is primarily remembered for his grasp on and defense of solid doctrine, he also spoke powerfully regarding the work of the Holy Spirit. Hilary honored the role of the Holy Spirit in illuminating the mind of the believer as to the meaning of Scripture, trusting Him to unveil and reveal even the nuanced meanings of God's Word.

In praying to the Lord God Almighty, Hilary writes, "We look to you to give us that fellowship of that Spirit who guided the Prophets and the Apostles, that we may take their words in the right sense in which they spoke and assign its right shade of meaning to every utterance."[1]

Hilary also spoke of the operation and working of the gifts of the Holy Spirit; and in doing so, he repeatedly used the word "we," meaning that he and those of his generation were experiencing these gifts and their benefits. In his classic work, *On the Trinity*, Hilary writes:

> It is by these miraculous workings that the manifestation of the Spirit takes place. For the gift of the Spirit is manifest, where wisdom makes utterance and the words of life are heard, and where there is the knowledge that comes of God-given insight...or by faith in God, lest by not believing the Gospel of God, we should be outside His Gospel; or by the gift of healings, that by the cure of diseases we should bear witness to His grace Who bestows these things; or by the working of miracles, that what we do may be understood to be the power of God, or by prophesy, that through our understanding of doctrine we might be known to be taught

of God; or by discerning of spirits, that we should not be unable to tell whether any one speaks with a holy or a perverted spirit; or by kinds of tongues, that the speaking in tongues may be bestowed as a sign of the gift of the Holy Spirit; or by the interpretation of tongues, that the faith of those that hear may not be imperiled through ignorance, since the interpreter of a tongue explains the tongue to those who are ignorant of it. Thus in all these things distributed to each one to profit withal there is the manifestation of the Spirit, the gift of the Spirit being apparent through these marvelous advantages bestowed upon each.[2]

Then, after listing the gifts of the Spirit found in 1 Corinthians 12:8-10, Hilary states, "Clearly these are the Church's agents of ministry and work of whom the body of Christ consists; and God has ordained them."[3] He also remarks, "How truly is the manifestation of the Spirit seen in the bestowal of such useful gifts!"[4]

Martin of Tours (AD 316-397)

Originally from Pannonia in modern-day Hungary and western Austria, Martin became a Christian at young age; and after a stint in the Roman army, he departed and studied under Hilary in Poitiers. He was eventually appointed as the pastor of the church in Tours, around sixty-four miles from Poitiers; but even before that, Martin had gained a reputation as one mightily used in healing and exorcism. Even though he was a monk prior to assuming his pastoral role, Martin did not isolate himself from the world. Noted scholar F. F. Bruce observes:

Martin did not use his monastic preferences as a pretext for complete withdrawal from the world. On the contrary, he made Tours the center of an intensive campaign for the evangelization of the heathen Gauls, as a result of which the frontiers of his bishopric were greatly extended.[5]

As a close associate of Martin's, Sulpicius Severus chronicled many events from Martin's life, speaking admirably of both his character and his work.

Severus speaks of Martin "displaying a kind of heavenly happiness in his countenance,"[6] and said, "no language can ever be capable of describing his inner life and daily conduct, and his mind always bent upon the things of heaven."[7] In addition to describing Martin's peaceful demeanor and diligence in prayer, Severus highlighted supernatural power that was expressed through Martin's ministry. For example, he writes:

> The gift of accomplishing cures was so largely possessed by Martin, that scarcely any sick person came to him for assistance without being at once restored to health.[8]
>
> This fact, too, ought not to be passed over in silence, that threads from Martin's garment, or such as had been plucked from the sackcloth which he wore, wrought frequent miracles upon those who were sick. For, by either being tied round the fingers or placed about the neck, they very often drove away diseases from the afflicted.[9]

In this biography, numerous healings and deliverances are documented, and Severus also notes that Martin often perceived things before they happened and "disclosed the things which had been revealed to him to the brethren."[10] As he cites various supernatural works that God did through Martin, he states that he is only communicating a "few out of a multitude"[11] and indicates he chose to report only a limited number of divine interventions because he did not want to wear out his readers with too many examples.

Martin's biographer also notes the effectiveness of Martin's ministry in communicating the gospel of Christ and establishing churches. He writes:

> Certainly, before the times of Martin, very few, nay, almost none, in those regions had received the name of Christ; but through his virtues and example that name has prevailed to such an extent, that now there is no place thereabouts which is not filled either with very crowded churches or monasteries. For wherever he destroyed heathen temples, there he used immediately to build either churches or monasteries.[12]

Bernard of Clairvaux (1090-1153)

Born in eastern France, Bernard was a prolific and eloquent writer. He was an abbot (the head of a Cistercian monastery) who exerted tremendous influence. One of Bernard's colleagues said, "His life is full of things admirable and worthy of praise. Some admire his teaching, others his character, others his miracles, and I render honor to all these."[13] When a minister has supernatural works operating through his life, he can become prideful, but Bernard maintained great humility and godly character throughout his life. One of Bernard's contemporaries writes:

> And when his actions and his words were supported even by miracles, which is a thing still more glorious, he was never thrown off his balance, never thought of himself more highly than he ought. On the contrary, he always thought humbly of himself, considered himself not the author, but

the instrument, of mighty works; and when in the universal judgment he was raised above all, he was the lowest of all in his own.[14]

Of Bernard's miraculous works, it is said, "the possessed, the blind, the deaf and dumb, the fever stricken, and even the dying, he cured by the laying on of his hands." It was also noted, He is said to have once performed thirty-six miraculous cures in a single day; and it was calculated that during this Rhineland mission he healed an average of thirty persons daily."[15]

Bernard demonstrated highly developed insights into the person and work of the Holy Spirit. In a sermon, "On the Two Operations of the Holy Spirit," he writes:

> For He not only fortifies us interiorly with virtues, unto our own salvation, but He also adorns us exteriorly with His gifts, unto the salvation of others. The former are bestowed upon us for our own sakes, the latter with a view to our neighbor's advantage. For instance, we obtain faith, hope, and charity for ourselves, as without them salvation is impossible. On the other hand, the word of wisdom and knowledge, the grace of healing, the gift of prophecy, and the like, which are in no sense necessary to the saving of our own souls, are communicated, doubtless, to be employed in promoting the spiritual interests of others. These operations or graces of the Holy Spirit, experienced in ourselves or in others, I will, if you allow me, call Infusion and Effusion, respectively, deriving the names from the ends for which they are bestowed.[16]

At the end of that same message, Bernard affirms, "Behold now how much has to be poured into us in order that we may venture to pour out."[17] As a young Bible school student, I heard teachings about "the Spirit within" and "the Spirit upon," and while such messages were derived from Scripture, I did not realize that medieval church leaders like Bernard were powerfully and clearly articulating the same ideas many centuries before.

The presence of spiritual gifts operating in the Cistercian order, of which Bernard was a key influencer, is reflected in remarks made to them in a letter from Pope Eugenius. Referring back to historical and biblical saints, he writes:

> Truly they received the first fruits of the Spirit, and their pleasant ointment has run down even to us. If you have received diversities of tongues, grace for working healings, knowledge of prophesying, if your words are more fragrant than the most costly ointments, if the world honors you and takes pleasure in running in the odor of your ointments, it is all nothing but the work of Him who says, "My Father has been working until now, and I have been working" (John 5:17).[18]

Such a statement reflects a very mature understanding of the reason the gifts were given, and a commitment to holding fast to their divine purpose. These were the gracious workings of the Holy Spirit and were not intended to exalt a person or a group.

Bernard also recognized that the more subtle workings of the Holy Spirit are to be appreciated, not just the more dramatic or sensational operations. He wisely writes:

Be neither slow nor slack in expressing your gratitude; learn to render thanks for every favor bestowed. "Consider diligently what is set before your face," so that none of the gifts of God, the ordinary no more than the extraordinary, the least no more than the greatest, may fail to be duly and gratefully acknowledged. Remember that we are ordered to "gather up the fragments, lest they be lost." That is to say, we are required to return thanks for even the very smallest of God's favors. For we always lose the benefit of divine graces when we neglect to requite them with thanksgiving. Ingratitude is the enemy of the soul, the extinguisher of merits, the destroyer of virtues, the waster of benefits. Ingratitude is a burning wind that dries up the fountains of piety, and the dews of mercy, and the springs of grace.[19]

Bernard clearly advocated glorifying God and having a heart full of gratitude for everything God does. He was not dismissive of the nuanced expressions of God's kindness.

Peter Waldo (1140-1218)

Born just thirteen years before the death of Bernard of Clairvaux, Peter Waldo was a wealthy merchant from the city of Lyons, France, the same city where Irenaeus had ministered around a thousand years earlier. Deeply moved by a gospel presentation on the street, Waldo liquidated his earthly assets, gave extravagantly to the poor, and funded the translation of Scripture into the language of his people.

Waldo and his followers—known as the Waldensians—not only believed that the Bible should be available in one's native tongue, but that Scripture should be the standard of authority in determining truth. As

Waldo studied the Bible, he was astonished that many of the beliefs taught by the institutional church were not supported in Scripture. Noting the excommunication and eventual persecution of the Waldensians by the established church, theologian Gregg Allison explains:

> Among the beliefs and practices for which the Waldensians were condemned were a refusal to submit to bishops and to obey the pope, whom they denied was the head of the Catholic Church because of his corruption; a denial of masses for the dead, prayer by the saints for Christians on earth, and the doctrine of purgatory; establishment of their own hierarchy; and a ministry in which even laypeople could pray, hear confessions of sin, and administer the sacraments.[20]

Peter Waldo was not the first to find fault with teachings and practices in the institutional church. Bernard before him expressed his disagreement with the Immaculate Conception; he believed that only Jesus—not Mary—was born sinless. After Waldo, other voices of dissent would arise such as Jan Hus, John Wycliffe, Girolamo Savonarola, and Martin Luther.

Waldo was also a strong proponent of voluntary poverty and preaching God's Word in public. With the Waldensians' commitment to the authority of Scripture, it is not surprising that when they released a confession of faith in 1431, it included a strong and distinct reference to divine healing through the anointing of oil.

> Therefore, concerning this anointing of the sick, we hold it as an article of faith, and profess sincerely from the heart, that sick persons, when they ask it, may lawfully be anointed with the anointing oil, by one who joins with them in praying that

it may be efficacious to the healing of the body, according to the design and end and effect mentioned by the Apostles, and we profess that such an anointing, performed according to the Apostolic design and practice, will be healing and profitable.[21]

Endnotes

1. Hilary, *On the Trinity*, in *The Complete Works of the Church Fathers*, ed. Philip Schaff (Seattle, WA: Amazon Digital Services, 2016), loc. 307025, Kindle.

2. Ibid., loc. 310322, Kindle.

3. Ibid., loc. 310359, Kindle.

4. Ibid., loc. 310374, Kindle.

5. Bruce, *The Spreading Flame*, loc. 8030, Kindle.

6. Sulpicius Severus, *The Life of St. Martin*, in *The Complete Ante-Nicene, Nicene and Post-Nicene Collection of Early Church Fathers*, ed. Philip Schaff (Seattle, WA: Amazon Digital Services), loc. 479623, Kindle.

7. Ibid., loc. 479613, Kindle.

8. Ibid., loc. 479439, Kindle.

9. Ibid., loc. 479479, Kindle.

10. Ibid., loc. 479530, Kindle.

11. Ibid., loc. 479492, Kindle.

12. Ibid., loc. 479407, Kindle.

13. Bernard, *Life and Works of Saint Bernard*, vol. 1, in *The Saint Bernard of Clairvaux Collection* (New York: Aeterna Press, 2016), loc. 2694, Kindle.

14. Ibid., loc. 2701, Kindle.

15. Ibid.

16. Bernard, *Sermons on the Canticle of Canticles*, vol. 1, Sermon XVIII, On the Two

Operations of the Holy Ghost, in *The Saint Bernard of Clairvaux Collection* (New York: Aeterna Press, 2016), loc. 25482, Kindle.

17. Ibid., loc. 22570, Kindle.

18. Eugenius, *A Letter of Pope Eugenius to the Cistercian Chapter*, in *The Saint Bernard of Clairvaux Collection* (New York: Aeterna Press, 2016), loc. 12927 and 12936, Kindle.

19. Bernard, *Sermons on the Canticle of Canticles*, vol. 1, Sermon LI in, *The Saint Bernard of Clairvaux Collection* (New York: Aeterna Press, 2016), loc. 30013, Kindle.

20. Gregg Allison, *Historical Theology: An Introduction to Christian Doctrine* (Grand Rapids, MI: Zondervan, 2011), loc. 17502, Kindle. Used by permission of Zondervan. www.zondervan.com

21. Thomas Boys, *The Suppressed Evidence: Proofs of the Miraculous Faith and Experience of the Church of Christ in All Ages* (London: Hamilton, Adams, and Company, 1832), 56.

CHAPTER EIGHT

THE SPIRIT'S FLAME IN THE REFORMATION

The Holy Spirit has called me through the Gospel, enlightened me with his gifts, and sanctified and preserved me in true faith, just as he calls, gathers, enlightens and sanctifies the whole Christian church on earth and preserves it in union with Jesus Christ in the one true faith.

—**Martin Luther**

Martin Luther (1483-1546)

PERHAPS no other name is as well known in the history of the Church as that of the boisterous and disruptive reformer, Martin Luther. A brilliant student of law, Luther had a terrifying experience in a thunderstorm, and vowing to become a monk, he joined the Augustinians. Perpetually troubled by guilt and fearful of the judgment of God, Luther applied himself most rigorously to achieve salvation by religious works, confession of sins with accompanying acts of penance, and by receiving the sacraments. All of this represented his attempt to earn the favor of God; and Luther said that if anyone could have earned Heaven by the life of a monk, it would have been him.

His rigorous ascetic practices included self-flagellation, self-imposed sleep deprivation, extreme fasting, and denying himself personal comfort, such as deliberately sleeping in the cold without a blanket. Luther had serious internal problems later in life, and this could have been brought on by damage he did to his own system during this season of his life. He said, "If I had kept on any longer, I would have killed myself with vigils, prayers, readings, and other good works."[1]

After years of spiritual struggle, Luther eventually found in Scripture the peace and assurance of salvation he had desperately sought. While a professor of theology at Wittenberg University, he came to understand salvation and forgiveness in a radically different way than through the lens of religious works. The key verse in Luther's personal transformation was Romans 1:17, which reads, *"For in it* [the gospel] *the righteousness of God is revealed from faith to faith; as it is written, 'The just shall live by faith.'"* Luther had always been distressed regarding the righteousness of God, because he knew that he fell far short of it. But now, a new understanding came. Luther writes:

> At last, by the mercy of God meditating day and night...I began to understand that the righteousness of God is that through which the righteous lives by a gift of God, namely by faith. Here I felt that I was altogether born again and had entered paradise itself through open gates.[2]

This scriptural insight would soon fuel a movement that would radically change the world.

Matters went public on October 31, 1517. Luther had become increasingly grieved with a form of church fundraising that involved the selling of indulgences, and Luther posted what are called the 95 *Theses* on the door of the Wittenberg church. In these propositions, Luther argued against the practice of the church selling these documents that purportedly authorized the release of individuals—the purchaser, or someone the purchaser designated—from time in purgatory.

Even though Luther wrote these grievances in Latin to invite discussion and debate among scholars, the 95 *Theses* were soon translated into German and other European languages and were distributed throughout the continent. Luther questioned the authority of the pope to sell indulgences, and argued that if the pope actually had such authority, why did he not grant that forgiveness based on love as opposed to doing it for money.

Eventually, Luther, the German priest, pastor, and professor, was condemned and excommunicated from the church, but Luther's influence was felt far and wide. His writings inspired many other reformers who would preach the same types of truth throughout Europe.

THE FIVE SOLAS

Critics of Luther can rightly cite his flaws, but he did an incalculably beneficial service in calling the church back to its biblical roots. The effects of Luther's ministry and that of other reformers can be summarized by the five *solas*:

- *Sola Scriptura*: The Bible alone is our highest authority— Scripture alone is the infallible guide in matters of God's revelation to man. Anything taught by man that contradicts Scripture is to be rejected.

- *Sola Gratia*: We are saved by the grace of God alone— salvation is given by God's grace and is not earned by the merits or works of man. Salvation is initiated entirely by God and what He did in sending Jesus.

- *Sola Fide:* We are saved through faith alone in Jesus Christ—God's grace-based salvation is received only by faith and not by works. Salvation cannot be earned by man's religious activities.

- *Solus Christus:* We trust in the Lord Jesus Christ alone for our salvation—He alone is the mediator between God and man—there is salvation in no one else. Salvation comes through Christ alone, not from any other man.

- *Soli Deo Gloria:* We are to live for the glory of God only—every part of the Christian life should express God's glory. Glorifying God, not pursuing the approval of man, is the purpose of our existence.

While Luther is primarily known for the message of justification by faith—that man enters into right standing with God by faith and not by works—the German monk-turned-reformer had various experiences that were supernatural in nature.

Theologically, Luther and other reformers had a problem with alleged healings and miracles in their day because, at least in part, so many of these claims were related to what they believed were grievous errors of the institutional church. Many healings, legitimate or not, were connected to relics, which in turn were usually connected to financial offerings. Miracles were often connected to unbiblical superstitions and prayers to the saints. Also, miracles were leveraged to defend the veracity of the institutional church and its doctrines.

Craig Keener makes note of the religious clutter that existed in Luther's time:

Some medieval practices pervasive by the time of the Protestant Reformation, such as traffic in authentic relics for pecuniary [financial] motives.... Medieval relics of various sorts include a piece of the bread from which Jesus fed the five thousand; competing sites' claims to hold Jesus's robe; the (strangely multiplying) remains of the "true cross" its somehow multiplying nails; the crown of thorns; multiple versions of the holy lance that pierced Jesus' side; his holy tears; some of his hair; some of the Savior's mopped-up blood; still more splendid, one of Jesus's baby teeth; his newborn umbilical cord; and last but not least, eight sites' claims to possess the holy prepuce left over from his circumcision.[3]

A contemporary of Luther named Erasmus satirically said that there were enough pieces of the true cross in Europe to rebuild Noah's Ark. Luther himself said:

> What lies there are about relics! One claims to have a feather from the wing of the angel Gabriel, and the Bishop of Mainz has a flame from Moses' burning bush. And how does it happen that eighteen apostles are buried in Germany when Christ had only twelve?[4]

In spite of Luther's disdain for counterfeit claims, as a pastor he was often moved with compassion and faith to pray for people to be healed and to recover. In one instance, Luther visited a woman who had long suffered severe seizures. *Table Talk* records, "Luther sighed and said: 'God rebuke thee, Satan, and commend thee that thou suffer this, his divine creature to be at peace.'"[5] After further prayer, it is noted, "The night following she took rest, and the next day was graciously delivered from her disease and sickness."[6]

In one case, Luther writes to a pastor in a nearby town and shares the advice on how to minister to a man in his congregation who was suffering from what Luther said was "not a case of ordinary melancholy." He tells the pastor:

> This must be counteracted by the power of Christ and with the prayer of faith. This is what we do—and we have been accustomed to it, for a cabinet maker here was similarly afflicted with madness, and we cured him by prayer in Christ's name.[7]

In addition, powerful testimonies remain of the dramatic and remarkable healing of two of Luther's associates, Philip Melanchthon and Friedrich Myconius, both of whom were gravely ill when Luther prayed for their recoveries.

Melanchthon's biographer writes of his serious illness, when death seemed certain. Luther was called and traveled immediately to his friend's bedside where he found Melanchthon in very bad shape. "His eyes were already dim, his reason was gone, he could not speak nor hear, and his countenance was loose and fallen."[8] In addition, "He recognized no one, and could neither eat nor drink."[9] Shocked by the condition in which he found Melanchthon, Luther prayed, and afterwards took him by the hand, saying, "Be of good cheer, Philip, you will not die!"[10]

After exhorting his friend, Melanchthon roused a bit, but told Luther not to intervene; that he was ready for and desirous of death. Luther responded, "By no means Philip; you must serve the Lord still longer."[11] As he became increasingly alert, Luther ordered that food be prepared, but Melanchthon refused to eat. Luther told him that if he did not eat, he would be excommunicated, and Melanchthon ate and regained strength. He later said of Luther, "If he had not come I should have died"[12] Luther also wrote, "Master Philip has been restored to life, as it were from the grave."[13]

Friedrich Myconius was another colleague and co-laborer of Luther's. Myconius was near death due to tuberculosis, and he wrote his friend, telling him of his soon-approaching death. Here is what transpired:

> Myconius was in the last stage of consumption, and already speechless. Luther wrote to him that he must not die: "May God not let me hear, so long as I live, that you are dead, but cause you to survive me. I pray this earnestly, and will have it granted, and my will will be done herein. Amen." "I was so horrified," said Myconius afterwards, "when I read what the good man had written, that it seemed to me as though I had heard Christ say, 'Lazarus, come forth.'" And from that time Myconius was, as it were, kept from the grave by the power of Luther's prayer, and did not die till after Luther's death.[14]

In a 1523 sermon, Luther was speaking about signs, and made some interesting remarks. On one hand, he indicates that not all Christians will do signs, but that the performance of signs is based on necessity. Then he states, "If it were necessary and conducive to the spreading of the Gospel, we could do easily the signs...."[15] Though Luther did not particularly see the necessity of signs in his day, he proceeds to reference John 14:12, "...*he who believes on Me, the works that I do he will do also; and greater works than these he will do*," and asserts:

> Therefore, we must allow these words to remain and not gloss over them, as some have done who said that these signs were manifestations of the Spirit in the beginning of the Christian era and that now they have ceased. That is not right; for the same power is in the church still. And though it is not exercised, that does not matter; we still have the power to do such signs.[16]

Martin Luther also honored the Holy Spirit in the fourth stanza of his great hymn, "A Mighty Fortress Is Our God," which contains the phrase, "The Spirit and gifts are ours through Him who with us sideth."

The Anabaptists

While Luther was leading the Reformation in Germany, Ulrich Zwingli (1484-1531) was doing the same in Geneva, Switzerland. Shortly afterward, John Calvin (1509-1564) furthered the work of the Reformation in Geneva, Switzerland, as did John Knox (1513-1572) in Scotland. These were known as the magisterial reformers because they believed in and cultivated a close relationship between the church and the civil government—the magistrates. The term magisterial can also refer to the teaching element that existed in the Reformation movement.

Other believers, however, thought the church should be entirely separate from government involvement and control. These radical reformers were called Anabaptists by the magisterial reformers. The name Anabaptist refers to being baptized again, because they rejected infant baptism, which the magisterial reformers embraced. These radical reformers believed that only those who had reached the age of accountability should be baptized and only upon a profession of faith. They rejected the idea that they were baptizing *again*, because they believed that baptizing infants was not valid to begin with. Unfortunately, there was great conflict between these two groups, and various government entities and the magisterial reformers often persecuted the Anabaptists brutally. Between four and five thousand Anabaptists were executed during the Reformation.

One of Martin Luther's disciples, Thomas Müntzer, believed that Luther was not going far enough in certain regards of church reform and aligned himself instead with more radical elements of the movement.

Stanley Burgess notes, "Müntzer contends that Christians are to experience the Holy Spirit as powerfully in postbiblical times as they did at the time of the prophets and apostles. He insists on a Baptism of the Holy Spirit."[17] Other early Anabaptists also felt the magisterial reformers did not go far enough relative to emphasizing the Holy Spirit.

Pilgram Marpeck wrote that Scripture does not exclude divine miracles and signs, and states, "God has a free hand even in these last days. He has performed miracles and signs before, and even does so today for him who has eyes to see."[18] Marpeck then spoke of people in his day who had been raised from the dead:

> Moreover, one also marvels when one sees how the faithful God (who, after all, overflows with goodness) raises from the dead several such brothers and sisters of Christ after they were hanged, drowned, or killed in other ways. Even today, they are found alive and we can hear their own testimony. Here and there one can find the same thing happening, even today, it takes place among those who are powerfully moved and driven by the living Word of God and the Spirit of Christ.[19]

Marpeck strongly emphasized the community of believers in his writings and saw the gifts of the Holy Spirit operating in the context of the overall body. He writes, "Thus, the gifts of the Spirit manifest themselves not only for private, but also for common benefit, service, and improvement."[20]

Marpeck also recognized the diversity of gifts that have been bestowed upon different individuals. "*Not all are apostles, nor prophets, not all perform miracles, not all are teachers* (1 Corinthians 12:29). "But none of these gifts of faith will be lacking to the believers in their need."[21]

He also stated that believers were to proactively cultivate the gifts of God: "The diversity of the gifts of grace each one must, in the fear of God, intensively and zealously discover and heed for himself…."[22]

Differences between Anabaptists and the magisterial reformers were highlighted in a dispute that took place in Zofingen, Switzerland, in 1532. Theologians who followed Luther and Zwingli challenged the Anabaptists as to why they refused to attend the Reformed church services. The Anabaptist ministers cited 1 Corinthians 14—the chapter that deals with the spiritual gifts of tongues, interpretation of tongues, and prophecy—and said, "A listener is bound by Christian love (if something to edification is given or revealed to him) that he should and may speak of it also in the congregation…."[23] A similar dialogue involved Marpeck, and when he was asked a similar question by a Reformed preacher as to why Anabaptists did not attend Reformed services, Marpeck responded that they did not attend because "Individual members are not permitted to exercise their gifts for the edification of the congregation."[24]

Every movement seems to have its aberrations, and the Anabaptists were no different. There were various streams or branches of Anabaptists in the sixteenth century, and different groups held conflicting views on a number of topics, including the gifts and operations of the Holy Spirit. Unfortunately, some considered direct, personal revelation to be more important than Scripture. There was also a radical, militant group of Anabaptists that tried to forcibly establish the earthly kingdom of God—the New Jerusalem—in the German city of Münster.

The visions and revelations that prompted this endeavor proved to be false, and the ruling Anabaptists there were overthrown in 1535. When the city fell, the leaders of the rebellion were executed. Even though the actions and beliefs of these few did not represent the majority, it still badly tarnished the Anabaptist reputation. Bruce Shelley notes, "For centuries thereafter, Europeans upon hearing 'Anabaptist' thought of the Munster rebellion. It stood for wild-eyed religious fanaticism."[25]

Moderate Anabaptists would find stable leadership from Menno Simons (1496-1561), a former Dutch Catholic priest for whom his followers would eventually be named—Mennonites. Simons believed the Bible was authoritative and also honored the person and work of the Holy Spirit. He writes, "To receive the Holy Ghost is to be a partaker of his gifts and power, to be taught, assured, and influenced by him, as the Scriptures teach."

Endnotes

1. Walther von Loewenich, *Martin Luther: The Man and His Work* (Minneapolis, MN: Augsburg Publishing House, 1982), 72.

2. Ibid., 84.

3. Craig S. Keener, *Miracles: The Credibility of the New Testament Accounts*, Volumes 1 and 2 (Grand Rapids, MI: Baker Academic, 2011), loc. 7476, Kindle.

4. Martin Luther quoted in Roland H. Bainton, *Here I Stand: A Life of Martin Luther* (Nashville, TN: Abingdon Press, 1978), loc. 4117, Kindle.

5. Martin Luther, *The Table Talk of Martin Luther*, trans. William Hazlitt, ed. Thomas S. Kepler (Mineola, NY: Dover Publications, 1566), loc. 2032, Kindle.

6. Ibid., loc. 2037, Kindle.

7. Martin Luther quoted in Bengt R. Hoffman, *Luther and the Mystics* (Minneapolis, MN: Augsburg Publishing House, 1976), 199.

8. Karl Friederich Ledderhose, *The Life of Philip Melanchthon*, trans. G. F. Krotel (Philadelphia: Lindsay and Blakiston, 1855), loc. 2081, Kindle.

9. Ibid.

10. Ibid.

11. Ibid., loc. 2088, Kindle.

12. Ibid., loc. 2096, Kindle.

13. Ibid., loc. 2103, Kindle.

14. Christoph Ernest Luthardt, *Apologetic Lectures on the Moral Truths of Christianity*, trans. Sophia Taylor (Edinburgh; T. and T. Clark, 1873), loc. 3764, Kindle.

15. Martin Luther, "Day of Christ's Ascension into Heaven," in *Sermons of Martin Luther*, vol. III, ed. and trans. John Nicholas Lenker (Grand Rapids, MI: Baker Book House, 1983), 190.

16. Ibid.

17. Stanley Burgess, ed. *Christian Peoples of the Spirit: A Documentary History of Pentecostal Spirituality from the Early Church to the Present* (New York: New York University Press, 2011), 142.

18. Pilgram Marpeck, *A Clear Refutation*, in *The Writings of Pilgram Marpeck*, trans. and ed. William Klassen and Walter Klaassen (Walden, NY: Plough Publishing House, 1531), loc. 891, Kindle.

19. Ibid., loc. 900, Kindle.

20. Ibid., loc. 1312, Kindle.

21. Ibid.

22. Ibid., loc. 1248, Kindle.

23. Charles Hannon Byrd II, *Pentecostal Aspects of Early Sixteenth-Century Anabaptism* (Eugene, OR: Wipf and Stock Publishers, 2019), loc. 5389, Kindle.

24. Ibid., loc. 5372, Kindle.

25. Bruce L. Shelley, *Church History in Plain Language* (Nashville, TN: Thomas Nelson Publishers, www.thomasnelson.com, 2008), 252, Kindle. Used by permission of Thomas Nelson.

CHAPTER NINE

FAITH GETS PERSONAL AND POWERFUL

(Fox, Spener, and Zinzendorf)

It is not enough that we hear the Word with our outward ear, but we must let it penetrate to our heart, so that we may hear the Holy Spirit speak there, that is, with vibrant emotion and comfort feel the sealing of the Spirit and the power of the Word.[1]

—**Philipp Jacob Spener**

WHILE the Protestant Reformation focused heavily on getting doctrine and theology right, others would come later who would place more emphasis on the heartfelt side of faith—the experiential side of relating to God. While good doctrine is very important, it is also important to *"taste and see that the Lord is good"* (Psalm 34:8). Intellectual assent to proper doctrine is not the same as having a living, vibrant, and personal relationship with God.

George Fox (1624-1691)

In his autobiography, George Fox speaks repeatedly of the power of the Lord. He describes God's power being upon him, breaking forth in meetings and dramatically affecting the people who heard the preaching of God's Word. In some cases, God's workings even thwarted the devices of his enemies. Born in the small English village of Leicestershire in 1624, Fox's followers became known as the Quakers, but he preferred to simply call his adherents *Friends*. Some say the name of Quaker came from people shaking under the power of God in their meetings, but others attribute it to Fox telling a magistrate that he should tremble, quake, before the judgment of God.

Fox believed that God's involvement in each believer's life was to be so personal—something he referred to as the "inner light"—that he strongly rejected external formalities of worship, including baptism and communion. Instead of hymns, creeds, and pre-planned sermons, Fox promoted gatherings where the people waited on God and only spoke when the Spirit moved them.

One time he wrote, "Friends, keep your meetings in the power of the Lord God, that hath gathered you; and none quench the spirit, nor despise prophesying."[2] In another place he admonished believers to not quench the Spirit's movings in the least degree, but neither to go beyond them.[3] Clearly, Fox was committed to the involvement and influence of the Holy Spirit in every aspect of ministry.

One of Fox's biographers noted both his unwavering tenacity and the supernatural element of his ministry. Rufus M. Jones writes that Fox "preached in cathedrals, on hay stacks, on cliffs of rock, from hill tops, under apple trees and elm trees, in barns and in city squares, while he sent epistles from every prison in which he was shut up."[4] He further states that "Diseases were cured through him; he foretold coming events; he often penetrated states and conditions of mind and heart; he occasionally had a sense of what was happening in distant parts."[5]

The descriptions that Fox gives of the Lord's work through his ministry are most impressive. He describes many healings and deliverances, often giving great detail. He reports people coming under tremendous conviction of their sin through the preaching of God's Word. In one case, he states, "The power of the Lord was so strong, that it struck a mighty dread amongst the people."[6] When asked about a specific healing that had taken place under his ministry, Fox responded, "I told him we did not glory in such things, but many such things had been done by the power of Christ."[7] In yet another situation, when Fox was challenging a civil official to repent and come to the Light, he writes, "As I admonished him, I laid my hand upon him, and he was brought down by the power of the Lord; and all the watchmen stood amazed."[8]

Fox provides many accounts of supernatural workings, but here are four notable ones:

- A report went abroad of me, that I was a young man that had a discerning spirit; whereupon many came to me, from far and near, professors, priests, and people. The Lord's power broke forth, and I had great openings and prophecies, and spoke unto them of the things of God, which they heard with attention and silence, and went away and spread the fame thereof.[9]

- The Lord opened my mouth, and the everlasting truth was declared amongst them, and the power of the Lord was over them all. For in that day the Lord's power began to spring, and I had great openings in the Scriptures. Several were convinced in those parts and were turned from darkness to light, from the power of Satan unto God, and many were raised up to praise God.[10]

- Many great and wonderful things were wrought by the heavenly power in those days; for the Lord made bare His omnipotent arm, and manifested His power, to the astonishment of many, by the healing virtue whereby many have been delivered from great infirmities. And the devils were made subject through His name; of which particular instances might be given, beyond what this unbelieving age is able to receive or bear.[11]

- After some time I went to a meeting at Arnside, where was Richard Myer, who had been long lame of one of his arms. I was moved of the Lord to say unto him amongst all the people, "Stand up upon thy legs," for he was sitting down. And he stood up, and stretched out his arm that had been lame a long time, and said, "Be it known unto you, all people, that this day I am healed."[12]

These types of descriptions make it clear why Fox repeatedly refers to the power of God in his writings. In one case, he shares about a particular prayer meeting in Mansfield. "The Lord's power was so great," he writes, "that the house seemed to be shaken…some of the professors said it was now as in the days of the apostles, when the house was shaken where they were.[13]

Fox did not believe that this power belonged to him—he knew it was God's power, and that it was to confirm the preaching of the gospel. Fox told his fellow ministers, "So, in the power of the Lord Jesus Christ preach the everlasting gospel, that by his power the sick may be healed, the leprous cleansed, the dead raised, the blind eyes opened, and the devils cast out."[14]

Edward Burrough, a fellow Quaker evangelist who knew and worked with Fox, speaks of the powerful nature of some of the early Quaker meetings. Burrough writes:

> While waiting upon the Lord in silence, as we often did for many hours together, with our hearts toward Him, being stayed in the light of Christ from all fleshy motions and desires, we often received the pouring down of His Spirit upon us, and our hearts were made glad, and our tongues loosened, and our mouths opened, and we spoke with new tongues, as the Lord gave us utterance, and His Spirit led us, which was poured upon sons and daughters. Thereby things unutterable were made manifest, and the glory of the Father was revealed. Then we began to sing praises to the Lord God Almighty, and to the Lamb, who had redeemed us to God, and brought us out of the bondage of the world, and put an end to sin and death.[15]

While the bulk of Fox's ministry took place in England, he also traveled and ministered in Scotland, Ireland, Wales, Holland, the Caribbean, and North America. William Penn, the founder of the state of Pennsylvania, was a Quaker himself and was most impressed with the character and ministry of George Fox. Penn writes that Fox was "a discerner of others' spirits" and that he had "an extraordinary gift in opening the Scriptures." Penn also said of Fox, "Above all, he excelled in prayer."[16]

The growth and expansion of the early Quakers was remarkable. Eddie Hyatt notes:

> In one generation, the people called Quakers became the fastest-growing movement in the Western world. By 1656, Fox had at least fifty-six associates who were traveling

preachers, and by 1660, the movement could boast forty thousand to sixty thousand adherents. This impressive sixteenth-century movement was, indeed, a Charismatic movement. Their opposition to externals in religion and their emphasis on the interior life are characteristics of such a movement. Their own testimony confirms the importance that they attached to miraculous healings and other charismatic gifts.[17]

Philipp Jacob Spener (1635-1705)

While the controversial George Fox was stirring things up in England, another voice was speaking in Germany, calling for continuing reform in the Church. Philipp Jacob Spener was called "the Spiritual Counselor of All Germany," and today, he is often referred to as the Father of German Pietism. Spener was different from Fox in many regards, but he strongly asserted that faith was not merely an intellectual, academic, or theological exercise. Rather, faith is to be an issue of the heart, a matter of devotion, and is to result in genuine fruitfulness and practical application in one's daily life.

Spener had seen fervency and spirituality decline in the church, and he had witnessed formality and ritualism increasing. He agreed essentially with the doctrines that came out of the Protestant Reformation, but believed clergy and believers alike need to experience a deep inner-working of the Holy Spirit in their lives; mental assent to doctrine is no substitute for true spirituality. The following statements from Spener reveal his observations and perspectives:

- Most distressing of all, however, is the fact that the lives of many such preachers and the absence in them of the fruits of faith indicate that they are themselves wanting in faith.

What they take to be faith and what is the ground of their teaching is by no means that true faith which is awakened through the Word of God, by the illumination, witness, and sealing of the Holy Spirit, but is a human fancy. To be sure, as others have acquired knowledge in their fields of study, so these preachers, with their own human efforts and without the working of the Holy Spirit, have learned something of the letter of the Scriptures, have comprehended and assented to true doctrine, and have even known how to preach it to others, but they are altogether unacquainted with the true, heavenly light and the life of faith.[18]

• It is certain that a young man who fervently loves God, although adorned with limited gifts, will be more useful to the church of God with his meager talent and academic achievement than a vain and worldly fool with double doctor's degrees who is very clever but has not been taught by God. The work of the former is blessed, and he is aided by the Holy Spirit. The latter has only a carnal knowledge, with which he can easily do more harm than good.[19]

In addition to Spener's emphasis on the need for believers to personally experience the working of the Holy Spirit within, he also emphasized the need for them to grow spiritually through meaningful interaction and communication among themselves. Thus, he promoted fellowship groups to meet in homes that would enable believers to discuss the sermons they had heard in church with a view toward applying those truths in their lives.

Spener is probably best remembered for his highly impacting book, *Pia Desiderada—The Piety We Desire*. In this landmark work, Spener strongly appeals for:

- *A more extensive use of the Bible.* He writes, "The more at home the Word of God is among us, the more we shall bring about faith and its fruits."[20]

- *The establishment and diligent exercise of the spiritual priesthood.* Calling for the church to revisit and reinvigorate Luther's emphasis on the priesthood of the believer, Spener called for all believers to be actively engaged in Christian ministry. He recognized that not everyone would be a preacher, but he advocated believers to instruct, admonish, correct, and comfort one another.

Encouraging believers to be active and not passive toward the things of God, Spener writes:

> Every Christian is bound not only to offer himself and what he has, his prayer, thanksgiving, good works, alms, etc., but also industriously to study in the Word of the Lord, with the grace that is given him to teach others, especially those under his own roof, to chastise, exhort, convert, and edify them, to observe their life, pray for all, and insofar as possible be concerned about their salvation.[21]

In other words, Spener wanted every believer to be an active participant, not a passive spectator, in spiritual and church matters.

- *The practical application of the Christian faith.* This was to be expressed primarily through fervent love among believers, as well as to those outside the church. Spener advocated believers actively pursuing opportunities to do good to others, and promoted the idea of companionable accountability to stimulate the pursuit of godliness.

- *Civility and charity in theological disputes.* While Spener believed that wrong doctrine was to be challenged and corrected, he believed that hateful, harsh attitudes and personal insults were wrong. He stated that we should exercise "a practice of heartfelt love toward all unbelievers and heretics" and that "A proper hatred of false religion should neither suspend nor weaken the love that is due the other person."[22] It is helpful to keep in mind that civility in religious disputes was not necessarily the norm in Spener's day. Martin Luther had been quite harsh in his denunciations of theological opponents, and John Calvin had even been in agreement with the execution of a heretical teacher in Geneva, though he later regretted it. Many needed to regain a sense of civility and kindness in Spener's day.

- *The promotion of spirituality and godliness in the training of ministers; not just intellectual and theological education.* Spener writes that, "students should unceasingly have it impressed upon them that holy life is not of less consequence than diligence and study, indeed that study without piety is worthless."[23]

- *Sermons that promote the edification of the hearers and lead to practical application in the life of the believer.* Spener was against sermons that merely showcased the intellectualism and learning of the preacher. He argues, "The pulpit is not the place for an ostentatious display of one's skill. It is rather the place to preach the Word of the Lord plainly but powerfully."[24]

These emphases would become influential trends that would significantly impact and shape Christianity, especially in the eighteenth century. As a matter of fact, Spener's name would not be as well remembered as those of two individuals he dramatically influenced, his godson, Nicholas von Zinzendorf, founder of the Moravians, and John Wesley, the founder of Methodism.

Even though Spener's ministry was not marked by "spectacular" manifestations of the Holy Spirit, the wisdom of the Holy Spirit was expressed through him to direct and promote healthy and godly developments in the Body of Christ. The maturity and stability Spener promoted would also facilitate a strong foundation for the church to be able to better manage the supernatural workings of the Holy Spirit that were approaching on the horizon.

Nikolaus Zinzendorf (1700-1760)

Born into wealth, Count Nikolaus von Zinzendorf was Philipp Spener's godson, and a student of Spener's successor, August Hermann Francke. Demonstrating a sensitive heart to God at an early age, Zinzendorf wrote simple statements of devotion to God when he was four years old. At the age of ten, he recognized a call to preach the gospel; and as a teenager, he and five other boys formed "The Order of the Mustard Seed." These young people dedicated themselves fully to God and to fellowship with one another, renounced worldliness, and consecrated themselves to the mission of God in the earth.

In 1722, Zinzendorf welcomed a group of religious refugees to his estate in Saxony in eastern Germany. The first residents of this new community were Moravians; they were the spiritual descendants of the passionate Czech reformer, John Hus (1373-1415), who preceded Luther by one hundred years. Hus had been burned at the stake as a heretic because of his commitment to the authority of Scripture and to the doctrine of justification by faith. These believers—Hussites, as they were sometimes called—had been persecuted generation after generation. They had also been known as *Unitas Fratrum,* which is Latin for United Brethren. They named their new community *Herrnhut,* meaning "The Lord's Watch."

Other persecuted believers also joined the Moravians at Zinzendorf's estate; for various reasons, conflict and strife began to develop. Through Zinzendorf's care, guidance, and spiritual influence, unity was established and the community began to diligently seek God. Their unified prayer and hungry hearts positioned them to receive a great outpouring of the Holy Spirit—what would be referred to as their Pentecost.

Moravian historian Ami Bost describes a service in 1727 where God's power was dynamically experienced:

> On Lord's day, the 10th of August, the minister Roth was seized in the midst of the assembly at Herrnhut, with an unusual impulse. He threw himself upon his knees before God, and the whole assembly prostrated themselves with him under the same emotions. An uninterrupted course of singing and prayer, weeping and supplication, continued till midnight. All hearts were united in love.[25]

Describing events three days later at Herrnhut, author John Greenfield relates the remarks of a Moravian historian:

> Church History also abounds in records of special outpourings of the Holy Ghost, and verily the thirteenth of August 1727 was a day of the outpouring of the Holy Spirit. We saw the hand of God and His wonders, and we were all under the cloud of our fathers baptized with their Spirit. The Holy Ghost came upon us and in those days great signs and wonders took place in our midst. From that time scarcely

a day passed but what we beheld His almighty workings amongst us. A great hunger after the Word of God took possession of us so that we had to have three services every day—5:00 and 7:30 a.m. and 9:00 p.m. Everyone desired above everything else that the Holy Spirit might have full control. Self-love and self-will as well as all disobedience disappeared and an overwhelming flood of grace swept us all out into the great ocean of Divine Love.[26]

Not only did the assembled believers at Herrnhut experience this dynamic outpouring on August 13, but two members of their community also experienced the same type of outpouring at the same time that day, even though they were working around twenty miles away. Also, the children were full partakers of what God was doing. After stating that a "remarkable revival took place among the children," Bost writes:

No words can express the powerful operation of the Holy Spirit upon these children. These days were truly days of Divine love at Herrnhut, in which they forgot every thing but heavenly enjoyments and longed to attain them.[27]

As the work of God progressed at Herrnhut, displays of heavenly power began to be seen and experienced. Zinzendorf's assistant and eventual successor, August Gottlieb Spangenberg describes what happened:

About this time, various gifts and spiritual powers manifested themselves in the church at Herrnhut; and, in particular, many miraculous cures. Its members believed, in filial simplicity, the words which the Saviour spoke respecting the hearing of prayer; and when any particular affair pressed itself upon them, they spoke with him concerning it, and expected every good thing from him; and it was done unto them according to their faith.[28]

And how did Zinzendorf respond to these spiritual gifts and miraculous healings?

> He acknowledged this confidence in our Lord Jesus Christ, as a fruit of the Holy Spirit, which ought reasonably to be esteemed, and not prove a stumbling-block to any. However, he did not wish that the brethren and sisters should regard such things as extraordinary, and thus attach themselves to them; but whenever they occurred, as, for instance, when any one experienced an instantaneous cure, either by a word spoken in faith, or by prayer, were it even from the most dangerous injuries or the most painful illnesses—he regarded it as a thing that was known, and spoke little about it. He also frequently asserted, both in public and in private, that wonders were not granted for the sake of believers, but of unbelievers—that wonder-working faith was a gift, which did not make its possessor a better child of God, but that he might even be inferior to others who did not possess such gifts....[29]

Zinzendorf appreciated the real purpose of why spiritual gifts were given. He writes, "Every gift, which our Savior bestows upon us for this purpose, we possess for use, and not for display, or to excite attention."[30]

Zinzendorf saw other workings of God throughout his life. On one occasion, he was about to set sail on a ministry trip, but was sick. He wrote in his diary, "I talked to my Savior and told Him it would not be convenient to be sick on the ship, so He healed me before we sailed."[31]

In another instance, Zinzendorf was aboard a ship on the Atlantic Ocean that was being violently battered by a storm. The situation was so intense that the captain assumed the ship was going to sink, but Zinzendorf informed him that the storm would subside in two hours, and it happened exactly as the Moravian preacher predicted. The mystified captain inquired as to how Zinzendorf so accurately predicted the end of the storm, and he replied:

> All my life I had a trusting relationship with my Savior. In any predicament I first ask myself, am I to blame? If I find sin in my life I fall at His feet to ask for forgiveness. My Savior forgives me, and He lets me know how my trying situation will end. If He keeps silent I conclude it is better for me not to know. However, this time He assured me that the storm will end in two hours.[32]

Leaders with lesser maturity and insight might have made miracles and supernatural phenomenon the major focus, but Zinzendorf did not. He declares, "I have but one passion; it is the love of Him, nothing but Him!"[33] Prayer became a major focus for the leader of the Moravians, and their prayers spawned a missionary emphasis that seems, in some way, to have resembled that of the first century apostles.

A Century of Prayer

Shortly after the "Moravian Pentecost" on August 13, 1727, the believers at Herrnhut responded to the leading of the Holy Spirit and committed to pray twenty-four hours a day, seven days a week. This consecration led to an around-the-clock prayer vigil that lasted more than one hundred years. There seems to be an undeniable connection between the prayers of the Moravians, and the initiation of a major missionary movement that would follow.

Into the Harvest

Zinzendorf himself possessed a great missionary heart, and his many followers embraced the same heavenly mandate to preach the gospel to every creature. The Count said, "May the Lamb that was slain receive the reward of His suffering" and "That land is henceforth my country which most needs the gospel." Zinzendorf had a very simple, straightforward approach to preaching the gospel on the mission field. He described what did not produce results, and then said:

> Preach Jesus Christ as the Lamb of God, that takes away the sin of the world, and as the propitiation for the sins of the whole world, with demonstration of the Spirit and with power; and when poor lost men come to Christ, and find grace and the forgiveness of their sins in his blood—their hearts are then filled with the Holy Spirit and the love of Christ, and they obtain a desire and power to follow him, and to live according to his will.[34]

Responding to the compassion and the call of God, the Moravians became, in the words of church historian Mark A. Noll, "the most dedicated Protestant missionaries in the whole of the eighteenth century." Noll went on to report:

> During the first century after the Moravians were reconstituted as a church under the leadership of Count von Zinzendorf in the early 1720s, approximately two thousand

(one-fourth of them women) volunteered for cross-cultural missionary service.[35]

It has often been suggested that the health and strength of a church is not found in its *seating* capacity, but in its *sending* capacity. In the light of this definition, the Moravians were one of the healthiest and strongest movements of all time. Church historian Alvin L. Reid states, "Whereas the ratio of Protestant laity to missionaries as a whole was 5000:1, the Moravian ratio was 60:1."[36]

What could have turned a disparate group of religious refugees into such world changers? In reviewing their history, it is clear that a profound outpouring of the Holy Spirit equipped, mobilized, and launched these believers into the world in the same way that the disciples of the first century had been. The book of Acts finds once-divided individuals coming into unity, giving themselves to prayer, and receiving the mighty baptism of the Holy Spirit. The very same thing happened with the Moravians under the leadership of Count Zinzendorf. Miracles and mighty signs accompanied both movements.

Many modern believers may not have heard of Philipp Jacob Spener or even of Nikolaus von Zinzendorf, but what God did through these men and their followers set the stage for and heavily influenced the life and ministry of John Wesley. The Church was beginning to take on more and more of its first century traits, and Wesley and the Methodists would continue to build on this foundation and experience increasingly powerful momentum.

Endnotes

1. Philipp Jacob Spener, *Pia Desideria*, trans. and ed. Theodore G. Tappert (Minneapolis, MN: Fortress Press, 1964), loc. 1957, Kindle.

2. George Fox, "Epistle 248," in *The Sermons and Articles of George Fox* (Seattle, WA: Amazon Digital Services, 2016), loc. 3308, Kindle.

3. George Fox, "Writing, Printing, and Speaking," in *The Sermons and Articles of George Fox* (Seattle, WA: Amazon Digital Services, 2016), loc. 11807, Kindle.

4. George Fox, *George Fox: An Autobiography*, ed. Rufus M. Jones (Jawbone Digital, 2015), loc. 238, Kindle.

5. Ibid., loc. 314, Kindle.

6. Ibid., loc. 1144, Kindle.

7. Ibid., loc. 5144, Kindle.

8. Ibid., loc. 1233, Kindle.

9. Ibid., loc. 708, Kindle.

10. Ibid., loc. 687, Kindle.

11. Ibid., loc. 939, Kindle.

12. Ibid., loc. 1613, Kindle.

13. Ibid., loc. 720, Kindle.

14. George Fox, "Epistle 114," in *The Sermons and Articles of George Fox* (Seattle, WA: Amazon Digital Services, 2016), loc. 625, Kindle.

15. William Evans, *A Memoir of the Life and Religious Labors of Edward Burrough: An Eminent Servant of Christ and Minister of the Gospel in the Society of Friends* (Philadelphia, PA: Friend's Book Store, 1890), 13.

16. William Penn, *A Brief Account of the Rise and Progress of the People Called Quakers* (Good Press, 2019), loc. 667, Kindle.

17. Hyatt, *2000 Years of Charismatic Christianity*, 94.

18. Philipp Jacob Spener, *Pia Desideria*, loc. 768, Kindle.

19. Ibid., loc. 1831, Kindle.

20. Ibid., loc. 1512, Kindle.

21. Ibid., loc. 1612, Kindle.

22. Ibid., loc. 1693, Kindle.

23. Ibid., loc. 1773, Kindle.

24. Ibid., loc. 1940, Kindle.

25. Ami Bost, *History of the Bohemian and Moravian Brethren* (London: The Religious Tract Society, 1848), 222.

26. John Greenfield and Mark Mirza (www.markmirza.com), *Power From on High: The Two Hundreth Anniversary of the Great Moravian Revival 1727-1927* (Atlanta, GA: CTM Publishing, 2017), loc. 247, Kindle.

27. Bost, *History of the Bohemian and Moravian Brethren*, 230-231.

28. August Gottlieb Spangenberg, *The Life of Nicholas Lewis, Count Zinzendorf, Bishop and Ordinary of the Church of the United (or Moravian) Brethren*, trans. Samuel Jackson (Miami, FL: Hardpress, 2017), loc. 2932, Kindle.

29. Ibid.

30. Bost, *History of the Bohemian and Moravian Brethren*, 381.

31. Paul Wemmer, *Count Zinzendorf and the Spirit of the Moravians* (Maitland, FL: Xulon Press, 2013), loc. 2068, Kindle.

32. Wemmer, *Count Zinzendorf*, loc. 2297, Kindle.

33. Bost, *History of the Bohemian and Moravian Brethren*, 413.

34. Spangenberg, *The Life of Nicholas Lewis, Count Zinzendorf*, loc. 3789, Kindle.

35. Mark A. Noll, *Turning Points: Decisive Moments in the History of Christianity* (Grand Rapids, MI: Baker Academic, 2012), 268.

36. Malcolm McDow and Alvin L. Reid, *Firefall 2.0: How God has Shaped History Through Revivals* (Wake Forest, NC: Gospel Advance Books, 2014), 170, Kindle.

CHAPTER TEN

JOHN WESLEY AND THE METHODISTS

> *The Holy Spirit began to move among us with amazing power when we met in his name…. These unusual works of the Holy Spirit continued to follow and bless my ministry.*
>
> —John Wesley

FEW names in church history carry as much influence as that of John Wesley (1703-1791) of England. He traveled about 250,000 miles ministering the Word of God, much of that on horseback. When he died in 1791, there were 72,000 Methodists in his home country, and an additional 43,000 adherents in America. He had preached 42,000 sermons and authored 250 books and pamphlets. As impressive as those numbers are, statistics alone do not begin to convey how powerfully the Holy Spirit worked through Wesley, dynamically and profoundly impacting people's lives.

Wesley's life parallels that of the apostle Paul in that both men were devoutly religious, seeking righteousness and holiness through good works. Both discovered that their own righteousness was entirely inadequate, and that only the righteousness of Christ, received by faith, could truly place them in right standing with God. The son of an Anglican priest, and a graduate and faculty member of Oxford University, Wesley's religious disciplines were extremely stringent. At Oxford, he and friends, including his brother Charles, as well as George Whitefield, were part of the "Holy Club" as they sought to deepen their piety. Wesley and his followers were later called Methodists because of their methodical and systematic approach to religious devotion.

In 1735, John and Charles boarded a ship sailing to the American colony of Georgia to engage in missionary work. In transit, their vessel was battered by a severe storm, and John found himself fearing for his life. Aboard the same ship was a group of Moravian missionaries—from Zinzendorf's ministry—and their calm, confident faith made a significant impression on Wesley. These missionaries joyfully sang psalms while Wesley, the ship's chaplain, was anxious and fearful. Wesley was deeply religious, but this gnawing agitation forced him to recognize that he lacked the peace and assurance they so gloriously possessed.

Following more than two difficult years on the mission field, Wesley returned to England, still struggling with his faith. He writes in his journal, "I went to America to convert the Indians, but oh, who will convert me? Who, what is he that will deliver me from this evil heart of unbelief?"[1] Five days later, he again expressed his angst, "I who went to America to convert others was never myself converted to God."[2] Back in England, Wesley began interacting with Peter Boehler, a young Moravian preacher who admonished him regarding his need for the new birth. He writes that Boehler "amazed me more and more by the account he gave of the fruits of living faith—the holiness and happiness which he affirmed to attend it."[3] Wesley acknowledged that he lacked faith, but Boehler told him, "Preach faith until you have faith, then you will preach it because you have it."

On May 24, 1738, a great breakthrough event occurred in Wesley's life that he describes in his journal:

In the evening, I went very unwillingly to a society in Aldersgate Street, where one was reading Luther's preface to the Epistle to the Romans. About a quarter before nine, while he was describing the change which God works in the heart through faith in Christ, I felt my heart strangely warmed. I felt I did trust in Christ, Christ alone for salvation, and an assurance was given me that he had taken away *my* sins, even *mine*, and saved *me* from the law of sin and death.[4]

A few days before John's experience, his brother Charles also received "the living faith," as John called it.

Because of the Moravians' influence on his life, John traveled to Germany and spent a couple of months with believers in Herrnhut. As Wesley witnessed the strong work of the Holy Spirit in the lives of the Moravians, it reinforced his blossoming perspective that salvation was to be truly experienced. Returning to England, he began seeing tremendous demonstrations of God's power:

Those who had received this new living faith through the Holy Spirit continued to meet together. About sixty of us were holding a love feast on New Year's Eve on Fetter Lane. At about three in the morning, as we were continuing in prayer, the power of God came mightily upon us. Many cried out in complete joy. Others were knocked to the ground. As soon as we recovered a little from that awe and amazement at God's presence, we broke out in praise. "We praise you, O God; we acknowledge you to be the Lord."[5]

From this time forward, Wesley spoke periodically of people who would sink, or fall to the ground under the power of the Holy Spirit while he was preaching. Sometimes he used the word "thunderstruck" to describe people who fell as their physical strength succumbed to God's power. He also described many crying out for mercy as they came under the conviction of the Holy Spirit.

These types of events did not happen all of the time, and there seemed to be seasons where they were more frequent than other. However, it is clear from Wesley's own writings that powerful expressions of the Holy Spirit often occurred. For example, on Thursday, April 26, 1739, Wesley writes that while he was preaching, "Immediately one, and another, and another sunk to the earth: They dropped on every side as if thunderstruck."[6]

The point with Wesley was never simply the phenomenon of people falling, but rather, that God was working mightily in their hearts to bring them into conviction, repentance, faith, and into right relationship with himself. To Wesley, outward manifestations were simply indicators of inward workings of the Holy Spirit. On May 9 of the same year, Wesley writes:

> In the evening, while I was declaring that Jesus Christ had "given himself a ransom for all," three persons, almost at once, sunk down as dead, having all their sins set in array before them. But in a short time they were raised up, and knew that "the Lamb of God who takes away the sin of the world," had taken away their sins.[7]

At the encouragement of his friend and fellow evangelist, George Whitefield, Wesley had begun preaching in open fields and on highways. At first, this seemed inappropriate to Wesley, but it proved to be a tremendously effective method. Not only was preaching outdoors necessary because many churches had closed their doors to him, but buildings could not handle the massive crowds that Wesley and Whitefield were drawing.

Just as Wesley was initially unsure about preaching outdoors, Whitefield was uncertain about some of the manifestations that were happening in Wesley's meetings. The two men had a most interesting exchange about the "outward signs" that were happening in Wesley's meetings, and interestingly, Whitefield had the opportunity to witness these himself. Wesley writes:

> I had an opportunity to talk with him [Whitefield] of those outward signs which had so often accompanied the inward work of God. I found his objections were chiefly grounded on gross misrepresentations of matter of fact. But the next day he had an opportunity of informing himself better: for no sooner had he begun (in the application of his sermon) to invite all sinners to believe in Christ, than four persons sank down close to him, almost in the same moment. One of them lay without either sense or motion. A second trembled exceedingly. The third had strong convulsions all over his body, but made no noise unless by groans. The fourth, equally convulsed, called upon God with strong cries and tears. From this time, I trust, we shall all suffer God to carry on His own work in the way that pleaseth Him.[8]

A few years later, Wesley was visiting Epworth where he had grown up. Because he was not welcome to speak to the congregation where his father had pastored, Wesley took the unusual action of preaching from his father's tombstone. His description of what happened while in Epworth is similar to what happened at other times throughout his ministry. Wesley writes:

> I preached on the righteousness of the law and the righteousness of faith. While I was speaking, several

dropped down as dead and among the rest such a cry was heard of sinners groaning for the righteousness of faith as almost drowned my voice. But many of these soon lifted up their heads with joy and broke out into thanksgiving, being assured they now had the desire of their soul—the forgiveness of their sins.[9]

While Wesley often mentioned the phenomenon of people falling, crying out, etc., this was never his goal. Rather, Wesley focused on what he called "the inward work of God." He sought to see people receive forgiveness and come to a "living faith." He desired to see people's lives transformed. One time Wesley reported that the moral character of Arbroath, a community in Scotland, had been radically changed because people there had responded to the gospel:

In this town there is a change indeed! It was wicked... remarkable for sabbath-breaking, cursing, swearing, drunkenness, and a general contempt of religion. But it is not so now. Open wickedness disappears...no drunkenness seen in the streets. And many have not only ceased from evil and learned to do well, but are witnesses of the inward kingdom of God, "righteousness, peace, and joy in the Holy Ghost."[10]

Healing Accounts

Wesley wrote often of people being healed and delivered from demonic power as a result of prayer. Regarding a New Year's Day service, Wesley writes, "We met, as usual, to renew our covenant with God. It was a solemn season wherein many found His power present to heal and were enabled to urge their way with strength renewed."[11]

Shortly before Christmas in 1742, both Wesley and a coworker, Mr. Meyrick, caught a "violent cold" due to preaching and riding in very cold weather. Wesley recovered, but Mr. Meyrick continued to decline. A few days later, Wesley writes:

> When I came home they told me the physician said he did not expect Mr. Meyrick would live till the morning. I went to him, but his pulse was gone. He had been speechless and senseless for some time. A few of us immediately joined in prayer: (I relate the naked fact:) Before we had done, his sense and his speech returned. Now he that will account for this by natural causes, has my free leave; but I choose to say, this is the power of God.[12]

After his initial recovery, Mr. Meyrick faced a setback. Five days later, on Christmas day, Wesley reports:

> The physician told me he could do no more; Mr. Meyrick could not live over the night. I went up and found them all crying about him; his legs being cold, and (as it seemed) dead already. We all kneeled down and called upon God with strong cries and tears. He opened his eyes and called for me; and, from that hour he continued to recover his strength, till he was restored to perfect health. I wait to hear who will either disprove this fact or philosophically account for it.[13]

After this healing event occurred in 1742, Mr. Meyrick lived decades longer and died in 1770 after a long and fruitful ministry.

Some might wonder why, after what seemed like an initial recovery, Mr. Meyrick became sick again. Why was it necessary for Wesley to pray for him on two different occasions? It would be good to recall that even Jesus laid hands twice on the blind man in Bethsaida. The first time Jesus laid hands on him, the man reported that he saw *men like trees, walking.* The manifestation of the healing was initiated, but not complete. The very next verse describes what Jesus did next: *"Then He put His hands on his eyes again and made him look up. And he was restored and saw everyone clearly"* (Mark 8:25).

Wesley was a learned and intelligent man, and yet he had no difficulty attributing these and other healings to supernatural interventions by God. Wesley wrote more than once of experiencing healing in his own life. For example, he speaks of a time when his horse had become "exceedingly lame" and also of the problems he himself encountered after a time of riding. He states:

> I was thoroughly tired, and my head ached more than it had done for some months…I then thought, "Cannot God heal either man or beast, by any means, or without any?" Immediately my weariness and headache ceased, and my horse's lameness in the same instant. Nor did he halt any more either that day or the next. A very odd accident this also![14]

Clearly, Wesley was being facetious when he referred to these as "accidents."

In yet another situation, Wesley speaks of symptoms being relieved while he preached and then experiencing complete healing manifesting in his body afterward:

> I found myself much out of order. However, I made shift to preach in the evening; but on Saturday my bodily strength

quite failed so that for several hours I could scarcely lift up my head. I was obliged to lie down most part of the day, being easy only in that posture. Yet in the evening my weakness was suspended while I was calling sinners to repentance. But at our love-feast which followed, beside the pain in my back and head and the fever which still continued upon me, just as I began to pray I was seized with such a cough that I could hardly speak. At the same time came strongly into my mind, "These signs shall follow them that believe" [Mark 16:17]. I called on Jesus aloud to "increase my faith" and to "confirm the word of his grace." While I was speaking my pain vanished away; the fever left me; my bodily strength returned; and for many weeks I felt neither weakness nor pain. "Unto thee, O Lord, do I give thanks."[15]

At one point in his ministry, Wesley was accused by a Mr. Church of being an "enthusiast" and of having claimed that healings and supernatural deliverances had happened under his ministry. Wesley's eloquent response demonstrates his firm belief in the supernatural power of God:

As it can be proved by abundance of witnesses that these cures were frequently (indeed almost always) the instantaneous consequences of prayer, your inference is just. I cannot, dare not, affirm that they were purely natural. I believe they were not. I believe many of them were wrought by the supernatural power of God.[16]

In the same response to Mr. Church, Wesley was firm in articulating his position that he had personally witnessed things that could not be explained by natural means. He writes:

> I acknowledge that I have seen with my eyes, and heard with my ears, several things which, to the best of my judgment, cannot be accounted for by the ordinary course of natural causes; and which I therefore believe ought to be "ascribed to the extraordinary interposition of God." If any man choose to style these *miracles*, I reclaim [object] not. I have diligently inquired into the facts. I have weighed the preceding and following circumstances. I have strove to account for them in a natural way. I could not, without doing violence to my reason.[17]

Wesley gave examples of supernatural works he had seen, including a supernatural deliverance of John Haydon from demonic power, and a dramatic healing he himself experienced. He states, "I cannot account for either of these in a natural way. Therefore I believe they were both supernatural."[18]

Wesley was no stranger to objections and criticism; and while some celebrated the works of God taking place, others certainly did not. Joseph Butler, the Bishop of Bristol, was disturbed at what he had heard about the different manifestations taking place in Wesley's ministry, and told him, "The pretending to extraordinary revelations and gifts of the Holy Ghost is a horrid thing, a very horrid thing." This rebuke came to Wesley in spite of them having met to discuss matters on three separate occasions. Wesley, though, was well aware of the possibility of false signs, and addressed the issue thoroughly.

Decently and in Order

What we call extremes or excesses today, Wesley called *extravagance*. Wesley always welcomed the working of the Spirit of God, but he was also keenly aware of fleshly activity that could distract from the gospel. Wesley gladly acknowledged the operation of God's power in the lives of people, but he was also a major proponent of the truth Paul communicates in 1 Corinthians 14:40, *"Let all things be done decently and in order."*

Wesley spoke of believers in one place who had experienced great blessings from God, but then expressed concern, "...even while they are full of love, Satan strives to push many of them to extravagance."[19] He then gave examples of meetings where chaos and confusion reigned. Wesley referred to people screaming, to the "Jumpers in Wales," and even to a group of people who would repeatedly fall and get back up in meetings—it sounds like they were falling for the sake of falling. Wesley states that these types of extravagances "bring the real work [of God] into contempt." He proceeds to admonish, "Yet whenever we reprove them, it should be in the most mild and gentle manner possible."[20]

Wesley was known for his strictness, so it is impressive for him to be calling for correction "in the most mild and gentle manner possible." Perhaps Wesley was basing this on an understanding that if people are corrected with unnecessary harshness, they will be afraid to ever yield to the Holy Spirit, even in the right way. Correction done in love will certainly yield the best results. Twentieth century Pentecostal leader Donald Gee spoke of showing kindness and humility even when people are not expressing the Holy Spirit in the best way possible.

> The true servant of God will ever have his eye and his heart open to help forward a genuine movement of the Spirit of God, though at first he may find it wrapped in the swaddling clothes of the weakness and the foolishness of our poor human nature.[21]

Wesley also spoke of preaching in a place where "outward signs" were not as pronounced as they had been at previous times, and Wesley was fine with that; he recognized that it was a different season for the people in that location. On an earlier visit by Wesley, people had been tremendously convicted of sin, with dramatic, accompanying signs. At this later time, Wesley states, "God was eminently present with us, though rather to comfort than convince" and "Many were refreshed with the multitude of peace."[22] In speaking of some of the more dramatic manifestations such as falling, trembling, etc., Wesley writes elsewhere, "Now these circumstances are common at the dawn of a work, but afterwards, very uncommon."[23]

Wesley did not believe that the same manifestations had to happen all the time, and he realized that there was always the possibility of fleshly counterfeits happening. He states that in some cases, "Satan mimicked this work of God in order to discredit the whole work," but that God "will enable us to discern how far, in every case, the work is pure and where it mixes or degenerates."[24]

Why Had the Gifts Diminished?

While Wesley had seen many manifestations of the Holy Spirit, he was curious as to why the gifts and demonstrations of the Holy Spirit, so prevalent in the early church, had diminished so greatly over the centuries. Referring back to the time of Constantine and the increasing institutionalization of the Church, he addresses this issue head-on:

> The cause of this was not (as has been vulgarly supposed) that there was no more need or occasion for them, because all the world had become Christian. This is a miserable mistake. Not a twentieth part of the world was then nominally Christian. The real cause of the loss was that the love of many, almost all the so-called Christians had grown

cold. The Christians had no more of the Spirit of Christ than the other heathens. The Son of Man, when He came to examine His church, could hardly find faith on earth. This was the real cause why the extraordinary gifts of the Holy Spirit were no longer to be found in the Christian church after that time. It was because the Christians had turned heathen again, and had only a dead form left. So, when this faith and holiness were nearly lost, dry, formal, orthodox men began even then to ridicule whatever gifts they did not have themselves. They belittled and discredited all the gifts of the Spirit as either madness or fraud.[25]

In another communication, Wesley responded to a Dr. Middleton, an anti-supernaturalist who claimed that the gift of tongues had not been heard of since the Reformation. Wesley counters by referring to the French Protestants, who in recent times had claimed to exercise tongues and other miraculous powers.[26]

Wesley actually bemoaned the overall condition of the church relative to the Holy Spirit and His wonderful gifts. Though Wesley witnessed numerous expressions of God's power, he realized that the church, generally speaking, was unaccustomed to and uncomfortable with the third member of the Godhead. He writes:

Who of you is, in any degree, acquainted with the work of his Spirit, his supernatural work in the souls of men? Can you bear, unless now and then, in a church, any talk of the Holy Ghost? Would you not take it for granted, if one began such a conversation, that it was hypocrisy or enthusiasm [extremism]?[27]

Organization and Lasting Influence

The power of God's Spirit working through Wesley has often been ignored, but what has been noted frequently is his organizational prowess. George Whitefield was actually considered to be the better preacher of the two, but Wesley's skills in organization helped perpetuate and maintain the fruit of his labors. Whitefield said:

> My brother Wesley acted wisely. The souls that were awakened under his ministry he joined in class [discipleship groups], and thus preserved the fruits of his labor. This I neglected, and my people are a rope of sand.[28]

Wesley organized his followers into groups that promoted discipleship, accountability, and spiritual growth. Lay preachers were developed and utilized, and women took on leadership roles in overseeing classes for other women. Wesley's programs were designed to supplement the Church of England, not to conflict with it. His lay preachers would not administer communion, as the members of the groups were expected to maintain their membership and involvement in the established church.

Eventually, the Methodists would ordain their own clergy and the societies became fully functioning congregations separate from the Church of England, but that was not Wesley's original intention. Today, Wesley's influence is felt far beyond the Methodist Church. Wesleyan groups, Nazarenes, Holiness groups, Pentecostal churches, Evangelical and Charismatic groups, as well as many "revival" oriented groups and movements all look to Wesley as a significant catalyst to their works.

A Prophetic Warning

Wesley not only grasped the spiritual climate of his own day, he was also a keen student of church history. He was fully aware of how different movements had started in revival but eventually degenerated into lifeless formalism and ritualism. His understanding of these matters prompted him to write:

> I am not afraid that the people called Methodists should ever cease to exist either in Europe or America. But I am afraid lest they should only exist as a dead sect, having the form of religion without the power. And this undoubtedly will be the case, unless they hold fast both the doctrine, spirit, and discipline with which they first set out.[29]

Wesley's prophetic concern was not just valid for his own followers but is a vital admonition to every movement that is birthed in the power of God's Spirit. Even Jesus mentioned the potential of the mighty first-century church of Ephesus losing its lampstand (Revelation 2:5). A church, once aflame with the power of God's Spirit, can lose its influence. It has happened repeatedly throughout church history.

Wesley's knowledge of human nature and of revival itself prompted him to state, "Therefore do I not see how it is possible, in the nature of things, for any revival of true religion to last long."[30] He reasoned that when God works deeply in the heart of people (he called Methodism a "religion of the heart") they become more industrious and prudent, which inevitably leads to prosperity.

Wesley had observed over many decades—he wrote this when he was 83 years old—that when people become more prosperous, they tend to become less reliant on God and digress into carnality. When this happens, Wesley observes, the outward structure of religion will remain, but "the spirit is swiftly vanishing away."[31]

While Wesley was not without hope, he saw only one way for people to experience meaningful, perpetuating revival. Though he saw wrong attitudes toward money as a significant stumbling block, he did not advocate poverty as the means to continuing spiritual vibrancy. Instead, he writes:

> We must exhort all Christians to gain all they can, and to save all they can; that is, in effect, to grow rich! What way, then, (I ask again,) can we take, that our money may not sink us to the nethermost hell? There is one way, and there is no other under heaven. If those who "gain all they can," and "save all they can," will likewise "give all they can;" then, the more they gain, the more they will grow in grace, and the more treasure they will lay up in heaven.[32]

So to Wesley, abundant, overflowing generosity was the only way that a person who had received the outward effects of inward grace would stay on track with God. Wesley's heart had been "strangely warmed" by the Holy Spirit, and he desired all followers of Jesus to stay fervent and passionate toward the things of God.

Endnotes

1. John Wesley, *Journal*, January 24, 1738, vol. 1 of *The Works of John Wesley* (Grand Rapids, MI: Baker Book House, 1986), 74.

2. John Wesley, *Journal*, January 29, 1738, vol. 1 of *The Works of John Wesley* (Grand Rapids, MI: Baker Book House, 1986), 75-76.

3. John Wesley, *Journal*, March 23, 1738, vol. 1 of *The Works of John Wesley* (Grand

Rapids, MI: Baker Book House, 1986), 89.

4. John Wesley, *Journal*, May 24, 1738, vol. 1 of *The Works of John Wesley* (Grand Rapids, MI: Baker Book House, 1986), 103.

5. John Wesley, *Journal*, January 1, 1739, vol. 1 of *The Works of John Wesley* (Grand Rapids, MI: Baker Book House, 1986), 170.

6. John Wesley, *Journal*, April 26, 1739, vol. 1 of *The Works of John Wesley* (Grand Rapids, MI: Baker Book House, 1986), 188.

7. John Wesley, *Journal*, May 9, 1739, vol. 1 of *The Works of John Wesley* (Grand Rapids, MI: Baker Book House, 1986), 193.

8. John Wesley, *Journal*, July 7, 1739, vol. 1 of *The Works of John Wesley* (Grand Rapids, MI: Baker Book House, 1986), 210.

9. John Wesley, *Journal*, June 12, 1742, vol. 1 of *The Works of John Wesley* (Grand Rapids, MI: Baker Book House, 1986), 379.

10. John Wesley, *Journal*, May 5, 1772, vol. 3 of *The Works of John Wesley* (Grand Rapids, MI: Baker Book House, 1986), 462.

11. John Wesley, *Journal*, January 1, 1777, vol. 4 of *The Works of John Wesley* (Grand Rapids, MI: Baker Book House, 1986), 91.

12. John Wesley, *Journal*, December 20, 1742, vol. 1 of *The Works of John Wesley* (Grand Rapids, MI: Baker Book House, 1986), 406.

13. John Wesley, *Journal*, December 25, 1742, vol. 1 of *The Works of John Wesley* (Grand Rapids, MI: Baker Book House, 1986), 406.

14. John Wesley, *Journal*, March 17, 1746, vol. 2 of *The Works of John Wesley* (Grand Rapids, MI: Baker Book House, 1986), 10.

15. John Wesley, *Journal*, May 8, 10, 1741, vol. 1 of *The Works of John Wesley* (Grand Rapids, MI: Baker Book House, 1986), 310.

16. John Wesley, "The Principles of a Methodist Farther Explained," vol. 8 in *The Works of John Wesley* (Grand Rapids: Baker, 1978), 457.

17. Ibid., 460.

18. Ibid.

19. John Wesley, *Journal*, April 3, 1786, vol. 8 in *The Works of John Wesley* (Grand

Rapids, MI: Baker Book House, 1986), 329.

20. Ibid.

21. Donald Gee, *Is It God? Tests for Evaluating the Supernatural* (Springfield, MO: Gospel Publishing House, 1972), 30.

22. John Wesley, *Journal*, November 25, 1759, vol. 2 in *The Works of John Wesley* (Grand Rapids, MI: Baker Book House, 1986), 519.

23. John Wesley, *Journal*, June 5, 1772, vol. 3 in *The Works of John Wesley* (Grand Rapids, MI: Baker Book House, 1986), 472.

24. John Wesley, *Journal*, November 25, 1759, vol. 2 in *The Works of John Wesley* (Grand Rapids, MI: Baker Book House, 1986), 519.

25. John Wesley, "The More Excellent Way," Sermon 89, vol. 7 in *The Works of John Wesley* (Grand Rapids, MI: Baker Book House, 1986), 26-27.

26. John Wesley, "A Letter to the Reverend Dr. Conyers Middleton," vol. 10 in *The Works of John Wesley* (Grand Rapids, MI: Baker Book House, 1978), 55-56.

27. John Wesley, "Scriptural Christianity," Sermon IV, vol. 5 in *The Works of John Wesley* (Grand Rapids, MI: Baker Book House, 1986), 51-52.

28. George Whitefield quoted in Ian J. Maddock, *Men of One Book: A Comparison of Two Methodist Preachers, John Wesley and George Whitefield* (Eugene, OR: Pickwick Publications, 2011), 83.

29. John Wesley, "Thoughts Upon Methodism," vol. 13 in *The Works of John Wesley* (Grand Rapids, MI: Baker, 1978), 258.

30. Ibid., 260.

31. Ibid.

32. Ibid., 260-261.

CHAPTER ELEVEN

GREAT AWAKENINGS IN AMERICA

(Edwards and Finney)

> *I received a mighty baptism of the Holy Ghost. The Holy Spirit descended upon me in a manner that seemed to go through me, body and soul. I could feel the impression, like a wave of electricity, going through and through me. Indeed it seemed to come in waves and waves of liquid love.*
>
> **—Charles Finney**

Jonathan Edwards (1703-1758)

JOHN Wesley was not the only great spiritual leader born in the year 1703. Across the Atlantic, another child—born in East Windsor, Connecticut—would have tremendous influence during a season called the Great Awakening. This was an extended period of revival and outpouring of the Holy Spirit that radically impacted the American colonies.

Jonathan Edwards enrolled in Yale University at the age of thirteen, and after earning two degrees, began serving as an assistant pastor to his grandfather, Solomon Stoddard in Northampton, Massachusetts.

Edwards had not only excelled in his educational pursuits, but had also experienced God's presence and goodness in a profoundly personal and heartfelt way.

> I began to have a new kind of apprehensions and ideas of Christ, and the work of redemption, and the glorious way of salvation by him. I had an inward, sweet sense of these things, that at times came into my heart; and my soul was led away in pleasant views and contemplations of them. And my mind was greatly engaged, to spend my time in reading and meditating on Christ; and the beauty and excellency of his person, and the lovely way of salvation, by free grace in him... And [I] found, from time to time, an inward sweetness, that used...to carry me away in my contemplations; in what I know not how to express otherwise, than by a calm, sweet abstraction of soul from all the concerns of this world.... The sense I had of divine things, would often of a sudden... kindle up a sweet burning in my heart; an ardor of my soul, that I know not how to express.[1]

Following a sixty-year tenure of ministry in Northampton, Edwards' grandfather passed away in 1728, and at the age of twenty-five, Jonathan Edwards assumed spiritual oversight of a congregation with more than six hundred members. Edwards was aware of five different "waves" or seasons of revival that had occurred during his grandfather's pastorate, but at the time Edwards assumed leadership of the Northampton congregation, it was a dry season, a period of spiritual recession. Edwards describes it as "a time of extraordinary dullness in religion" and said there was significant carnality and ungodliness in the community.[2]

In 1733, Edwards begins to describe a moving of God's Spirit that produced an unusually high number of people coming to a saving knowledge of the Lord Jesus Christ. He writes, "The Spirit of God began extraordinarily to set in, and wonderfully work among us."[3] Edwards explains that people of all ages were spiritually impacted, and asserts that the awakening was so profound that "There was scarcely a person in the town, old or young, left unconcerned about the great things of the eternal world."[4] Then, describing the momentum of God's work in the lives of people, he writes, "The work of conversion was carried on in a most astonishing manner, and increased more and more; souls did come as it were by flocks to Jesus Christ."[5]

Edwards paints the following beautiful picture of the awakening as it progressed:

> This work of God, as it was carried on, and the number of true saints multiplied, soon made a glorious alteration in the town: so that in the spring and summer following, anno 1735, the town seemed to be full of the presence of God: it never was so full of love, nor of joy, and yet so full of distress, as it was then. There were remarkable tokens of God's presence in almost every house. It was a time of joy in families on account of salvation being brought to them; parents rejoicing over their children as new born, and husbands over their wives, and wives over their husbands. The doings of God were then seen in His sanctuary, God's day was a delight, and His tabernacles were amiable. Our public assemblies were then beautiful: the congregation was alive in God's service, every one earnestly intent on the public worship, every hearer eager to drink in the words of the minister as they came from his mouth; the assembly in general were, from time to time, in tears while the word was preached; some weeping with sorrow and distress, others

with joy and love, others with pity and concern for the souls of their neighbors.[6]

Edwards estimated that more than 300 persons came to Christ in his community alone in a period of six months, and remarkably, this divine outpouring was not restricted exclusively to Northampton. "Many places in Connecticut," he notes, "have partaken in the same mercy."[7]

Edwards also marveled at the rapidity with which God worked in the lives of people, stating that God was doing in a matter of a couple of days what would normally take an entire year. He states:

> God has also seemed to have gone out of His usual way, in the quickness of His work, and the swift progress His Spirit has made in His operations on the hearts of many. It is wonderful that persons should be so suddenly and yet so greatly changed. Many have been taken from a loose and careless way of living, and seized with strong convictions of their guilt and misery, and in a very little time old things have passed away, and all things have become new with them. God's work has also appeared very extraordinary in the degrees of His influences; in the degrees both of awakening and conviction, and also of saving light, love, and joy, that many have experienced. It has also been very extraordinary in the extent of it, and its being so swiftly propagated from town to town.[8]

Edwards not only witnessed a great working of God's Spirit, but he also gave deep and considerable thought to it. God had given him a great intellect and a strong sense of discernment, and Edwards made many tremendous observations.

Many of the people converted in Northampton and other parts of New England exhibited certain "outward signs" as they came under conviction from the Holy Spirit. Throughout his writings, Edwards identifies weeping and tears, trembling, groans, loud outcries, agonies of body, sighing, fainting, and the failing of bodily strength as some of the expressions he witnessed.[9] He did not take the position that these types of manifestations, which typically took place during the preaching of God's Word, were automatically and always the work of God's Spirit, but neither did he discount them as necessarily being counterfeit or out of order.

In 1741, Edwards wrote *Distinguishing Marks of a Work of the Spirit of God* to help believers understand the difference between the work of the Holy Spirit, flesh-based excesses, and demonic counterfeits. Edwards believed he had witnessed many evidences of genuine works of the Holy Spirit and did not believe that counterfeits or excesses invalidated the authentic. He states, "The devil's sowing such tares is no proof that a true work of the Spirit of God is not gloriously carried on."[10] In other words, Edwards advocated not "throwing out the baby with the bathwater."

Edwards believed that God sometimes revealed His wrath or His love to people present in the church services, and this often led to what he called "bodily effects." The revealing of God's wrath to individuals was not designed to leave them hopeless or condemned, but rather, to bring them to a place of sober repentance where they would reach out to receive the grace and mercy of God unto salvation. Edwards saw many people react to impressions from the Spirit of God in fairly dramatic ways, and he wrote, "No wonder that the wrath of God, when manifested but a little to the soul, overbears human strength."[11]

Edwards did not believe—in many cases of people being overcome and overwhelmed—that it was mere emotionalism, or *enthusiasm*, according to the popular term of that day. Rather, he believed there were many legitimate occasions where the Spirit of God enabled an individual to perceive something very powerful of the eternal world. When this happened, a bodily response is readily understood. He writes of people who were overwhelmed by a Spirit-given encounter with God's love:

> It may easily be accounted for, that a true sense of the glorious excellency of the Lord Jesus Christ, and of his wonderful dying love, and the exercise of a truly spiritual love and joy, should be very much as to overcome the bodily strength.... Therefore, it is not at all strange that God should sometimes give his saints such foretastes of heaven, as to diminish their bodily strength.[12]

Like Wesley in England, Edwards sometimes saw people sink to the ground as they were overcome by convicting power of the Spirit of God. As a matter of fact, Wesley had read reports of the Great Awakening in the American colonies and was greatly inspired by them.

Edwards was well aware that several critics disliked outward expressions in church services, but he defended what he felt were legitimate manifestations by using biblical examples. For example, he points out that when there was a supernatural working of God, the Philippian jailer *"when he, in utmost distress and amazement, came trembling and fell down before Paul and Silas... and said, 'Sirs, what must I do to be saved?'"* (Acts 16:29-30).[13] He also cited examples of the Queen of Sheba being overwhelmed when she beheld the glory of Solomon (1 Kings 10:4), the disciples crying out for fear when they saw Jesus walking on the water (Matthew 14:26), and even the bride being faint with lovesickness (Song of Solomon 2:5) as scriptural examples that illustrated and paralleled the bodily effects experienced by Christians who were having encounters with the Holy Spirit. Having cited these and other examples, Edwards writes, "We may at least argue, that such an effect may well be supposed to arise, from such a cause in the saints in some cases, and that such an effect will sometimes be seen in the church of Christ."[14]

Edwards also countered the criticism that many were receiving strong "impressions" during spiritual experiences and encounters. He writes:

> It is no argument that a work is not of the Spirit of God, that some who are the subjects of it have been in a kind of ecstasy, wherein they have been carried beyond themselves, and have had their minds transported into a train of strong and pleasing imaginations, and a kind of visions, as though they were rapt up even to heaven, and there saw glorious sights. I have been acquainted with some such instances.[15]

Edwards refuted those who said such ecstatic experiences were demonic in origin, and he also denied that such experiences were of the same authoritative nature as those that Paul and other biblical figures had. He simply did not think it strange that "persons under a true sense of the glorious and wonderful greatness and excellency of divine things, and soul-ravishing views of the beauty and love of Christ, should have the strength of nature overpowered."[16]

After addressing and countering many of the arguments that others made against outward signs that accompany a work of God's Spirit, Edwards articulates five major points of criteria that should be considered in evaluating whether a true work of God is taking place. The foundational Scripture Edwards used for his book, *Distinguishing Marks of a Work of the Spirit of God*, is 1 John 4:1, which reads, "*Beloved, do not believe every spirit, but test the spirits, whether they are of God; because many false prophets have gone out into the world.*" Beginning with that verse, and continuing through the next several verses, Edwards proposes the following five points as a means of testing whether a work is of God. I have paraphrased the gist of each of his points as section headings.

TESTING THE SPIRITS

1. A true work of God exalts Jesus.

Edwards believed strongly that any operation of the Holy Spirit always brings the focus to Jesus Christ, exalting Him as the Son of God and as the Savior of all. Edwards laid special emphasis upon the importance of Jesus being truthfully presented according to what the Scripture teaches of Him. The devil's work will never exalt Jesus truthfully because:

> The devil has the most bitter and implacable enmity against that person, especially in his character of the Savior of men; he mortally hates the story and doctrine of his redemption; he never would go about to beget in men more honorable thoughts of him, and lay greater weight on his instructions and commands.[17]

2. A true work of God works against Satan's kingdom, sin, and worldly lust.

Edwards cites 1 John 4:4, "*You are of God, little children, and have overcome them, because He who is in you is greater than he who is in the world*," and expounds on the fact that when the Spirit of God works in our lives, He gives believers victory over the fleshly and demonic elements at work in the world.

3. A true work of God respects the divine authority of Scripture.

Contrary to other influences that would devalue Scripture or direct people to other sources of guidance and authority, the Holy Spirit will always direct us to God's Word—the Bible. A wrong spirit, Edwards argues, will not direct people to or promote Scripture.

> The devil has ever shown a mortal spite and hatred towards that holy book the Bible: he has done all in his power to extinguish that light; and to draw men off from it: he knows it to be that light by which his kingdom of darkness is to be overthrown.[18]

4. A true work of God promotes the "Spirit of Truth" against the "spirit of error."

Referencing 1 John 4:6, Edwards asserts that the Holy Spirit will lead people into the great truths that bring them to an awareness of sin and redemption, and to an accurate understanding of themselves and of the nature of God. The Holy Spirit "represents things as they truly are."[19]

5. A true work of God produces love for God and love for people.

Having addressed issues of discernment from 1 John 4:1-6, Edwards proceeds to highlight the apostle John's emphasis throughout the rest of the chapter on divine love as the most significant factor in recognizing a true work of God. Edwards acknowledges that there is "counterfeit love, that often appears among those who are led by a spirit of delusion,"[20] but is confident that what Scripture says of love will clearly delineate God's love from the counterfeit. Edwards writes:

> The surest character of true divine supernatural love— distinguishing it from counterfeits that arise from a natural self-love is, that the Christian virtue of humility shines in it; that which above all other renounces, abases, and annihilates what we term self. Christian love or, or true charity, is an humble love (1 Corinthians 13:4-5).[21]

ANOTHER WAVE OF REVIVAL (1740-1742)

Following an initial season of revival (1735-36), Edwards reports that there was a lull, of sorts, that occurred. In 1743, he wrote an account of a subsequent wave that took place—*An Account of the Revival of Religion in Northampton 1740-1742.* In this, he speaks of a very positive alteration that had taken place in the community in the wake of the previous revival season, and noted evidences of another resurgence of spiritual hunger that took place beginning in 1740. This momentum was greatly enhanced when George Whitefield, the famed British evangelist, came and preached in the Northampton church. Edwards remarks that "the congregation was extraordinarily melted by every sermon; almost the whole assembly being in tears for a great part of the sermon time."[22]

In the second wave, Edwards specifically notes that many children and young people were powerfully affected by the move of God's Spirit. In one situation, Edwards describes a scenario where several "appeared to be overcome with a sense of the greatness and glory of divine things, and with admiration, love, joy, and praise, and compassion"[23] and at the same time, many others:

> were overcome with distress about their sinful and miserable estate and condition; so that the whole room was full of nothing but outcries, faintings, and the like. Others soon heard of it in several parts of the town, and came to them; and what they saw and heard there was greatly affecting to them, so that many of them were overpowered in like manner, and it continued thus for some hours; the time being spent in prayer, singing, counseling, and conferring.[24]

Edwards indicates that the spiritual momentum continued powerfully and reports that many fell under conviction and that many were converted. He writes, "It was a very frequent thing to see a house full of out-cries, faintings, convulsions, and such like, both with distress, and also with admiration and joy."[25] He also observes that it was not customary to have meetings that went late into the evening hours, nevertheless "there were some that were so affected, and their bodies so overcome, that they could not go home, but were obliged to stay all night where they were."[26]

Edwards even notes:

> There were some instances of persons lying in a sort of trance, remaining perhaps for a whole twenty-four hours motionless, and with their senses locked up; but in the meantime under strong imaginations, as though they went to heaven and had there a vision of glorious and delightful objects.[27]

He remarks that in these very intense cases, some had problems maintaining their balance and spiritual equilibrium, and that efforts were made to "keep the people, many of them, from running wild."[28]

AFTER THE REVIVALS

Jonathan Edwards saw many outstanding expressions of God's Spirit, during his pastorate, and he provided a great analysis and articulation of what he had witnessed. In spite of his brilliance, he was dismissed from his church in 1750. When his tenure in Northampton ended, Edwards and his wife relocated to Stockbridge, Massachusetts, and he served as missionary pastor to Native Americans. He also used this time to continue writing. After a few years in Stockbridge, he became the president of the College of New Jersey, which would later become Princeton. He died shortly after his installation.

Charles Finney (1792-1875)

The year after John Wesley died in England, Charles Grandison Finney was born in Connecticut. When Finney was a toddler, his family moved to New York, and this lawyer-turned-preacher would eventually make an indelible mark on revivalism and evangelicalism in the United States. As a young man, he was disinterested in religion, but scriptural references in law books piqued his curiosity, so he purchased a Bible in order to study it for himself. He began to attend church and was exposed to hyper-Calvinism, a theology that Finney would soundly reject. Of his pastor, Finney writes, "I was rather perplexed than edified by his preaching."[29]

After being involved in church, Finney recognized a spiritual deficiency in his life. He states, "I became very restless. A little consideration convinced me I was by no means in a state of mind to go to heaven if I should die" and "still my mind was not made up as to the truth or falsehood of the Gospel and of the Christian religion."[30] The Holy Spirit worked on Finney's heart; and in the autumn of 1821, he diligently sought to know the truth. After much wrestling in his soul, Finney came into saving faith and describes the assurance he received in these words: "The repose of my mind was unspeakably great. I never can describe it in words. The thought of God was sweet to my mind, and the most profound spiritual tranquility had taken full possession of me."[31] He also said, "There was a great sweetness and tenderness in my thoughts and feelings."[32]

Finney was very soon to experience another dimension of the Holy Spirit's work in his life beyond salvation and assurance. After an encounter where "it seemed as if I met the Lord Jesus Christ face to face," Finney says:

I received a mighty baptism of the Holy Ghost. Without any expectation of it...the Holy Spirit descended upon me in a manner that seemed to go through me, body and soul. I could feel the impression, like a wave of electricity, going through and through me. Indeed it seemed to come in waves and waves of liquid love, for I could not express it in any other way. It seemed like the very breath of God. I can recollect distinctly that it seemed to fan me, like immense wings. No words can express the wonderful love that was shed abroad in my heart. I wept aloud with joy and love; and I do not know but I should say, I literally bellowed out the unutterable gushings of my heart. These waves came over me, and over me, and over me, one after the other, until I recollect I cried out, "I shall die if these waves continue to pass over me." I said, "Lord, I cannot bear any more;" yet I had no fear of death. How long I continued in this state, with this baptism continuing to roll over me and go through me, I do not know.[33]

From that time forward, Finney was empowered as a witness for the Lord Jesus, and many with whom he interacted on a personal basis came under conviction and were gloriously saved.

AN UNSAVED WOMAN HEALED AND SAVED

In addition to abundant evangelistic fruit that sprang from Finney's life, he also began learning about cooperating with the Holy Spirit in prayer. He relates that the Lord taught him "in those early days of my Christian experience, many very important truths in regard to the spirit of prayer."[34] He then shares of hearing about an unsaved woman he knew who had fallen sick and was not expected to live through the night.

He speaks of the intense burden of prayer that came upon him and how challenging it was to respond. He writes, "I struggled, but could not say much. I could only groan with groanings loud and deep."[35]

After an evening of agonizing prayer, Finney sensed the Lord's peace and assurance and became fully persuaded that the woman would recover. By the next day, the woman had already begun to improve. Finney told her husband that his wife would not die of this sickness, nor would she die in her sins. True to what Finney had prayed through and boldly said, the woman recovered and came to faith in Christ. This experience was new to Finney and mystified him somewhat, but he said a Christian brother explained to him that his time in prayer was merely the travail of his soul, and Finney states, "A few minutes conversation, and pointing me to certain scriptures, gave me to understand what it was."[36]

EARLY EXPERIENCES

In the very early days of his preaching, Finney faced a resistant, somewhat hostile congregation. Instead of backing down from the obstinate crowd, Finney writes:

> The Spirit of God came upon me with such power that it was like opening a battery upon them. I took it for granted that they were committed against the Lord, and for an hour and a half the Word of God came through me as a fire and a hammer breaking the rock, and a sword piercing to the dividing asunder of soul and spirit.[37]

Instead of a negative reaction, Finney noted that many were under such conviction that they could not raise their heads, and different ones were calling upon Finney throughout the evening to pray for them. Finney's biographer writes, "A woman was on the floor speechless and helpless, and remained so for sixteen hours, when she came out with the song of salvation upon her lips."[38]

One of the dramatic conversions that took place under Finney's ministry was that of a woman whose husband had previously led her into Universalism. She was dying, but Finney led her to faith in Jesus, and the husband was enraged. The man took a loaded pistol to the church where Finney was preaching, intending to kill him. Instead of carrying out his murderous plan, the gospel and the power of God radically impacted the man, and he spent the night agonizing over his fallen and sinful condition. The next morning, he "met Finney in the street, lifted him from his feet, and swung him around in a Christian embrace."[39]

IN SODOM, NEW YORK

Finney traveled and preached in many locations in the northeastern part of the United States, calling people to repentance and to faith in the Lord Jesus Christ. In one location, Finney observed that the people were particularly profane, and he preached about the judgment that came upon biblical Sodom, not realizing that the community he was in was itself called Sodom in New York. In spite of initial resistance, Finney writes:

> In a few moments there seemed to fall upon the congregation an instantaneous shock. I cannot describe the sensation that I felt, nor that which was apparent in the congregation; but the word seemed literally to cut like a sword. The power from on high came down upon them in such a torrent that they fell from their seats in every direction. In less than a minute nearly the whole congregation were either down on their knees, or on their faces, or in some position prostrate before God. Everyone was crying or groaning for mercy upon his own soul.[40]

This type of spiritual outpouring happened frequently when Finney preached the gospel, especially in his earlier years of preaching, and Finney addressed such outward, physical manifestations. He writes:

> In every age of the Church, cases have occurred in which persons have had such clear manifestations of Divine truth as to prostrate their physical strength entirely. This appears to have been the case with Daniel. He fainted and was unable to stand. Saul of Tarsus seems to have been overwhelmed and prostrated under the blaze of Divine glory that surrounded him. I have met with many cases where the physical powers were entirely prostrated by a clear apprehension of the infinitely great and weighty truths of religion.[41]

Finney was clear in his assessment that there were both legitimate and fanatical physical manifestations that occurred in revival meetings. He states that legitimate expressions occur when, "the soul is shut up to God," when there is "a simple revelation of God to the soul by the Holy Ghost," and when there "is a calm, deep, sacred flow of the soul in view of the clear, infinitely important, and impressive truths of God."[42]

IN ROME, NEW YORK

One might wonder if Finney was a sensationalist who tried to make these outbursts happen. On the contrary, he did not want these outward expressions to be a distraction. For example, in Rome, New York, Finney says:

> The Spirit's work was so spontaneous, so powerful and so overwhelming, as to render it necessary to exercise the greatest caution and wisdom, in conducting all the meetings,

in order to prevent an undesirable outburst of feeling, that soon would have exhausted the sensibility of the people....[43]

Finney's goals were to see repentance and faith established in people's lives, but he understood that at times, genuine outward expressions did happen. However, he did not hype people or try to force such manifestations.

In one of his first meetings in Rome, Finney sensed the growing intensity of the spiritual atmosphere. He explains that "the feeling was so deep, that there was danger of an outburst of feeling, that would be almost uncontrollable" and he states, "nothing had been said or done to create any excitement in the meeting. The feeling was all spontaneous."[44] Not wanting to see an excessive outburst, Finney dismissed the congregation and asked them to be silent, not speaking to each other as they left the sanctuary. In spite of Finney's instruction, the people were so moved by the Spirit of God that the dismissal did not reflect the serenity Finney desired.

> One of the first young men in the place, so nearly fainted, that he fell upon some young men that stood near him; and they all of them partially swooned away, and fell together. This had well-nigh produced a loud shrieking; but I hushed them down, and said to the young men, "Please set that door wide open, and go out, and let all retire in silence." They did as I requested. They did not shriek; but they went out sobbing and sighing, and their sobs and sighs could be heard till they got out into the street.[45]

In the days that followed, people in the town were profoundly affected by the convicting power of the Holy Spirit, bringing many to repentance and salvation.

The night after the attempted "quiet dismissal," Finney notes that "We saw people hurrying, and some of them actually running to the meeting. They were coming from every direction."[46] He also writes:

> This meeting was very much like the one we had had the night before. The feeling was overwhelming. Some men of the strongest nerves were so cut down by the remarks which were made, that they were unable to help themselves, and had to be taken home by their friends.[47]

Finney preached for twenty nights in a row and twice on the Sabbath, and multiple salvations took place. The host pastor speculated that there were nearly five hundred conversions in those twenty days of outpouring. Finney's biographer notes that "that there was not a case of apostasy after eight months."[48]

Perhaps one of the reasons Finney witnessed such life-transforming expressions of God's power is because of his commitment to the genuine and his disdain for the counterfeit. Finney witnessed other ministers trying to hype congregations into acting certain ways and then claiming it was an expression of the power of God. In a chapter titled Excitement in Revivals, Finney describes a minister who stood before a group of women, clapping his hands, and shouting loudly, "POWER, POWER, POWER!"

He describes the event as "calculated" and states that even though people eventually did cry out and fall, there was no spiritual substance to it. He writes, "there was not a word of truth communicated; there was no prayer or exhortation" and states, "So far as such efforts to promote revivals are made, they are undoubtedly highly disastrous, and should be entirely discouraged."[49] It seems that Finney highly respected spontaneous responses that were a genuine response to the truth and the presence of God, but he had no use for coerced or manipulated attempts by ministers to manufacture similar reactions.

Finney understood that a certain level of excitement would accompany a true revival but expressed concern about superficiality in some revival works. He believed that too much emphasis on excitement created significant problems. In a chapter titled Unhealthy Revival Excitement, Finney writes:

> Now, just so much excitement is important in revivals as is requisite to secure the fixed and thorough attention of the mind to the truth, and no more. When excitement goes beyond this, it is always dangerous. When excitement is very great, so as really to carry the will, the subjects of this excitement invariably deceive themselves. They get the idea that they are religious in proportion as they are governed by their feelings.[50]

The reason Finney did not want people hyper-emotional or overly excited in his meetings is because he believed it distracted from the true work that God wanted to accomplish in people's lives. Finney writes, "The more calm the soul can be kept while it gazes on those truths, the more free is the will left to comply with obligation as it lies revealed in the intelligence."[51]

To Finney, the goal was always to preach the truth of the gospel with a view toward the conversion of the lost. He never advocated stirring people up emotionally for the sake of mere emotionalism, but he also encouraged ministers not to be consumed with suppressing emotions. He writes:

> It should be remembered that great revivals of religion can never exist without deep excitement of feeling; and yet it is

193

the revival of religion at which we ought to aim; and since some excitement is naturally and necessarily incidental to a revival of religion, let it come, and do not fear it.[52]

In effect, it seems as though Finney wanted believers to recognize the difference between the substance of revival and the effect of revival. The display of excitement and emotions may have been a legitimate effect, but the true substance and purpose of revival is the proclamation of Jesus and the transformation of lives by the Holy Spirit.

ROCHESTER, NEW YORK

The high-water mark of Finney's revival work took place in Rochester, New York, over a six-month period in 1830. While the city itself was the epicenter of this revival, it affected the entire northeast. Towns and Porter note, "According to one estimate, news of the Rochester Revival sparked revival fires in 1,500 towns and villages throughout New England."[53] Finney said, "the work spread like waves in every direction."[54]

During the Rochester Revival, Finney was also invited to come speak in a local high school. Finney was told years later by one of the school administrators that "more than forty persons that were then converted in that school had become ministers," and that "a large number of them had become foreign missionaries."[55]

Finney said that the work of God "made a great change in the moral state and subsequent history of Rochester," and that "The great majority of the leading men and women in the city were converted."[56] Crediting the influence of the revival, Rochester's district attorney told Finney years afterward, "the population of Rochester had increased two-thirds from the revival in 1830, but the crime rate reduced by two-thirds over the same span."[57]

BEHIND THE SCENES PRAYER

Finney also noted that there was a spirit of prevailing prayer behind the work in Rochester. He refers specifically to Mr. Abel Clary, who had been saved at the same time as Finney, and says that Clary was in Rochester for the entire time that Finney was. He says that Clary never attended the meetings but gave himself to continual prayer support for Finney and the work of God that was taking place. Finney writes of Clary:

> He had been licensed to preach; but his spirit of prayer was such, he was so burdened with the souls of men, that he was not able to preach much, his whole time and strength being given to prayer. The burden of his soul would frequently be so great that he was unable to stand, and he would writhe and groan in agony. I was well acquainted with him, and knew something of the wonderful spirit of prayer that was upon him. He was a very silent man, as almost all are who have that powerful spirit of prayer.[58]

Finney also refers to another brother in the Lord, Father Nash, "who in several of my fields of labor came to me and aided me." He said that Nash was "another of those men that had such a powerful spirit of prevailing prayer."[59]

One of the highest commendations of the revival in Rochester came from Lyman Beecher (1775-1863), the famed Boston preacher, whose daughter, Harriet Beecher Stowe, authored *Uncle Tom's Cabin*, and whose son, Henry Ward Beecher, became the most popular American preacher in the next generation. Lyman Beecher had initially criticized and opposed Finney's work so intensely that he wrote:

Finney, I know your plan, and you know I do; you mean to come into Connecticut and carry a streak of fire to Boston. But if you attempt it, as the Lord liveth, I'll meet you at the State line, and call out all the artillerymen, and fight every inch of the way to Boston, and then I'll fight you there.[60]

Beecher changed his views over time and later welcomed Finney to Boston, where Finney would preach in various churches for a year. Finney's one-time opponent, now friend, said of his Rochester meetings:

That was the greatest work of God, and the greatest revival that the world has ever seen in so short a time. One hundred thousand were reported as having connected themselves with churches as the results of that great revival. This is unparalleled in the history of the church.[61]

Finney was not afraid to break conventional molds. In a sense, he was a pragmatist, focusing on what worked, not simply following traditional models. Instead of a Sunday-only approach, Finney held extended meetings on consecutive evenings. He believed in directly confronting the spiritual needs of people, challenging them to respond to what he preached. He instituted the "anxious bench" where people could come for instruction and ministry and was also a proponent of altar calls.

Finney also prayed to God in common, everyday language, and encouraged women to pray publicly. Along with his overall message and these types of measures, Finney is often referred to as the "Father of Modern Revivalism."

Endnotes

1. Jonathan Edwards, *Letters and Personal Writings*, ed. George S. Claghorn, *The Works of Jonathan Edwards*, vol. 16 (New Haven, CT: Yale University Press, 1998), 792-793.

2. Jonathan Edwards, *A Faithful Narrative of the Surprising Work of God*, vol. 1, in *The Works of Jonathan Edwards* (Edinburgh, UK: The Banner of Truth Trusts, 1834), 347.

3. Ibid., 348.

4. Ibid.

5. Ibid.

6. Ibid.

7. Ibid., 349.

8. Ibid., 350.

9. Jonathan Edwards, *Distinguishing Marks of a Work of the Spirit of God*, vol. 2, in *The Works of Jonathan Edwards* (Edinburgh, UK: The Banner of Truth Trusts, 1834), 261.

10. Ibid., 265.

11. Ibid., 261.

12. Ibid., 261-262.

13. Ibid., 262.

14. Ibid.

15. Ibid., 263.

16. Ibid.

17. Ibid., 266-267.

18. Ibid., 267.

19. Ibid., 268.

20. Ibid.

21. Ibid.

22. Jonathan Edwards, *Narrative of the Revival at Northampton in 1740-1742 (Memoirs)* vol. 1, in *The Works of Jonathan Edwards* (Edinburgh, UK: The Banner of Truth Trusts, 1834), lvii.

23. Ibid.

24. Ibid.

25. Ibid.

26. Ibid.

27. Ibid., lix.

28. Ibid.

29. Charles G. Finney, *Memoirs of Revivals in Religion*, vol. 1, in *The Works of Charles Finney* (New York: A.S. Barnes & Company Publishers, 1876), loc. 12905, Kindle.

30. Ibid., loc. 12927, Kindle.

31. Ibid., loc. 13050, Kindle.

32. Ibid., loc. 13052, Kindle.

33. Ibid., loc. 13074, Kindle.

34. Ibid., loc. 13291, Kindle.

35. Ibid., loc. 13296, Kindle.

36. Ibid., loc. 13308, Kindle.

37. Charles G. Finney, in A. M. Hills, *Biography of Charles Finney*, vol. 1, in *The Works of Charles Finney* (Cincinnati, OH: Mount of Blessings, 1902), loc. 502, Kindle.

38. Ibid., loc. 505, Kindle.

39. Ibid., loc. 512, Kindle.

40. Charles Finney, *Power From on High*, vol. 1, in *The Works of Charles Finney* (Classic Christian E-Books, c. 1871), loc. 2916, Kindle.

41. Charles Finney, *Revival Fire*, vol. 1, in *The Works of Charles Finney* (Classic Christian E-Books), loc. 11920, Kindle.

42. Finney, *Revival Fire*, loc. 11952, Kindle.

43. Finney, *Memoirs*, loc. 15045, Kindle.

44. Ibid., loc. 14920, Kindle.

45. Ibid., loc. 14934, Kindle.

46. Ibid., loc. 14953, Kindle.

47. Ibid., loc. 14955, Kindle.

48. A. M. Hills, *Biography of Charles Finney*, vol. 1, in *The Works of Charles Finney* (Cincinnati, OH: Mount of Blessings, 1902), loc. 88, Kindle.

49. Finney, *Revival Fire*, loc. 11976, Kindle.

50. Ibid., loc. 11643, Kindle.

51. Ibid., loc. 11680, Kindle.

52. Ibid., loc. 12674, Kindle.

53. Elmer Towns and Douglas Porter, *The Ten Greatest Revivals Ever: From Pentecost to the Present* (Ann Arbor, MI: Servant Publications, 2000), loc. 102, Kindle.

54. Finney, *Memoirs*, loc. 16788, Kindle.

55. Ibid., loc. 16689, Kindle.

56. Ibid., loc. 16697, Kindle.

57. McDow and Reid, *Firefall 2.0*, 222, Kindle.

58. Finney, *Memoirs*, loc. 16739, Kindle.

59. Ibid., loc. 16749, Kindle.

60. Lyman Beecher, *Autobiography, Correspondence, Etc. of Lyman Beecher*, ed. Charles Beecher (New York: Harper & Brothers, 1864), loc. 8946, Kindle.

61. Finney, *Memoirs*, loc. 16797, Kindle.

CHAPTER TWELVE

SPIRIT-EMPOWERED EVANGELISM

(Spurgeon and Moody)

If we think to succeed without the Spirit, we are not after the Pentecostal order. If we have not the Spirit which Jesus promised, we cannot perform the commission which Jesus gave.

—Charles H. Spurgeon

Charles Spurgeon (1834-1892)

KNOWN as the "Prince of Preachers," Charles Spurgeon brought a degree of eloquence to the pulpit that perhaps has never been rivaled. At the age of nineteen, Spurgeon preached his first message at London's New Park Street Chapel to the eighty people in attendance. He became their pastor, and the church experienced continuous growth for years. In 1861, the congregation relocated to the new Metropolitan Tabernacle that seated a staggering 5,600 people. Though Spurgeon did not have a college degree, his personal library ultimately contained more than 12,000 volumes.

When Spurgeon died in 1892, close to 60,000 people came to pay respects at the Metropolitan Tabernacle as his body lay in state. In addition to preaching for forty years, Spurgeon had published 140 books and had established a large orphanage, homes for the poor, and a school for pastors. It is hard not to be impressed with some of the externals of Spurgeon's ministry, but the fruit is most understandable when his spiritual foundation and values are examined.

Spurgeon was known for preaching Christ-centered, Christ-exalting, Bible-based messages, and he vigorously defended the faith in the midst of various controversies throughout his life. In addition to being a man of "The Book," he continuously acknowledged the enablement and empowerment of the Holy Spirit in his ministry.

Theologically, Spurgeon was a Calvinist, as was George Whitefield and Jonathan Edwards, whereas John Wesley and Charles Finney held to Arminian views. Simplistically stated, Calvinists emphasize God's sovereignty, predestination, and election. Arminian theology, on the other hand, stresses free will and human responsibility. Interestingly, God worked powerfully through all of them as they proclaimed Jesus as Savior and Lord.

Spurgeon made certain statements that expressed his belief that certain gifts of the Spirit had ceased, and yet many statements he made also show his deep reliance upon the Person of the Holy Spirit. Ironically, several of Spurgeon's experiences seem to fit the description of what modern Pentecostals or Charismatics would call gifts of the Spirit, even though Spurgeon did not classify them that way. Is it possible that genuine gifts of the Holy Spirit can operate through a person even if he or she doesn't label them as such, or that they are the very gifts described in the New Testament?

A gift exists because of the power behind it, not because of the label we give it. It would be well to remember Shakespeare's words as conveyed through his character Juliet: "What's in a name? That which we call a rose by any other name would smell as sweet." While cessationists—those who believe certain operations of the Holy Spirit have ceased—and continuationists—those who believe all of the gifts the Holy Spirit are still available—may differ in their interpretations of what Spurgeon experienced, Spurgeon clearly believed that the Holy Spirit was working through his ministry to confirm the gospel and bring people to the saving knowledge of Jesus Christ.

Spurgeon's father and grandfather were both pastors, but Charles did not enter ministry simply because it was the "family business." Rather, he had a very distinct and unique call of God upon his own life. Spurgeon refers to a great soul-winning minister named Richard Knill. This minister was visiting Spurgeon's grandfather's home, and he perceived a strong calling upon young Charles. When Spurgeon was around ten years old, Knill laid hands on and prayed for the young boy. He spoke these words over him, "This child will one day preach the gospel, and he will preach it to great multitudes. I am persuaded that he will preach in the chapel at Rowland Hill, where (I think he said) I am now the minister."[1]

One of Spurgeon's biographers was Russell H. Conwell, the founder and first president of Temple University in Philadelphia, Pennsylvania. He was also the pastor of the distinguished Grace Baptist Church in Philadelphia, and was personally acquainted with Spurgeon. Conwell believed that Knill's words spoken over young Spurgeon reflect "...a supernatural foresight, and that a gleam of divine light opened to him the future of this servant of God."[2]

Conwell also writes, "We believe Mr. Knill's prophecy was supernatural." While Spurgeon's call came from God, and was merely acknowledged by Knill, those words represent a powerful recognition of God's call. It is easy here to remember the exhortations given by the apostle Paul to his protégé and to see the parallels with what Spurgeon would experience centuries later as a ten-year-old.

> *This charge I commit to you, son Timothy, according to the prophecies previously made concerning you, that by them you may wage the good warfare* (1 Timothy 1:18).

> *Do not neglect the gift that is in you, which was given to you by prophecy with the laying on of the hands of the eldership* (1 Timothy 4:14).

> *I remind you to stir up the gift of God which is in you through the laying on of my hands* (2 Timothy 1:6).

A MINISTRY BIRTHED IN PRAYER

When Spurgeon first preached at the church he would pastor in London, he quickly discovered that the congregation was greatly given to prayer. Though it was not the large congregation it would ultimately become, Spurgeon commented upon the earnestness of their prayers and acknowledged the presence of God that was tangibly present. He observes:

> More than once, we were all so awestruck with the solemnity of the meeting, that we sat silent for some moments while the Lord's power appeared to overshadow us; and all I could do on such occasions was to pronounce the Benediction, and say, "Dear friends, we have had the Spirit of God here very manifestly tonight; let us go home, and take care not to lose His gracious influences."[3]

Spurgeon notes that tremendous outcomes resulted from the prayers of these believers. He writes, "Then down came the blessing; the house was filled with hearers, and many souls were saved" and that "soon the blessing came upon us in such abundance that we had not room to receive it."[4] Though Spurgeon was no doubt a gifted and talented individual, he fully recognized that the source of blessing was not himself, but God, and that it was the prayers of all the people that made power-producing results available.

SPURGEON AND DIVINE HEALING

In his biography on Spurgeon, Conwell has a fascinating chapter titled Wonderful Healing in which he recounts numerous examples of Spurgeon praying for sick members in his church and the recoveries that followed. He writes that Spurgeon had diligently studied, with great interest, the topic of divine healing. Spurgeon, he said, had many experiences of people not recovering from their illnesses after prayer, but notes:

> Such experiences would have discouraged him entirely in the theory that there was any use in prayer, had it not been for the wonderfully direct recovery of other people under circumstances which showed that there was no other possible solution to the mystery but in saying that the prayer had a definite and miraculous influence.[5]

Conwell proceeds to note the extensiveness of people who benefitted from Spurgeon's prayers for them while they were on the sickbed. Writing in 1893, he states:

> There are now living and worshipping in the Metropolitan Tabernacle hundreds of people who ascribe the extension of their life to the effect of Mr. Spurgeon's personal prayers. They have been sick with disease and nigh unto death, he

has appeared, kneeled by their beds, and prayed for their recovery. Immediately the tide of health returned, the fevered impulse became calm, the temperature was reduced, and all the activities of nature resumed their normal functions within a short and unexpected period.[6]

Conwell notes that even though many people were greatly impacted by Spurgeon's prayers, he was very reluctant and hesitant to draw attention to himself in such matters. Twice he spoke of himself "as unworthy of possessing the gift of healing,"[7] yet people were healed nonetheless.

Regardless of the terminologies used or not used relative to these recoveries, God's power was obviously at work. One young girl who doctors said would die was healed when Spurgeon prayed for her. The little girl told her mother afterward that during the prayer, she felt "a strange sensation running all over her, as though the fever began to decline at her head and gradually passed off at her feet."[8]

THE WORD OF KNOWLEDGE

Throughout Scripture, in both the Old and New Testament, God would supernaturally reveal certain information to individuals that would further His own plan and purpose. Those who received such insights from God were not omniscient, nor could they just randomly turn the gift on and off at their discretion. Many believe that this operation of the Holy Spirit is what is called "the word of knowledge" that Paul identifies in 1 Corinthians 12:8. R. T. Kendall writes "this gift could refer to theological and biblical knowledge, but it may also be understood as being a 'special word' that a person needs urgently: a timely and relevant message from the Spirit that assures one that God and not man has spoken."[9]

Kenneth E. Hagin defines this as a "supernatural revelation by the Holy Ghost of certain facts in the mind of God."[10] Similarly, Rick

Renner refers to this gift as "a fragment of special knowledge that one supernaturally receives."[11] Renner also states that the revelatory gifts of the Holy Spirit, which include the word of wisdom and the discerning of spirits, as well as the word of knowledge, "cause a person to supernaturally receive understanding from Heaven of something that could not be naturally obtained."[12]

Though Spurgeon never used the term "word of knowledge" to describe various events that occurred periodically in his ministry, his descriptions of those happenings certainly fit these cited definitions. For example, Spurgeon relates a time when he was preaching, and in the midst of the sermon, he suddenly pointed to a section of the congregation and announced that there was a young man present who was wearing a pair of gloves that were not rightfully his, and that he had stolen them from his employer. When the service was over, a young man who was under great conviction came to the back room desiring to meet with Spurgeon. He confessed his sin of stealing the gloves, repented profoundly, and begged Spurgeon not to tell his mother about his misdeed. Spurgeon, reflecting on this event, said, "the arrow had struck the target for which God intended it."[13]

Spurgeon biographer W. Y. Fullerton reports a time when Spurgeon stated that there was a man in the congregation with a bottle of gin in his pocket. Fullerton reports, "It so happened, there was such a man, and he was startled into conversion."[14] In yet another setting, Spurgeon pointed to a specific man in the congregation and identified his occupation— he was a shoemaker—and described some very specific details about his recent business practices that needed to be adjusted. The man was alarmed and said, "It struck me that it was God who had spoken to my soul through him…. At first, I was afraid to go again to hear him…but afterwards I went, and the Lord met with me, and saved my soul."[15] This type of thing happened on more than these few occasions. Spurgeon writes:

> I could tell as many as a dozen similar cases in which I pointed at somebody in the hall without having the slightest knowledge of the person, or any idea that what I said was right, except that I believed I was moved by the Spirit to say it; and so striking has been my description, that the persons have gone away, and said to their friends, "Come, see a man that told me all things that ever I did; beyond a doubt, he must have been sent of God to my soul, or else he could not have described me so exactly." And not only so, but I have known many instances in which the thoughts of men have been revealed from the pulpit. I have sometimes seen person's nudge their neighbors with their elbow, because they had got a smart hit, and they have been heard to say, when they were going out, "The preacher told us just what we said to one another when we went in at the door."[16]

In the midst of this quote, Spurgeon refers to what the woman at the well said of Jesus, *"Come, see a man that told me all things that ever I did"* (John 4:29). Jesus had said things to her that He could have only known by the Spirit of God who had revealed it to Him. This is the same type of thing that happened often in Spurgeon's ministry and he freely acknowledged that the Spirit of God moved him to say such things.

In an article written in 1865, Spurgeon states that his spiritual journey had been "frequently directed contrary to our own design and beyond our own conception by singularly powerful impulses, and irresistibly suggestive providences" and validates the idea "that God occasionally grants to his servants a special and perceptible manifestation of his will for their guidance, over and above the strengthening energies of the Holy Spirit, and the sacred teaching of the inspired Word."[17]

Spurgeon was cautious, though, in these matters, and he fully recognized the need for discernment in evaluating the validity of such leadings. He acknowledged the danger of abuses and the potential problems of unstable individuals arbitrarily following misguided notions. He soundly rejected any type of impression that violated Scripture, common sense, or reason.

> But notwithstanding all the folly of hair-brained rant, we believe that the unseen hand may be at times assuredly felt by gracious souls, and the mysterious power which guided the minds of the seers of old may, even to this day, sensibly overshadow reverent spirits. We would speak discreetly, but we dare say no less.[18]

It is important to understand that how we label an operation of the Holy Spirit is less important than the operation itself. I might call what happened with Jesus and with Spurgeon a "word of knowledge" while others might refer to it as an "impression" given by the Holy Spirit. Either way, though, it is God supernaturally working through a yielded vessel to meet the needs of the person.

This raises a fascinating question: Is it possible that certain gifts of the Holy Spirit listed in 1 Corinthians 12 could operate through a person who believed that such "gifts" had ceased? I think it is entirely possible that certain believers who assume that gifts of the Spirit have ceased could actually experience those gifts and recognize that God was at work without ever realizing that, technically, there was a gift of the Holy Spirit in operation.

It is good to remember that while there might be certain norms, God doesn't always move in accordance with our preconceived ideas or expectations. For example, the high priest Caiaphas is certainly not portrayed as one of the good guys in the Bible; he had a part in orchestrating Jesus' crucifixion. He saw Jesus as a threat and said, *"it is expedient for us that one man should die for the people, and not that the whole nation should perish"* (John 11:50). In retrospect, the apostle John writes, *"He did not say this on his own; as high priest at that time he was led to prophesy that Jesus would die for the entire nation"* (John 11:51 NLT). It is not the norm for someone in spiritual darkness to prophesy, but that's what happened here. It's also not the norm for the Lord to open the mouth of a donkey either, but it happened in God's dealings with Balaam (Numbers 22:28-30).

THE SOURCE OF SPURGEON'S POWER

In addition to continually exalting the person and work of Jesus Christ, two things are very noticeable in reading about Spurgeon—his total reliance upon the Holy Spirit and his heartfelt commitment to prayer. Consider some of the statements Spurgeon made regarding his profound dependency upon the supernatural power and presence of God:

> We have felt the Spirit of God operating upon our hearts, we have known and perceived the power which He wields over human spirits, and we know Him by frequent, conscious, personal contact. By the sensitiveness of our spirit we are as much made conscious of the presence of the Spirit of God as we are made cognizant of the existence of the souls of our fellowmen by their action upon our souls, or as we are certified of the existence of matter by its action upon our senses.... We know that there is a Holy Ghost, for we feel Him operating upon our spirits. If it were not so, we should

certainly have no right to be in the ministry of Christ's church.[19]

To us, as ministers, the Holy Spirit is absolutely essential. Without Him our office is a mere name.... We believe ourselves to be spokesmen for Jesus Christ, appointed to continue His witness upon earth; but upon Him and His testimony the Spirit of God always rested, and if it does not rest upon us, we are evidently not sent forth into the world as He was. At Pentecost the commencement of the great work of converting the world was with flaming tongues and a rushing mighty wind, symbols of the presence of the spirit; if, therefore, we think to succeed without the Spirit, we are not after the Pentecostal order. If we have not the Spirit which Jesus promised, we cannot perform the commission which Jesus gave.[20]

In one place, Spurgeon describes what seems like a certain type of euphoria or ecstasy that he would sometimes experience while ministering. Though Spurgeon clearly had a great mind, he said:

The divine Spirit will sometimes work upon us so as to bear us completely out of ourselves. From the beginning of the sermon to the end we might at such times say, "Whether in the body or out of the body I cannot tell: God knoweth." Everything has been forgotten but the one all-engrossing subject in hand. If I were forbidden to enter heaven, but were permitted to select my state for all eternity, I should choose to be as I sometimes feel in preaching the gospel.[21]

While Spurgeon enjoyed the presence and empowerment of God while he ministered, he realized that the Holy Spirit was not given simply for his pleasure and benefit. Rather, the Holy Spirit anoints the minister in a human-divine partnership to produce results, to transform people's lives, and to bring much glory to God.

> Miracles of grace must be the seals of our ministry; who can bestow them but the Spirit of God? Convert a soul without the Spirit of God! Why, you cannot even make a fly, much less create a new heart and a right spirit. Lead the children of God to a higher life without the Holy Ghost! You are inexpressibly more likely to conduct them into carnal security, if you attempt their elevation by any method of your own. Our ends can never be gained if we miss the cooperation of the Spirit of the Lord.[22]

Two other statements by Spurgeon powerfully reveal his dependence on the Holy Spirit and on prayer. These certainly were great keys in the supernatural touch that rested upon his ministry.

> A very important part of our lives consists in praying in the Holy Ghost, and that minister who does not think so had better escape from his ministry. Abundant prayer must go with earnest preaching. We cannot be always on the knees of the body, but the soul should never leave the posture of devotion. The habit of prayer is good, but the spirit of prayer is better.[23]

> I hope, brethren, that none of you will say that I have kept back the glorious work of the Holy Spirit. I have tried to remind you of it, whenever I have read a chapter, by praying that God the Holy Spirit would open that chapter to our minds. I hope I have never preached without an entire dependence on the Holy Ghost. Our reliance upon prayer has been very conspicuous; at least, I think so. We have not

begun, we have not continued, we have not ended anything without prayer. We have been plunged into it up to the hilt. We have not prayed as we should; but, still, we have so prayed as to prevail; and we wish it to be on record that we owe our success, as a church, to the work of the Holy Spirit, principally through its leading us to pray.[24]

And how did Spurgeon pray? In one message, he states:

I must pour out my heart in the language which his Spirit gives me; and more than that, I must trust in the Spirit to speak the unutterable groanings of my spirit, when my lips cannot actually express all the emotions of my heart. Let none despise this prayer; it is matchless....[25]

In yet another sermon, Spurgeon declares:

The Spirit of God is not sent merely to guide and help our devotion, but He Himself "makes intercession for us" according to the will of God. By this expression it cannot be meant that the Holy Spirit ever groans or personally prays, but that He excites intense desire and creates unutterable groans in us and these are ascribed to Him.... He can enable us when we are on our knees to rise above the ordinary routine of prayer into that victorious persistence against which nothing can stand. He can lay certain desires so pressingly upon our hearts that we can never rest till they are fulfilled. He can make the zeal for God's house to eat us up, and the passion for God's glory to be like a fire within our bones, and this is one part of that process by which, in inspiring our prayers, He helps our infirmity.[26]

DID SPURGEON PROPHESY AN
END-TIME OUTPOURING?

Spurgeon believed that the outpouring of the Holy Spirit had been minimal in his era, but he anticipated a significantly greater work to come. While his theology did not seem to permit him to envision biblical types of miracles occurring, his expectations are still profoundly challenging and encouraging. In one particular message, he proclaimed:

> Another great work of the Holy Spirit, which is not accomplished, is the bringing on of the latter-day glory. In a few more years—I know not when, I know not how—the Holy Spirit will be poured out in a far different style from the present....
>
> I do hope that perhaps a fresh era has dawned upon us, and that there is a better pouring out of the Spirit even now. For the hour is coming, and it may be even now is, when the Holy Spirit shall be poured out again in such a wonderful manner, that many shall run to and fro, and knowledge shall be increased—the knowledge of the Lord shall cover the earth as the waters cover the surface of the great deep; when his kingdom shall come, and his will shall be done on earth even as it is in heaven.
>
> My heart exults, and my eyes flash with the thought that very likely I shall live to see the outpouring of the Spirit; when "the sons and the daughters of God again shall prophesy, and the young men shall see visions and the old men shall dream dreams." ...There shall be such a miraculous amount of holiness, such an extraordinary fervor of prayer, such a real communion with God, and so much vital religion, and such a spread of the doctrines of the cross, that every one

will see that verily the Spirit is poured out like water, and the rains are descending from above. For that let us pray; let us continually labor for it, and seek it of God.[27]

What about these "impressions" or words of knowledge that Spurgeon experienced? Can the Holy Spirit still guide people that way today? I once had an experience during a time of congregational prayer. After some instruction, the people were directed to pray. Some knelt, some stood, and some walked, but all prayed. At one point, my attention was drawn to a young man I had never seen before who was kneeling in prayer at the front of the sanctuary. All of a sudden, I had the distinct impression that this young man was dealing with temptation regarding suicide. My "perception" surprised me, and I wondered if it was just an overactive imagination on my part, but the impression persisted.

After deliberating briefly, I went over and knelt down beside the young man and asked if I could talk with him for a minute. He agreed, and I said to him, "As I was praying, I saw you, and I seemed to have an impression that perhaps you are dealing with suicidal thoughts. I could be wrong, but I wanted to see if maybe this is something you have been struggling with." His eyes widened, and with a sense of great surprise, he acknowledged that my impression was correct. He asked me how I knew that, and I explained to him that I felt the Lord had shown me that so he would know that God loved him and wanted to help him.

He allowed me to minister to him, we prayed together, and he had a real spiritual breakthrough. His hope was restored, and I encouraged him to stay in touch with me. He called me the very next day and was beginning to make new plans for his future. He advised that he was about to look for a job and asked if I "could do that thing I had done the night before." I asked what he meant, and he said, "You know, could you ask God and maybe He could tell you where I should go and apply for a job." I was touched by his sincerity, but I needed to explain to him that such happenings were not like a light switch—something that I can just turn on and off at will. I did pray with him, though, that God would give him wisdom in his job search and that God would give him favor with his potential employer.

We should never underestimate God's love or willingness to reach hurting people with His love and compassion. In some cases, it may be expressed through a high profile person such as Spurgeon, but God may work through any of His children who will make themselves available as a vessel He can work through. We don't necessarily have to have some kind of supernatural insight into people's lives to reach out to them with love and compassion, but such an insight from God can be one of many tools that can be used in ministering to others.

D. L. Moody (1837-1899)

God is a supernatural God, and you've got to have supernatural power to do His work. –D. L. Moody

Dwight Lyman Moody's life began with severe challenges. One of nine children, his father died when Dwight was only four years of age. He was raised in poverty and only attended a few years of elementary school. At the age of seventeen, he moved from his hometown of Northfield, Massachusetts, to Boston where he began working as a shoe salesman. A kind and compassionate Sunday School teacher named Edward Kimball took an interest in Dwight, even though he described the young man's mind as spiritually dark.

Kimball visited Moody while he was at work, and there, in the stock room, Kimball presented what he said later was a "very weak plea for Christ." But the love of God touched Moody's heart and he responded.

Kimball writes, "It seemed the young man was just ready for the light that then broke upon him, and there, in the back of that store in Boston, he gave himself and his life to Christ."[28] When Moody applied for church membership a month later, he was rejected because of his inability to answer certain questions by the examining committee, but was accepted into membership a year later.

In September 1856, at the age of nineteen, Moody moved to Chicago; and though he continued selling shoes for a season, Moody threw himself wholeheartedly into gospel work. He began reaching out to young men, inviting them to church, and teaching them the Bible in his Sunday School class. He eventually moved his burgeoning class into an abandoned building, and by 1859, he had one thousand students in his program. During the Civil War, Moody was a chaplain for the Union Army, ministering to the soldiers and making nine trips to the front lines.

Moody's later work included working with the Illinois State Sunday School Board, serving as president of the YMCA in Chicago and preaching as an itinerant evangelist both in America and in England; he made seven trips to England. He also founded a church and a Bible School that continue to this day. Even though Moody had no formal ministerial training and was never ordained as a minister, his work powerfully impacted both America and England. According to one estimate, Moody brought the gospel to 100 million people, and that was before the benefits of modern technology.

WHY GOD USED D. L. MOODY

R. A. Torrey was an associate of Moody's. He served as the second president of the Moody Bible Institute, following Moody, and was also the senior pastor of the Chicago Avenue Church, which would later be called the Moody Church. From his close and personal association, Torrey produced a wonderful piece titled *Why God Used D. L. Moody.*

He lists seven vital factors he believed were the basis of Moody's tremendously fruitful ministry. He writes that Moody:

1. Was a Fully Surrendered Man

2. Was a Man of Prayer

3. Was a Deep and Practical Student of the Bible

4. Was a Humble Man

5. Was Entirely Free from the Love of Money

6. Had a Consuming Passion for the Salvation of the Lost

7. Was Endued with Power from on High

As admirable and necessary as all of these traits are, this chapter will focus on Torrey's seventh point—the on-going fullness of God's power in Moody's life. Torrey notes that prior to 1871, Moody was a very diligent worker, but that he lacked spiritual power. Torrey actually asserts that Moody "worked very largely in the energy of the flesh."[29] This was about to change, though, because of two praying women who regularly attended the services where Moody regularly preached. They let him know that they were praying for him; and upon Moody's inquiry, they informed him specifically that they were praying for him "to get the power." Instead of taking offense, as some preachers might have, Moody began to diligently inquire and seek God regarding this heavenly empowerment.

According to Moody's son, a very intense hunger and thirst for spiritual power was aroused in him.[30] Of this hunger, Moody says, "I began to cry as I never did before. I really felt that I did not want to live if I could not have this power for service."[31] Torrey describes what happened to Moody shortly afterward as he was walking up Wall Street in New York City.

In the midst of the bustle and hurry of that city his prayer was answered; the power of God fell upon him as he walked up the street and he had to hurry off to the house of a friend and ask that he might have a room by himself, and in that room he stayed alone for hours; and the Holy Ghost came upon him, filling his soul with such joy that at last he had to ask God to withhold his hand, lest he die on the spot from very joy. He went out from that place with the power of the Holy Ghost upon him.[32]

Moody notes that the effects of his preaching after this encounter were significantly enhanced, that hundreds now began to be saved. He also said that this experience he had was beyond description, and that it was so sacred to him that he rarely spoke of it.[33]

THE SPIRIT WITHIN AND THE SPIRIT UPON

As a Spirit-anointed evangelist, Moody led untold thousands to Christ. He also shared frequently about the Source of divine power who was at work in his life, enabling him to be an effective ambassador of Heaven. He was adamant that it was one thing to have the Holy Spirit inwardly, in the sense of being a child of God, but that there is a definite and subsequent experience of being filled with the power of the Spirit for service. For example, in *Secret Power*, Moody writes:

> I think it is clearly taught in the Scripture that every believer has the Holy Ghost dwelling in him. He may be quenching the Spirit of God, and he may not glorify God as he should, but if he is a believer on the Lord Jesus Christ, the Holy Ghost dwells in him. But I want to call your attention to another fact. I believe today, that though Christian men and women have the Holy Spirit dwelling in them, yet He is not

dwelling within them in power; in other words, God has a great many sons and daughters without power.[34]

In this same work, Moody contends powerfully for ministers and the church to recognize and receive the Holy Spirit in His fullness.

> There has been much inquiry of late on the subject of the Holy Spirit. In this and other lands thousands of persons have been giving attention to the study of this grand theme. I hope it will lead us all to pray for a greater manifestation of His power upon the whole Church of God. How much we have dishonored Him in the past! How ignorant of His grace, and love and presence we have been?[35]
>
> Through His agency we are "born again," and through His indwelling we possess superhuman power... The Holy Spirit who inspired prophets, and qualified apostles, continues to animate, guide and comfort all true believers... I believe, and am growing more into this belief, that divine, miraculous creative power resides in the Holy Ghost.[36]

Around three years before Moody passed away, he preached in Boston—the city where he met Jesus as a teenager—and he spoke on the topic of "Power for Service." In this message he articulated that the Church should seek and anticipate another outpouring as was experienced at Pentecost.

> See the results when the disciples got the power! See how He came on the Day of Pentecost. It is not carnal to pray that He may come again, and that the place may be shaken... I think the Church has made this woeful mistake that Pentecost was a miracle never to be repeated. I believe

if we looked on Pentecost as a specimen day, and began to pray, we should have the old Pentecostal fire back in Boston. That's what we want! May God open our eyes and reveal it to us![37]

In addition to believing a reoccurrence of Pentecost was both possible and to be desired, Moody believed that the purpose of a new Pentecost would be the same as the purpose of the first. In Acts 1:8, Jesus instructs His disciples, *"But you shall receive power when the Holy Spirit has come upon you; and you shall be witnesses to Me in Jerusalem, and in all Judea and Samaria, and to the end of the earth."*

I firmly believe that if we had this building filled with men and women expecting the Pentecostal power, we would get it. I believe if this building was filled with men and women hungry for the Spirit of God, we would have this place shaken, and there would be an influence felt not only in this land, but in foreign lands. It wouldn't take long to reach the whole world. Talk about twenty years. It needn't take twenty years if the Church of God is baptized and quickened.[38]

You may have noticed that even though Moody placed great emphasis on preaching the gospel and the power of the Holy Spirit, he did not seem to give any attention to healings or miracles; they did not seem to occur in his ministry. While healing and supernatural works have been highlighted through various people throughout this book, it is important to realize that such works were not and are not hallmarks of every believer or minister.

John the Baptist, as important as his ministry was, did not minister healing or miracles. As people began to follow Jesus, some of the people said, "'John didn't perform miraculous signs,' they remarked to one another, 'but everything he said about this man has come true'" (John 10:41 NLT).

Even though Scripture makes no mention of such a happening, it is always possible that someone or some people received healing while listening to John preach, but that was not John's focus or objective. His was a message of repentance, admonishing people to turn their hearts toward God in expectation of the Messiah's coming. That is what the Holy Spirit anointed John the Baptist to do, and he was anointed in a most remarkable way. When the angel appeared to Zechariah announcing the birth of the forerunner of Jesus, the indications of the Holy Spirit's anointing are most evident:

> For he [John the Baptist] *will be great in the eyes of the Lord. He must never touch wine or other alcoholic drinks.* **He will be filled with the Holy Spirit, even before his birth.** *And he will turn many Israelites to the Lord their God.* **He will be a man with the spirit and power of Elijah.** *He will prepare the people for the coming of the Lord. He will turn the hearts of the fathers to their children, and he will cause those who are rebellious to accept the wisdom of the godly* (Luke 1:15-17 NLT).

Isn't that amazing? John was filled with the Holy Spirit even before he was born. He had *"the spirit and power of Elijah,"* and yet no one knew of him working any miracles.

Maybe this was a matter of people's preconceived ideas about the supernatural work of God. The fact that so many people repented and were baptized was indication of the working of God's Spirit, even though that was not classified as miraculous. Whatever people may call it or not call it, it is nonetheless the work of the Holy Spirit, and Jesus held John in tremendously high regard. Jesus said, *"Of all who have ever lived, none is greater than John the Baptist. Yet even the least person in the Kingdom of Heaven is greater than he is!"* (Matthew 11:11 NLT).

Some people seem to think that every New Testament character went around healing everyone all the time, but that is not the case. While many healings and miracles are recorded, none are mentioned regarding the ministries of Timothy, Titus, Mark, Luke, Apollos, Priscilla, or Aquila. The fact that none are mentioned does not mean that none occurred through them, simply that the New Testament is silent about it. In 1 Corinthians 12:29-30, the apostle Paul asks if all Christians are workers of miracles, or if all believers have gifts of healings, and the implied answer is "no." This does not mean that any believer might not see a person healed, for example, in response to the prayer of faith or anointing with oil. Rather, it means that not every believer is especially endowed by the Holy Spirit to minister that way as part of his or her calling.

God does not call and equip all of His children the same way. This is a truth that Paul emphasizes in 1 Corinthians 12:11 when he writes, *"But one and the same Spirit works all these things, distributing to each one individually as He wills."* Likewise, he tells believers in Rome that they have *"gifts differing according to the grace that is given to us"* (Romans 12:6). I remember hearing the story of Howard Carter, an early Pentecostal pioneer of the twentieth century. After a teaching session, an individual approached him and requested prayer for healing. He told the individual that he could certainly pray by faith, but that his wife had a stronger anointing to pray for healing—his anointing was more in the area of helping people receive the infilling of the Holy Spirit. He suggested that the person have his wife pray, since that was more her gifting.

In reading these last few chapters, a person who compares himself or herself to Wesley, Edwards, Finney, and Moody could get quite intimidated. After all, these people all had world-renowned ministries.

How could any of us ever measure up to them or the results they achieved? It is important to remember, though, that God does not want us to compare our gifts or our lives to those of others. In the first chapter, we addressed the topic of the spectacular as opposed to the supernatural. Not every supernatural gift is expressed spectacularly. Some gifts are quite subtle, and yet they are beautiful in their impact.

For example, right in the middle of the dynamic gifts of apostles, prophets, healings, and miracles in 1 Corinthians 12:28, Paul also lists helps and administrations. Where would the church be without those two valuable and essential gifts? The Holy Spirit inspires those gifts just as much as He does the more spectacular ones. Likewise, in Romans 12:8 Paul lists giving and mercy as grace-based activities of believers. We may classify and categorize some of these gifts and workings differently, but they are all given by God to equip us to serve others and glorify Him. We are to honor every gift, every expression, and every working of the Holy Spirit in and through every believer.

Endnotes

1. Charles Spurgeon, *Charles Spurgeon—An Autobiography: Diary, Letters, and Records* (Harrington, DE: Delmarva Publications, 2013), loc. 955, Kindle.

2. Russell H. Conwell, *The Life of Charles Haddon Spurgeon* (Philadelphia, PA: Edgewood Publishing, 1892), loc. 553, Kindle.

3. Spurgeon, *Charles Spurgeon—An Autobiography*, loc. 951, Kindle.

4. Ibid.

5. Ibid., loc. 1365, Kindle.

6. Ibid., loc. 1405, Kindle.

7. Ibid., loc. 1485, Kindle.

8. Ibid., loc. 1445, Kindle.

9. R. T. Kendall, *40 Days with the Holy Spirit: A Journey to Experience His Presence in a Fresh New Way* (Lake Mary, FL: Charisma House, 2014), 160, Kindle.

10. Kenneth E. Hagin, *The Holy Spirit and His Gifts* (Tulsa, OK: Faith Library Publications, www.rhema.org, 1991), 85.

11. Rick Renner, *Why We Need the Gifts of the Holy Spirit* (Shippensburg, PA: Harrison House, 2018), 37.

12. Ibid., 35.

13. Spurgeon, *Charles Spurgeon—An Autobiography*, loc. 17360, Kindle.

14. W. Y. Fullerton, *Charles Haddon Spurgeon: A Biography* (Harrington, DE: Delmarva Publications, 2014), loc. 3736, Kindle.

15. Spurgeon, *Charles Spurgeon—An Autobiography*, loc. 13091, Kindle.

16. Ibid., loc. 17360, Kindle.

17. Charles Spurgeon, "Two Episodes in My Life" in *Sword and Trowel*, October 1865 (Seattle, WA: Amazon Digital Services, 2010), loc. 2463, Kindle.

18. Ibid., loc. 2471, Kindle.

19. Charles Spurgeon, *Lectures to My Students* (Grand Rapids, MI: Zondervan, www.zondervan.com, 1875), 185, Kindle. Used by permission of Zondervan.

20. Ibid., loc. 186, Kindle.

21. Ibid., loc. 191, Kindle.

22. Ibid., loc. 195, Kindle.

23. Ibid., loc. 196, Kindle.

24. Spurgeon, *Charles Spurgeon—An Autobiography*, loc. 26691, Kindle.

25. Charles Spurgeon, "The Fatherhood of God," vol. 5, in *Spurgeon's Sermons* (Grand Rapids, MI: Baker Books, September 12, 1883), 97.

26. Charles Spurgeon, "The Holy Spirit's Intercession," in *Spurgeon's Teaching on the Holy Spirit* (Seattle, WA: Amazon Digital Services, 2017), loc. 169, Kindle.

27. Charles Spurgeon, "The Power of the Holy Spirit," in *Twelve Sermons on the Holy Spirit* (Seattle, WA: Amazon Digital Services, 2014), loc. 945, Kindle.

28. William R. Moody, *The Life of Dwight L. Moody: By His Son* (Harrington, DE:

Delmarva Publications, 2013), loc. 602, Kindle.

29. R. A. Torrey, *Why God Used D. L. Moody* (Seattle, WA: Amazon Digital Services, 2010), loc. 283, Kindle.

30. Moody, *The Life of Dwight L. Moody*, loc. 2094, Kindle.

31. Ibid., loc. 2104, Kindle.

32. R. A. Torrey, *Why God Used D. L. Moody*, loc. 291, Kindle.

33. Moody, *The Life of Dwight L. Moody*, loc. 2137, Kindle.

34. D. L. Moody, *Secret Power*, in *The Life and Works of Dwight L. Moody* (New York: Fleming H. Revell Company, 1881), loc. 8116, Kindle.

35. Ibid., loc. 7859, Kindle.

36. Ibid., loc. 7879, Kindle.

37. Dwight L. Moody, "Power For Service," in *The Life and Works of Dwight L. Moody* (Classic Christian Ebooks, 2012), loc. 29318, Kindle.

38. D. L. Moody, *The Home Work of D.L. Moody*, in *The Life and Works of Dwight L. Moody* (New York: Fleming H. Revell, 1886), loc. 41475, Kindle.

CHAPTER THIRTEEN

HEALING SPECIALISTS

> *At that moment I believed I was healed, the room was filled with the glory of God…and I was so overwhelmed with the power of God, I felt that everything like disease was removed; I felt as light as a feather, as if I could run through a troop, and leap over a wall. I leaped for joy into the other room, shouting victory in the name of Jesus, and I was not afraid to tell it that I was healed of some troubles I had for twenty years, I was relieved of them, praise the name of the Lord.*[1]
>
> —Sarah Mix (1832-1884)

IN the 1800s, a number of men and women arose who were convinced that God wanted to bring physical healing into the lives of people. They realized that a major part of Jesus' ministry involved healing the sick, and they believed that God could and would still bring help to hurting humanity through prayer and faith. People often think of the healings that took place through Peter and Paul in the book of Acts, but are dismissive because, they reason, they were apostles and such a gift was only for them.

However, it is important to realize that people other than apostles saw healings and miracles in the book of Acts. Stephen was a believer who had been appointed to wait on tables, and yet Scripture states that he was *"full of faith and power, did great wonders and signs among the people"* (Acts 6:8). Likewise, Philip was another servant in the New Testament church who traveled to Samaria and preached Christ to the people. Luke writes:

> And the multitudes with one accord heeded the things spoken by Philip, hearing and seeing the miracles which he did. For unclean spirits, crying with a loud voice, came out of many who were possessed; and many who were paralyzed and lame were healed. And there was great joy in that city (Acts 8:6-8).

The nineteenth century saw the emergence of various ministers who strongly emphasized the ministry of divine healing. God used them in such an effective way that the sick and the afflicted sought them out, and many were marvelously healed. This chapter will examine some of these "healing specialists."

Johann Christoph Blumhardt (1805-1880)

Johann Blumhardt was a Lutheran pastor from Germany who cared deeply for those under his spiritual oversight, and he went to great lengths to see that they received all that God had for them. While Blumhardt's overriding concern was the health of people's souls, he was also passionately interested in seeing them receive physical healing.

In 1841, Blumhardt encountered a young lady named Gottliebin Dittus. She was deeply tormented and had been experiencing a wide variety of bizarre demonic manifestations. Encountering someone so profoundly troubled was new territory for Blumhardt, yet he exhibited tremendous compassion and patience as he ministered to her through a two-year process he eventually called "the struggle."

Though often discouraged by a seeming lack of progress and setbacks, momentum shifted when Blumhardt instructed the young lady to pray, "Lord Jesus, help me! We have seen long enough what the devil can do; now we desire to see also what Jesus can do." Relief came, but so did further challenges.

Gottliebin's recovery was progressive, not instantaneous, and her sister Katharina also experienced a notable battle with demonic power. However, a great breakthrough occurred when Katharina, in Blumhardt's presence, cried out, "Jesus is the victor! Jesus is the victor!" Gottliebin eventually experienced complete liberation and eventually served as part of Blumhardt's ministry team.

The people of that community had been acutely aware of the severe nature of this young lady's problems, so when healing came to her, it had a profound effect. Charles E. Moore writes of what took place after Gottliebin's deliverance:

> Almost overnight the town of Möttlingen was swept up in an unprecedented movement of repentance and renewal. Stolen property was returned, broken marriages restored, enemies reconciled, alcoholics cured, and sick people healed. An entire village experienced what life could be like when God was free to rule.[2]

This revival, often referred to as "The Awakening," was so impacting that "by the Easter following, it was estimated that twenty people only in the village remained unconverted."[3] The healings recorded due to prayer throughout Blumhardt's ministry are impressive. Blumhardt himself, along with his baby and his wife all experienced healing. Numerous others received healing from such maladies as lameness, blindness, skin disorders, paralysis, and epilepsy.

Christoph Friedrich Blumhardt, Johann's son, also experienced divine healing and writes of a time when he broke his hand and was in bed in great pain:

> I laid my good hand over the bad one, and literally thanked the Lord for two whole hours, letting the power and blessings of God flow over. I thanked him for allowing me, alone and undisturbed, to accept his words of life and to center myself on him again. As I did this, I felt that my calling was being strengthened spiritually, and at the same time the pain I felt grew less and less. In those two hours I received more strength, more healing from God than words can ever express. A few weeks later a surgeon came to our house. When he happened to see my hand, he commented that it had been broken in two places but had obviously healed as well as if hours of prayer—in which I did nothing but thank God—the Lord himself healed my hand.[4]

The visit by the surgeon was consistent with Johann's view that there is nothing wrong with physicians, and that they should be allowed to do their job. He states, "To reject physicians out of hand not only amounts to loveless harshness toward their profession, but reveals an exaggerated insistence on faith—that faith has to accomplish everything."[5]

Blumhardt expressed an unwavering belief that Jesus is *"the same yesterday, today, and forever"* (Hebrews 13:8) and believed that healing was an expression of God's love and compassion toward His people. He writes:

> Has he changed any? Certainly not! He traveled from place to place doing good and healing just so that all subsequent generations could trust him, and so that all who are

miserable and afflicted might always know where to turn for help. Jesus still does wonderful things, "going around doing good and healing," even if it is in a more inconspicuous way. He draws close to anyone in need and pain so that we, too, might experience firsthand that he is the one who knows how to help us. Still today Jesus works good and heals. The question to us is: Will we come to him?[6]

Like many others who saw people healed, Blumhardt refused to focus exclusively on healing. He believed it was just one part of God's overall plan for humankind, but he always kept the major emphasis on the inward work of the Holy Spirit. He did not want people sensationalizing physical healing.

Jesus did not like it when people made a big to-do about his miracles. He always had something more in mind than the miracle itself. When Jesus performed a miracle, what mattered most to him was that it would arouse a deep, godly feeling. His acts of mercy were signs of something greater—something beyond the temporal. He touched the inner person.[7]

Even though outstanding results took place in and through his ministry, Blumhardt sensed that much more was possible, especially for the Body of Christ at large. He said:

I long for another outpouring of the Holy Spirit, another Pentecost. That must come if things are to change in Christianity, for it simply cannot continue in such a wretched state. The gifts and powers of the early Christian time—oh, how I long for their return! And I believe the Savior is just waiting for us to ask for them.[8]

Dorothea Trudel (1813-1862)

Raised in Männedorf, a small Swiss village beside Lake Zürich, Dorothea Trudel was born into a life of struggle. Her father, often angry and absent, had problems with alcohol, and he left her mother and ten siblings in regular financial distress. Dorothea's mother was devout, God-fearing, and given to much prayer. When challenges such as illness came to the family, Dorothea's mother turned to prayer, and young Dorothea saw God's hand move on their behalf. Dorothea writes:

> I was attacked by small pox at four years old and almost blinded by it, while my brother who was fourteen, was seized with epilepsy, our mother believed and trusted that the Lord would help, and in a short time we both recovered.[9]

When Dorothea was running a flower business in her mid-thirties, some of her workers became ill. She cared for them physically, but also searched the Scriptures and began to pray for them. One particular passage of Scripture was impressed upon her:

> *Is anyone among you sick? Let him call for the elders of the church, and let them pray over him, anointing him with oil in the name of the Lord. And the prayer of faith will save the sick, and the Lord will raise him up. And if he has committed sins, he will be forgiven* (James 5:14-15).

Dorothea not only took this Scripture to heart, but she put it into practice. Her workers all recovered, and word began to circulate about her faith-filled prayers. She first began praying for the sick in her community, then from the surrounding areas, and eventually, people were coming from other European nations to receive healing.

To accommodate those coming, Dorothea began to receive people into her home, and she later bought other homes to house those who had come to Männedorf. Even though she was ordered by government officials to shut down her work, she continually made appeals until the courts eventually ruled in her favor.

While the legal battle was challenging to Trudel, it provided the opportunity for a multitude of documented healing testimonies to be presented in the courts, and this included confirmations by doctors whose patients had been healed through prayer and faith. It was also communicated that any of those receiving ministry were welcome to be under the care of a physician as well—Trudel did not look down upon medical care.

In arguing that they were not "practicing medicine without a license," Trudel clearly articulated the methodology that she and her workers used:

> The mode of treatment is exceedingly simple. The first and main objective is to impress the heart; the cure of the body is secondary. There is a short service—a Bible hour—three times a day, and personal visitation of the patients besides. Prayer is made for them, hands are laid on them, and they are anointed with oil.[10]

Trudel was strongly motivated by compassion, and exhibited a great concern to help people be right with God spiritually and healthy in their souls. It was this kind of love that motivated all she did. In a letter to a pastor, she expresses her passion to see greater expressions of both the love of God and the power of God.

> If we speak with new tongues, the fruit of our lips will be the result of God's Spirit. We will pray with one another

for the tongues from God, to be able to cry out with loud voices…. We must be witnesses for God, witnesses who are constrained to do all for the love of Christ. I do not know anything better to ask for every one than this love. Let us pray with one accord that this Spirit may come upon all of us. I feel ashamed that in the Old Testament Elias could call down fire from heaven to consume the wood and stone, the earth and water, and that we, though children of the New Testament, cannot call for the Pentecostal fire to quicken our dead Christianity. A holy indignation seizes me when I read of the fire which burned unceasingly during day and night upon the altar of God.[11]

The healing work in Männedorf continued after Dorothea's passing through Samuel Zeller, his sister, four male coworkers, and a number of older women who had experienced healing through Dorothea's work. None of these claimed to have had any particular "gift" of healing, but simply acted on God's Word and encouraged others to believe the Bible. Neither did these devoted gospel workers believe that their particular ministry locale was the key for anyone's recovery. Zeller states:

People need not come to Männedorf in order to get well in body and mind. Let them unreservedly believe God's holy promises and they will experience the same blessed results in any part of the world.[12]

Charles Spurgeon, whom we studied in the previous chapter, said of Dorothea Trudel:

I do not know how far faith may still operate upon the bodily frame, for there is certainly an intimate connection between the soul and the body. Those wondrous cases recorded in the life of Dorothea Trudel of Zurich indicate the singular power of faith to assist in the cure of the body by its calming influence on the mind. That admirable woman, who has but just departed this life, became the founder of a hospital in which cures were worked mainly by the means of prayer and faith—cures which have been substantiated in the best possible manner, namely, by her enemies having dragged her before the law courts of Zurich for practicing medicine without a diploma, when she proved that the only medicine used was directing the mind to Christ, and proclaiming the gospel, by which a holy calm spread over the mind and the body derived manifest benefit. Such cases, and others which we have noticed, go to show that if we had more faith in the living God it might sometimes be possible for the soul to so overmaster the body that out of weakness we might still, in Hezekiah's fashion, be made strong.[13]

Dr. Charles Cullis (1833-1892)

Born and raised as an Episcopalian in Boston, Charles Cullis was sickly as a child and continued to face physical infirmity into young adulthood. He began experiencing success as a physician, but his world was shaken when his young wife died. He committed to giving any excess income beyond that required for his personal needs to charitable and religious works, and yet his heart was still unsettled. He began searching the Scripture, and his heart was stirred by its truth, especially its wonderful promises. He said, "I will take every promise in the Bible as my own, just as if my own name, Charles Cullis, were written in it."[14] Cullis began to grow spiritually and delight greatly in the Word of God.

In 1862, Cullis began to sense a desire to open a private hospital that would freely care for those suffering from consumption—now called Tuberculosis—the incurable, in particular. Then, in 1864, Cullis purchased a house for this very purpose. While a few did recover, the patients who came to the house did not come to be cured, but:

> They came there to die, and the treatment had far more relation to the future life than to the present. When, therefore, a patient had been brought to Christ, and had died in the triumphs of faith, that case was regarded as the largest possible success.[15]

Within a year, a second home was purchased and patients continued to be cared for. This was very much a faith venture, and finances were often very tight. In October 1865, Cullis noted that after paying the monthly bills, he had less than fifteen dollars left, and yet he expressed trust, saying, "I have no fear, for 'I know that my Redeemer liveth.'"[16] Additional homes were acquired and different projects were undertaken in the months and years that followed, and Cullis recorded increasing numbers of patients, provisions to meet the financial needs, and continuing salvations among the patients, a large number of whom went to Heaven.

At the beginning of the seventh year of his work, Cullis had a dynamic spiritual experience that took him to a richer, deeper level in his walk with the Lord. He writes, "Never has my own soul been so blessed and filled with the love of God, as since I surrendered self and all...to receive Christ in all his fullness...."[17] Another part of Dr. Cullis' spiritual journey was learning of the healing ministry of Dorothea Trudel in Switzerland. After reading the *Life of Dorothea Trudel*, he asked, "If God can perform such wonders in Switzerland, why not in Boston?"[18]

Shortly later, in January 1870, Cullis writes of Lucy Drake, a patient who came to him with a tumor "for which there was no human remedy but the knife."[19] He shared James 5:14-15 with her, and she consented to receive prayer and be anointed with oil according to the Bible. Cullis notes that afterward, Lucy walked three miles, and "from that time the tumor rapidly lessened, until all traces of it at length disappeared."[20] Two years later, Cullis noted that the woman was continuing in perfect health.

In the summer of 1873, Cullis and his wife traveled to Europe and visited different faith ministries, among them, George Mueller's orphanage in Bristol, England, and Dorothea Trudel's healing homes in Mannedorf, Switzerland. By this time, Trudel had passed away and the homes were under the direction of her successor, Samuel Zeller. What Cullis witnessed in Mannedorf was remarkable.

> Here they found about a hundred and fifty persons who had come to be healed in answer to prayer; including thirty insane persons, on which the prayer of faith seemed particularly efficacious. The presence of the Holy Ghost in this work was evidenced by the rich spiritual blessings which accompanied the physical ones.[21]

This visit and what Cullis observed made a great impact on him. He had been exercising faith in God for years as he and his team loved and cared for the sick with compassion, ministered salvation to many, and trusted for financial provision, but now a new element—faith and prayer for physical healing—was added to their approach.

In his 1875 report about the work in Boston, Cullis writes:

> During the past year many have come to me, and claimed the promise contained in James 5:14-15. Requests for prayer for the healing of the body have also reached me from hundreds,

afflicted in most cases with diseases that the physicians have given up as hopeless. A great proportion of these have been entirely healed.[22]

Cullis also expressed great joy at seeing people set free that were suffering the effects of alcohol, tobacco, and opium addiction. He writes:

It is quite the usual thing for lost men, utterly under the power of strong drink, to experience instant and complete deliverance from that awful bondage, in connection with their conversion to God. At the Lewis Street Mission, and in other such places where people of that description so often appear, salvation for the body is as fully expected as salvation for the soul: it is fully understood that these men need new nerves and new stomachs, as well as new hearts; and God seems to be just as willing to give the one as the other.[23]

The emphasis and results in the area of healing were pronounced enough that some former friends began to disassociate from Dr. Cullis. Some had been glad to support a work that emphasized physical care of the sick and concern for their spiritual well-being, but the idea of faith-filled prayers for healing was a bridge they were not willing to cross. Others, though, rejoiced in this new development and were glad to see the healing touch of God become a vital part of Dr. Cullis' work.

Two decades after anointing Lucy Drake and seeing her tumor disappear, Cullis writes:

From that day to this, nearly twenty years ago, I have prayed with tens of thousands of people suffering from all kinds of diseases, curable and incurable, with the consumptive and cancerous, the rheumatic, and those who had tumors of all kinds, and with many who had incurable diseases that I cannot mention, and they have been healed. I could tell you—but it would take the whole night and more—of some of the most wonderful of cases.[24]

It should be noted that Dr. Cullis continued treating patients medically when he incorporated faith and prayer into his care of the sick and hurting. In 1883, he remarks:

> While I have never relinquished my medical practice—recognizing my knowledge in this profession as belonging to God for the benefit of such as have not faith, and using it as the legitimate means for the support of my family—I have also declared my faith in the promises of God, and my willingness to claim the promise of healing for all such as are willing to trust God with me.[25]

Cullis was once challenged by a group of ministers as to whether everyone he prayed for was healed. Cullis responded by asking them, "Were all the sinners converted to whom you preached yesterday?"[26] He then summarized his sentiments of that encounter:

> How strange that those who are so familiar with failures in their own use of the universally accepted means of grace should demand unvarying success of those who are put forward by the Spirit to recall and recover one of the gospel gifts so long lying dormant in the Church![27]

In essence, Cullis was telling these ministers that if not everyone they preach to receives salvation, they should not be critical of the fact that not everyone he prays for is healed.

The Domino Effect
(William Boardman and Andrew Murray)

It is important to realize that Charles Cullis, or any of these figures throughout church history, were both influenced by others and in turn, influenced others. While a chapter may focus on a particular individual, there were typically a host of others who ministered the same types of truths around the same time, even if they were less known. This is certainly true in the case of Cullis, although there were also some well-known people that benefitted from, and to some degree, replicated his ministry.

William E. Boardman was a holiness preacher who established a close relationship with Cullis in the 1870s. Boardman took note of Lucy Drake's healing that took place under Cullis' ministry, and in 1873, Boardman and Cullis visited Europe. Together, they visited the healing homes established in Germany and Switzerland by Blumhardt and Trudel, as well as other ministry centers. With Cullis' encouragement, Boardman published a book in 1881 titled *The Lord That Healeth Thee*.

Boardman ended up establishing a ministry in London called Bethshan—Hebrew for House of rest, security, or tranquility—where healing services were regularly conducted and individuals stayed in homes provided by the ministry. Not only Boardman, but also teams of others helped in ministering to the sick.

One of those who received healing at Bethshan in London was the famed author and pastor Andrew Murray of South Africa. In 1879, Murray's voice became strained badly, and this condition continued for more than two years. During this time, "he was not often able to speak publicly. He would write out his message at times and it would be read to the congregation by others."[28] Murray sought and received medical assistance, but to little avail. He had also been inspired regarding divine healing by Cullis, Boardman, and others, and he ended up spending three weeks receiving ministry at Bethshan in London. There, Murray recovered, and "was taught that healing by faith was not just to heal the body, but to help one on to holiness and a life of consecration to God."[29]

In addition to the healing Murray received while at Bethshan, he writes of a healing he witnessed pertaining to a hopelessly ill lady. She had been bedfast for seven years and suffered from epilepsy, tuberculosis, and other sicknesses. As she listened to the Word of God—Matthew 8:17, *"He took our infirmities and bore our sicknesses"* in particular—she arose from the couch where she was reclining, and "from that moment her healing made rapid progress. At the end of a few weeks she no longer had the appearance of an invalid, and later her strength was such that she could spend many hours a day visiting the poor."[30]

After his time at Bethshan where he was taught, experienced, and observed healing, Murray both taught and wrote on the topic of divine healing in addition to numerous other biblical topics. Murray rejected the idea that miracles were no longer needed in modern times, as they had been in the first centuries of the church. He writes:

> If we think of the ignorance and unbelief that reign even in the midst of the Christian nations, aren't we driven to conclude that there is a need for manifest acts of the power of God to sustain the testimony of believers and to prove that God is with them?[31]

Murray taught that miracles were less frequent in his day because of the unbelief of the church, and that "The more the Spirit of God lives and acts in the souls of believers the more the miracles by which he works in the body will multiply. These miracles help the world recognize what redemption means."[32]

A.J. Gordon (1836-1895)

Being named after someone famous is no guarantee that a person will become influential, but it certainly turned out to be the case when John and Sally Gordon named their infant son Adoniram Judson, after the famed missionary to Burma. Commonly known as A.J. Gordon, this New Hampshire born pastor and scholar would ultimately share tremendous insights with the church world. He would enlighten many regarding present-day realities concerning divine healing and the work of the Holy Spirit.

Revered for his godly character and rich teaching, Gordon was not only acquainted with and preached for fellow Bostonian, Dr. Charles Cullis, he also enjoyed rich fellowship with famed evangelist, D. L. Moody. So great was Moody's affection for his friend that when Gordon passed away in 1895, Moody wrote his widow and not only offered loving condolences, but also requested that Gordon's remains be brought for burial at Moody's Northfield Campus in Massachusetts. Moody noted the tremendously rich deposits Gordon made during his various ministry visits, and expressed, "Northfield has never been stirred over anyone's death as it has been over his."[33] Gordon was also personally acquainted with Charles Spurgeon, and they highly respected each other's works and writings.

In the many years that Gordon preached at Moody's Northfield conferences, he frequently spoke on the importance of being filled with the Holy Spirit. He stressed that being filled with the Spirit is a distinct experience subsequent to salvation, and that it is a command Jesus gave for every believer. Of his own experience, Gordon relates, that receiving the Holy Spirit is a simple matter of faith. He writes:

> I simply knelt and said, "O God, Thou hast said by the lips of Jesus that Thou art more ready to give the Holy Spirit

to them that ask Thee than we are to give good gifts to our children. Father, I take Thee at Thy word. I ask Thee in Jesus' name for the Holy Spirit." Then I got up and went about my work. I can say this, that from that hour, as I have gone about my parish, and to and from hospitals and meetings, it has often seemed that my feet hardly touched the sidewalk.[34]

Clarendon Street Baptist Church, the Boston congregation that Gordon pastored, experienced significant progress over the years of his ministry. When he first assumed the pastorate, it was a very exclusive congregation. Prime pews were "sold" to the highest bidders, and one church worker was reprimanded for including the words "Strangers Welcome" on church advertising. Gordon disliked the wealthy receiving such preferential treatment, and he was also grieved that worship did not involve congregational singing. Professionals performed classical music *for* the congregation, but Gordon believed church members should worship personally and corporately.

Through much patience, the local church eventually changed, and Gordon celebrated the fact that the lost and hurting began to find a spiritual home where lives could be transformed and where people could worship God together as a spiritual family. He particularly delighted in two men who were instantaneously and supernaturally delivered from opium addiction and became solid members of the church. How were people's lives transformed, and how did the church transition from being rigid and exclusive to being spiritual and life giving? Gordon relates:

> If the Holy Ghost can only have men and women who are willing to be used, there is nothing that cannot be accomplished. Let me publicly say that when I awoke to this fact, and began to preach it, and called you to pray about

it, and put myself into the power of the Holy Ghost—then began the real progress in this church.[35]

In addition to his insights on the Person and work of the Holy Spirit, Gordon also had profound understanding on divine healing as an expression of God's love and care for His people.

Gordon had associations in circles that were strongly academic, and he recognized the prevalence of strong anti-supernatural biases. Referring to what was then a recent poll in a religious journal, Gordon states that "the respondents were well nigh unanimous in the opinion that the age of miracles was passed away with the apostolic period."[36] It was against this type of backdrop that Gordon masterfully argued—from Scripture, history, and reason—for the realities of the working of the Holy Spirit and for demonstrations of God's power in the present day. He writes, "Believing miracles to have existed in the days of Christ and the Apostles, is it reasonable for us to conclude that they may have continued to exist until our present time? It seems to us that it is."[37]

As noted earlier, Gordon taught consistently and emphatically that there is an empowerment—a baptism in the Holy Spirit—that is separate from and subsequent to salvation. He writes, "It seems clear from the Scriptures that it is still the duty and privilege of believers to receive the Holy Spirit by a conscious, definite act of appropriating faith, just as they received Jesus Christ."[38] This empowerment by the Spirit was not merely theoretical or doctrinal in Gordon's mind; it had a very tangible application in how ministry took place. He believed that God's servants were to be anointed to minister, and that such ministry was distinctly different from that done in the power of the flesh.

Let us set the popular preacher and the apostolic preacher side by side, and consider whose reward we would choose,

universal admiration or "God also bearing witness, both with
signs and wonders and with divers miracles, and gifts of the
Holy Ghost, according to his will" (Heb. 2:4)—the sermon
greeted with applause and the clapping of hands, or "the
word received with joy of the Holy Ghost" (1 Thess. 1:6)?—
admiration of the preacher possessing all who listen to the
discourse, or "the Holy Ghost fell on all them which heard
the word" (Acts 10:44)? Language cannot express the vital
moment of the question which we are here discussing. Our
generation is rapidly losing its grip upon the supernatural;
and as a consequence the pulpit is rapidly dropping to the
level of the platform. And this decline is due, we believe,
more than anything else, to an ignoring of the Holy Spirit as
the supreme inspirer of preaching.[39]

Elsewhere, Gordon asserts that the Lord had provided the Church
a supernatural power in order to accomplish a supernatural work, and
he calls for a "resumption of the Church's primitive endowments."[40] He
also states, "the Church in every direction needs to be reshaped to the
apostolic model and reinvested with her apostolic powers."[41] Gordon
also writes, "The gifts of tongues and of prophecy therefore do not seem
to be confined within the first age of the church."[42]

Gordon did not simply advocate the gifts of the Holy Spirit for the
modern church, but also believed that the very Person of the Holy Spirit
should be tangibly present and highly involved in gatherings of believers.

Honor the Holy Ghost as Master of assemblies; study
much the secret of surrender to him; cultivate a quick ear
for hearing his inward voice and a ready tongue for speaking
his audible witness; be submissive to keep silence when
he forbids as well as to speak when he commands, and we

shall learn how much better is God's way of conducting the worship of his house than man's way.[43]

Whereas Dr. Cullis prayed for the sick in simple faith, Gordon was more of a scholar in his approach. He did not believe, though, that one had to have great intellect or profound theological insights in order to receive or minister healing. Gordon said that if theologians would sit at the feet of Dorothea Trudel, they would "learn things which their utmost wisdom had failed to grasp."[44]

Gordon believed that both the forgiveness of sin and the healing of disease were established by the redemptive work of Christ, and he encouraged others to consider the rationality of such a proposal. He writes, "In the atonement of Christ there seems to be a foundation laid for faith in bodily healing," and while he was not excessively dogmatic, he asserts, "It is at least a deep and suggestive truth that have Christ set before us as the sickness-bearer as well as the sin-bearer of his people."[45] Of Matthew 8:17, "*He Himself took our infirmities and bore our sicknesses*," Gordon writes, "the passage seems to teach that Christ endured vicariously our diseases as well as our iniquities."[46]

Gordon was arguing, in effect, that healing is not randomly, arbitrarily, and mysteriously offered by God, but that there is a legal basis for God's children receiving healing. He states, "If now it be true that our Redeemer and substitute bore our sicknesses, it would be natural to reason at once that he bore them that we might not bear them."[47] Gordon understood that the ultimate manifestation of Christ's redemptive work relative to our bodies would be the resurrection, but that in the meantime, "Healing by the power of the Holy Ghost is the pledge and foretoken of this consummation."[48] He also asks, "Until the harvest shall come, is it reasonable to suppose that we are to be left entirely without the firstfruits of our redemption?"[49]

Endnotes

1. Mrs. Edward Mix, *Faith Cures and Answers to Prayer* (Springfield, MA: Press of Springfield Printing Co., 1882), 11.

2. Johann Christoph Blumhardt and Christoph Friedrich Blumhardt, *The God Who Heals: Words of Hope for a Time of Sickness*, ed. Charles E. Moore (Walden, NY: Plough Publishing House, 2016), 71, Kindle.

3. James Robinson, *Divine Healing: The Formative Years* (Eugene, OR: Pickwick Publications, 2011), 56, Kindle.

4. Blumhardt and Blumhardt, *The God Who Heals*, loc. 82-83, Kindle.

5. Ibid., loc. 46, Kindle.

6. Ibid., loc. 18, Kindle.

7. Ibid., loc. 103, Kindle.

8. Friedrich Zuendel, *The Awakening: One Man's Battle With Darkness* (Walden, NY: Plough Publishing House, 2014), loc. 541, Kindle.

9. Charles Cullis and Dorothea Trudel, *Dorothea Trudel: The Prayer of Faith* (Seattle, WA: Amazon Digital Services, 2013), loc. 598, Kindle.

10. Ibid., loc. 265, Kindle.

11. Ibid., loc. 1287-1295, Kindle.

12. Ibid., loc. 1710, Kindle.

13. Charles Spurgeon, "God's Cure for Man's Weakness," Sermon 697, June 24, 1866, in *The Metropolitan Tabernacle Pulpit*, 1866 (Pasadena, TX: Pilgrim Publications, 1974), 350-351.

14. Charles Cullis, *Have Faith in God*, ed. W. H. Daniels (New York: Willard Tract Repository, 1885), 6.

15. Ibid., 19.

16. Ibid., 25.

17. Ibid., 89.

18. Cullis and Trudel, *Dorothea Trudel*, loc. 48, Kindle.

19. Cullis, *Have Faith in God*, 339.

20. Ibid., 340.

21. Ibid.

22. Ibid., 341.

23. Ibid., 345-346.

24. Charles Cullis, *Faith and Healing* (Boston, MA: Willard Tract Repository), 10.

25. Cullis, *Have Faith in God*, 170.

26. Ibid., 130-131.

27. Ibid., 131.

28. Andrew Murray, *Divine Healing* (Abbotsford, WI: Aneko Press, 2016), loc. 1614, Kindle.

29. Ibid.

30. Ibid., loc. 866, Kindle.

31. Ibid., loc. 126, Kindle.

32. Ibid., loc. 147, Kindle.

33. Kevin Belmonte, *A.J. Gordon: An Epic Journey of Faith and Pioneering Vision* (Bloomington, IN: WestBow Press, 2017), loc. 4599, Kindle.

34. Ibid., loc. 3976, Kindle.

35. Ibid., loc. 4399, Kindle.

36. A.J. Gordon, *The Ministry of Healing: Miracles of Cure in All Ages* (Seattle, WA: Amazon Digital Services, 2010), 1, Kindle.

37. Ibid., 39, Kindle.

38. A.J. Gordon, *The Ministry of the Spirit* (Philadelphia, PA: American Baptist Publication Society, 1894), loc. 661, Kindle.

39. Ibid., loc. 1423, Kindle.

40. Ibid., loc. 1616, Kindle.

41. Gordon, *The Ministry of Healing*, loc. 2, Kindle.

42. Ibid., loc. 55, Kindle.

43. Gordon, *The Ministry of the Spirit*, loc. 1509, Kindle.

44. Gordon, *The Ministry of Healing*, loc. 15-16, Kindle.

45. Ibid., loc. 16, Kindle.

46. Ibid.

47. Ibid., loc. 17, Kindle.

48. Ibid., loc. 51, Kindle.

49. Ibid., loc. 56, Kindle.

CHAPTER FOURTEEN

THE TWENTIETH-CENTURY EXPLOSION

> *The Pentecostal power, when you sum it all up, is just more of God's love. If it does not bring more love, it is simply a counterfeit.*
> —William J. Seymour

IF streams of God's supernatural power flowed throughout history following the apostolic era, the twentieth century saw the emergence of mighty rivers. From the Reformation onward, key biblical truths that had largely been ignored and neglected by much of institutional Christianity began to be rediscovered, reclaimed, and reemphasized. Some of these foundational principles that came back into focus included justification by grace through faith, the authority of Scripture, sanctification, and the importance of experiencing faith in a meaningful, heartfelt way. The Church also began to recapture an urgency regarding evangelism and missions. In addition, there were various outpourings of God's Spirit, and the idea of "empowerment for ministry" was embraced, and to a certain degree, the healing ministry began to reemerge.

As the twentieth century dawned, there was much evidence of increasing spiritual hunger and stirring in many places around the world. Groups in America, England, India, Africa, Latin America, and the Far East were praying for revival. Mighty works of God, then, began to break out in such places as Japan, Australia, New Zealand, Scandinavia, and South Africa. The Welsh Revival under Evan Roberts had a particularly strong effect in Europe. Even Pyongyang in Korea—today, North Korea—experienced a great outpouring of God's Spirit in 1907.

In Western India, Pandita Ramabai (1858-1922) had embraced "the religion of Jesus Christ" during her schooling in England. Upon her return to India, she established homes for women and orphaned girls, and worked for social reform on many levels.

> Ramabai realized that some things only change through prayer, and she used her significant influence to encourage women to pray for spiritual and social change in India. In January 1905, she issued a call to prayer, and 550 women began meeting twice daily for intercessory prayer. That summer, Ramabai sent 30 young women out into the villages to preach the gospel. These young female preachers were successful, and they reported an outpouring of the Holy Spirit on June 29, 1905, which included several being "slain in the Spirit" and experiencing a burning sensation. This Indian revival continued for several years. By 1906, participants also began receiving the gift of speaking in tongues.[1]

There were other examples of Holy Spirit baptism with the evidence of speaking in tongues that took place in different parts of the world, but the traction and momentum of what happened in Los Angeles initiated a domino effect of spiritual blessing that impacted the church like few other revivals in history.

Azuza Street

Different waves of revival were also sweeping across the United States and Canada in the early 1900s, but the 1906 Azusa Street outpouring in Los Angeles was especially impactful. It was there that the Pentecostal experience was powerfully received by many, and from that place the influence of this movement was felt around the world. William J. Seymour (1870-1922), born of freed slaves in Louisiana, was the leader of the Azusa Street meetings. He had a background in holiness teaching, and had also been influenced by Charles Parham, who earlier led a small Bible School in Topeka, Kansas. Parham laid hands on Agnes Ozman on January 1, 1901, and she was filled with the Holy Spirit with the evidence of speaking in tongues.

In 1905, Seymour came under Parham's influence, who had since moved to Houston, Texas. After his time with Parham, Seymour moved to Los Angeles for what would become one of the most dynamic periods of ministry in the twentieth century. On April 9, 1906, after leading his congregation in weeks of diligently seeking God, Seymour and others were filled with the Holy Spirit and spoke in other tongues. Word spread rapidly about the revival in Los Angeles, and people hungry for God came from many parts of the nation and the world to partake of the experience.

Church historian Vinson Synan notes, "The Azusa Street Apostolic Faith Mission conducted three services a day, seven days a week, for three and one-half years. Thousands of seekers received the baptism in the Holy Spirit with tongues."[2] Many of these would take the Pentecostal message and blessing back to their home states and countries, and within a short time, Pentecostal works were springing up across the United States and in other parts of the world.

One who witnessed much of what happened at Azusa Street was Frank Bartleman, a preacher who, along with many others, had been praying for such an outpouring of God's Spirit. Bartleman had even corresponded with Evan Roberts, the leader of the Welsh Revival, soliciting prayer and guidance concerning needed revival in the States. Speaking of the spiritual support that came from Wales, Bartleman writes, "I feel their prayers had much to do with our final victory in California."[3] Evan Roberts spoke prophetically about what was fulfilled through Azusa Street and through many other events in the twentieth century:

> The world will be swept by His Spirit as by a rushing, mighty wind. Many who are now silent Christians will lead the movement. They will see a great light, and will reflect this light to thousands now in darkness. Thousands will do more than we have accomplished as God gives them power.[4]

Of special note at the Azusa Street Mission was the interracial makeup of both leadership and worshippers; this was not common in that day. Women also shared the pulpit with men. Stanley Burgess describes their meetings:

> At Azusa, services were long, and on the whole they were spontaneous. In its early days music was a cappella, although one or two instruments were included at times. Services included singing, testimonies given by visitors or read from those who wrote in, prayer, altar calls for salvation or sanctification or for baptism in the Holy Spirit, and of course, preaching. W.J. Seymour was clearly in charge, but much freedom was given to visiting preachers. Prayer for the sick was also a regular part of services. Many shouted.

Others were "slain in the Spirit" or "fell under the power." Sometimes there were periods of extended silence or of singing in tongues. No offerings were collected, but there was a receptacle near the door for gifts.[5]

While speaking in tongues was a notable element of the revival at Azusa Street and Seymour believed in it, he did not want that element to receive excessive or exclusive emphasis. He also desired that the fruit of the Spirit—as well as the gifts—receive appropriate attention. He admonished his followers, "Don't go out of here talking about tongues; talk about Jesus."[6]

What happened during those three years at Azusa Street was a landmark event, but continued workings of the Holy Spirit would cascade and multiply throughout the twentieth century in different parts of the country and the world. The gospel would continue to go forth as it had in centuries past, but many of those carrying the message would now be operating with additional spiritual tools and equipment. The resurrected Jesus would still be proclaimed, and the new birth would still be offered, but now ministers were also emboldened to pray for the sick, and believers would be encouraged to receive *"power from on high"* (Luke 24:49) and to operate in the gifts of the Holy Spirit.

Numerous Pentecostal denominations were established in the early 1900s to bring order and organization to the movement. Some of these groups include the Church of God in Christ, the Church of God (Cleveland), the Assemblies of God, the International Church of the Foursquare Gospel, the International Pentecostal Holiness Church, and Open Bible Churches.

Any attempt to list all of the workings of the Holy Spirit in the twentieth century, or in any century for that matter, is beyond human ability. Prominent, public figures did many things for God, and such works were often recorded for our benefit. Heaven alone, though, will tell all that God has done through His servants, many of them unsung, humble individuals who prayed for and ministered to others in relative obscurity. While many healings and works of the Spirit were accomplished from public platforms, countless more expressions of God's compassion and supernatural activity occurred far from the spotlights, through one-on-one, personal interactions. All of these are equally valuable in God's sight, though some are more widely known than others. A few notable elements in the twentieth century are described in the following pages of this chapter.

Women in Ministry

Women shared the pulpit at Azusa Street, with some citing the prophecy of Joel, quoted by Peter at Pentecost as a basis for this:

> *"'In the last days,' God says, 'I will pour out my Spirit upon all people. Your sons and **daughters** will prophesy. Your young men will see visions, and your old men will dream dreams. In those days I will pour out my Spirit even on my servants—men and **women** alike—and they will prophesy'"* (Acts 2:16-18 NLT).

Some of the notable women who were used by God to bring great blessing to multitudes in the twentieth century include Maria Woodworth-Etter (1844-1924), Lilian B. Yeomans (1861-1942), Carrie Judd Montgomery (1858-1946), Aimee Semple McPherson (1890-1944), and Kathryn Kuhlman (1907-1976).

Much has been written, and rightly so, about these and other pioneer preachers of the twentieth century. Not only did they have to face the oft-typical challenges of women in the pulpit, but they also were proclaiming what was—to some—a controversial message, that Jesus still heals and still fills people with the Holy Spirit. As beneficial as it would be to study all of these (and such studies are certainly encouraged), the story of Lilian B. Yeomans is particularly fascinating.

Lilian B. Yeomans (1861-1942)

Lilian B. Yeomans, MD, was a graduate of the University of Michigan Department of Medicine. As a young physician and surgeon, she began using morphine to cope with the pressures of her work, and became severely addicted. After many failed attempts, including unsuccessful treatment programs, Yeomans finally turned to the Word of God. When other attempts had failed miserably, God's power brought her complete deliverance. The following excerpts are from Yeomans' healing testimony.

> At last I drew my neglected Bible to me and plunged into it with full purpose of heart to get all there was for me, to do all that God told me to do, to believe all He said; and praise God, the insoluble problem was solved, the impossible was achieved, the deliverance was wrought!
>
> If anyone asks by what special Scripture verse I was healed, I feel as though I could almost say I was healed by the whole Book.
>
> The specific, irresistible, indescribable craving produced by demon power was gone.
>
> And the best of all is that this healing was no happy accident, no special miracle on my behalf but the working out in me of God's will for all of us—perfect soundness by faith in the name of Jesus of Nazareth.[7]

Yeomans went on to teach God's Word, devoting her life to helping others receive healing for the next four decades. In her latter years, she was a faculty member at L.I.F.E. Bible College under Aimee Semple McPherson.

Fred Francis Bosworth (1877-1958)

As a teenager, F. F. Bosworth was instantly healed of what had been diagnosed as terminal tuberculosis through the prayers of Miss Perry, a Methodist lady who traveled, selling Bibles and preaching the gospel. Bosworth's path led him into associations with numerous early twentieth century leaders. He spent time at Zion where he led the band for John Alexander Dowie, and received the Baptism of the Holy Spirit through the ministry of Charles Parham. Bosworth was also friends with John G. Lake, whose ministry powerfully impacted South Africa.

F.F. Bosworth moved to Dallas in 1910 and pioneered a church that served as a revival center, which included hosting of an extended healing revival conducted by Maria Woodworth-Etter. He also held large healing campaigns in many major cities, especially in the 1920s. In 1924, he published his classic work, *Christ the Healer*. Bosworth reported that they received a constant stream of testimonies of people who were healed while reading his book, even though they had been prayed for previously without success. He also delivered his salvation and healing message through radio over WJJD in Chicago. Speaking of healing testimonies, he writes, "We have received more than 225,000 letters from our radio listeners and their friends, most of whom we have never seen."[8]

Some of the healing reports that have been discussed throughout this book occurred when people were ministered to one-on-one, often through the laying on of hands or through anointing with oil. Bosworth, on the other hand, reports people being healed while reading his book or through listening to his messages on the radio. Bosworth's emphasis was not on his faith or any type of gift he might have had. Rather, he believed in getting the Word of God into people so that faith would arise in their hearts. He writes, "It is the Word of God, planted and watered and steadfastly trusted, which heals both body and soul."[9]

Bosworth encouraged believers to become fully persuaded of God's compassion, of the efficacy of Christ's redemptive work on the cross, and of God's will regarding healing. He encouraged people to let the Word of God build their faith, and then receive their healing by faith.

> The Bible tells us there is no Word of God without power. Psalm 107:20 tells us: "He sent his word, and healed them." This is His way of healing both our souls and our bodies. I have known of many who have been healed after reading the words in Isaiah 53:5, "With his stripes we are healed." They then said, "God says I am healed, and I am going to believe God and not my feelings."[10]

In 1952, when Bosworth was 75 years of age, when most ministers have retired or slowed down significantly, he engaged in international ministry for five years, preaching in South Africa and other nations. Bosworth's son said of his ministry:

> The saving of souls was paramount, and every other consideration, including the healing of the body, was secondary. Early in Dad's ministry, he discovered that the healing side of the Gospel had been given to the Church as its greatest evangelizing agency. This discovery guided him through more than fifty years of ministry.[11]

Bosworth himself said that the inner working of God in a person's soul was far more significant than the outward healing that he often witnessed:

> While we rejoice in these miracles, we remember that they are only external manifestations of a thousand times greater and more precious miracle that has transpired within the sacred chamber of the inner soul. The inner *cause* is so much more precious than the outward *effect*. External results from prayer are like figures in a bank book that show that you have gold deposited in the bank. The gold is more valuable than the figures.[12]

Tommy Lee Osborn (1923-2013)

One of several younger ministers that F. F. Bosworth was able to mentor was T. L. Osborn. Instead of praying individually for every single person in his large international evangelistic outreaches, Osborn began praying for the healing of people en masse. Acknowledging Bosworth's influence on his life and ministry, Osborn writes, "Tens of thousands of people have testified of receiving healing during our crusades by hearing and believing the word of God as we preached or taught it to the multitudes."[13]

Osborn began ministering to crowds en masse when he realized it was physically exhausting to pray individually for each sick person when thousands were present and in need. He also came to believe it was limiting God to think that a person could only be healed through individual ministry. Referring to a crusade in Puerto Rico, Osborn writes:

It was either healing en masse, or limit the scope of the campaign and of God's healing power. I chose to step aside and let God through to the people unhindered by my human limitations. Day after day, I instructed the multitudes in individual faith, urging every person to do his own asking, his own believing, and his own receiving. I taught the people to know their own rights in Christ, to claim what belonged to them individually, to act their own faith and to receive the answers to their own prayers. Instead of a few being blessed, thousands were healed every day.[14]

Osborn speaks of another great campaign in Africa and states that they had ministered for days to neglected people. His description of what happened is gripping. "As Christ was lifted up among them, thousands were saved and healed. Every conceivable type of disease and infirmity was healed miraculously. No one was ever prayed for individually."[15]

While most of Osborn's work was overseas, he preached and ministered stateside as well. He shares what happened when he was preaching once in New York on Romans 1:16—that the gospel is the power of God unto salvation to everyone who believes.

An old man who had been in a wheelchair for 16 years heard the gospel and believed it—acted upon it. The gospel stated that Jesus had already borne his diseases. He believed it and acted accordingly. He decided that he must arise and walk. He was instantly made whole. I was never able to finish my message or to pray for the sick that night. The people, with one accord acted upon the facts of the gospel; the cripples walked, the deaf heard, the lame exercised their faith and were healed, those with braces, canes, and trusses discarded them and a great mass-miracle occurred.[16]

Along with his wife, Daisy, T. L. Osborn ministered the gospel in nearly 100 nations, frequently bringing the gospel to countries that were predominantly non-Christian.

A Changing of the Guard

While the majority of Osborn's work took place overseas, a major outbreak of healing revival was percolating and being released in the United States as well. Three major leaders in the earlier healing movement had passed away—Aimee Semple McPherson, Charles Price, and Smith Wigglesworth—the last two died within a few days of each other in 1947. With the departure of these figures, a new crop of ministers emerged. Many of these would crisscross the nation, preaching and praying for the sick in large tents.

Kenneth E. Hagin describes this special season wherein the Holy Spirit was emphasizing divine healing:

> Then, in 1947…the wave of the healing revival started. You talk about healing! I got in on it, and to tell you the truth about it, it was the easiest thing in the world to get people healed. I have never seen anything like what we had then; it was easy to get people healed!"[17]

This season in American church history brought the supernatural working of God to the attention of the public perhaps more than at any other time.

Some of the ministers from this new era had experienced divine healing themselves before launching into their own ministries. Kenneth E. Hagin (1917-2003) had been healed of a deformed heart and an incurable blood disease, while Lester Sumrall (1913-1996) had been healed of tuberculosis. Oral Roberts (1918-2009) the most famous evangelist from this era, had been healed as a teenager of tuberculosis and of stuttering through the prayers of a healing evangelist. Ministering the Word of God to the sick was an integral part of all of their ministries. Those three men, along with Osborn, had great longevity too, and enduring fruit from their ministries. Unfortunately, this was not the case with many of the ministers of that era.

David Edwin Harrell Jr. documents this major surge of healing revivalism in his book, *All Things Are Possible: The Healing and Charismatic Revivals in America*. The first half of his book chronicles "The Healing Revival, 1947-1958." While dozens of evangelists preached and prayed for the sick during this era, Gordon Lindsay held an extremely important role, but not so much because of his preaching. Harrell describes him and his role:

> More than any single man, Gordon Lindsay brought system and unity to the healing revival. Lindsay contributed to the revival an orderly mind, a keen business sense, boundless energy, badly needed literary skills, and an ecumenical spirit. He very quickly surmised that the revival needed a coordinator and publicist more than another evangelist. Lindsay's calm temperament, his career as an itinerant evangelist in the 1930s, and a well-deserved reputation for integrity pushed him quickly to the foreground.

Lindsay resigned his pastorate in Oregon in 1947 to manage revival meetings for William Branham. After publishing one issue of *The Voice of Healing* magazine to promote Branham's ministry, Branham took an extended leave of absence from ministry. As a result, Lindsay expanded the purpose of the publication, using the new magazine to represent many of the healing evangelists of the day.

During the next ten years, *VoH* became the primary voice of the worldwide salvation healing revivals, featuring the crusades and schedules of numerous evangelists and publishing photographs and documented accounts of miracles that occurred in these services (healings of the blind, deaf, crippled, and those with other ailments).[18]

Lindsay also headed up a ministerial fellowship utilizing the same name, The Voice of Healing, to provide fellowship, encouragement, and guidance for revivalists with healing and deliverance ministries. Using these tools, Lindsay was a steadying influence as he sought to promote unity among ministers and to encourage high ethical standards in ministerial conduct and practices.

Lindsay was empathetic toward the special challenges and pressures faced by those with supernatural ministries, and he stood up for those who were falsely and unfairly attacked. At the same time, he strongly urged high-profile preachers to resist and avoid the common pitfalls and temptations often associated with their type of ministries. For example, he admonished the revivalists to avoid pride, exaggeration, extremism, and wrong attitudes and practices toward money. He gave a stark warning regarding one minister who "promises the people that God has given him the gift to make them wealthy, if only they will give him a good offering. Such assertions approach to the crime of blasphemy."[19]

Lindsay also writes:

Some spiritual moves have been blessed of God, and then suddenly faded away because of the presumptuous and erratic conduct of certain of the leaders. One such move occurred some years ago in America. We shall not identify it, for some very devoted Christians were associated with it.

At first, we rejoiced in this outpouring of the Spirit. But very soon we saw something develop that alarmed us. Some of the leaders were claiming that they were the "Powerhouse" and all other churches were "dried up." They said that people should come to them to get recharged. When we saw such bold pretensions, we realized that the usefulness of such leaders could not last long.[20]

Other seasoned voices joined Lindsay in calling for purity within the movement.

The British minister, Donald Gee, was an elder statesman in the Pentecostal movement and was a great proponent of ministers walking in wisdom and maturity. He urged the revivalists to keep their motives right: "Over-desire is only another term for lust, and there can be an unhealthy lusting after signs and wonders that desires them for their own sake rather than for the glory of God and the work of the Gospel."[21]

As the season featuring a special emphasis on healing subsided in the late 1950s, Lindsay pointed the Body of Christ to continue its outward focus of taking the gospel to the world. He noted that many of the evangelists had become pastors, and that others now had their own publications. Lindsay explained the evolution of the organization in these terms:

While the policy of The Voice of Healing will always be to emphasize evangelism, the scope of its ministry has broadened to include all the gift ministries of the Church. The Voice of Healing seeks to encourage cooperation and unity between all members of the Body of Christ. God's people have a great task to accomplish before Jesus returns— the evangelization of the nations....[22]

Endnotes

1. Darrin J. Rogers, "This Week in AG History—April 1, 1916," *Assemblies of God*; https://news.ag.org/en/Features/This-Week-in-AG-History-April-1-1916; accessed January 2, 2020.

2. Vinson Synan, *The Century of the Holy Spirit: 100 Years of Pentecostal and Charismatic Renewal, 1901-2001* (Nashville, TN: Thomas Nelson Publishers, www.thomasnelson.com, 2001), loc. 141, Kindle. Used by permission of Thomas Nelson.

3. Frank Bartleman, *How Pentecost Came to Los Angeles: The Story Behind the Azusa Street Revival*, ed. Cecil M. Robeck Jr. and Darrin Rodgers (Springfield, MA: Gospel Publishing House), loc. 848, Kindle.

4. Ibid., loc. 863, Kindle.

5. Stanley Burgess, ed., *The New International Dictionary of Pentecostal and Charismatic Movements* (Grand Rapids, MI: Zondervan, www.zondervan.com, 2003), 346.   Used by permission of Zondervan.

6. Craig Borlase, *William Seymour: A Biography* (Lake Mary, FL: Charisma House, 2006), xi.

7. Lilian B. Yeomans, *Healing from Heaven*, in *His Healing Power* (Shippensburg, PA: Harrison House, 2003), loc. 185-206, Kindle.

8. F. F. Bosworth, *Christ the Healer* (Grand Rapids, MI: Chosen Books, 1948), loc. 16, Kindle.

9. Ibid.

10. Ibid., loc. 128, Kindle.

12. Ibid., loc. 8, Kindle.

13. Ibid., loc. 16, Kindle.

14. T. L. Osborn, *Healing the Sick* (Shippensburg, PA: Harrison House, 1956), loc. 469, Kindle.

15. T. L. Osborn, *Healing En Masse* (Tulsa, OK: A T. L. Osborn Publication, 1956), 17.

16. Ibid., 22.

17. Ibid., 49-50.

18. Kenneth E. Hagin, *Plans, Purposes, and Pursuits* (Tulsa, OK: Faith Library Publications, www.rhema.org, 1988), 71.

19. J. A. Hewitt, "Voice of Healing," in *International Dictionary of Pentecostal and Charismatic Movements*, ed. Stanley Burgess (Grand Rapids, MI: Zondervan, www.zondervan.com, 2003), 1178-1179.   Used by permission of Zondervan.

19. Gordon Lindsay, *God's 20th Century Barnabas* (Dallas, TX: Christ for the Nations, 1982), 276.

20. Ibid., 277-278.

21. Donald Gee, "Attitudes Toward the Supernatural," *Pentecost*, no. 38 (December 1956), 17.

22. Lindsay, *God's 20th Century Barnabas*, 278.

CHAPTER FIFTEEN

EXPANSION, RECOGNITION, AND INTEGRATION

In Pentecostalism, poor and broken people discover that what they read in the Gospels is happening now in their midst.
—Richard Shaull

THERE have been times in recent history when Pentecostal and charismatic Christians have been denigrated and marginalized, not only by society, but also by established forms of Christianity. Frank Bartleman references the response to the 1906 outpouring at Azusa Street: "There was much persecution, especially from the press. They wrote us up shamefully, but this only drew the crowds. Some gave the work six months to live."[1] Bartleman also notes, "The newspapers here are very venomous, and most unfair and untrue in their statements. The pseudo systems of religion are fighting hard also."[2]

There was also opposition from academia. For example, respected scholar, B. B. Warfield (1851-1921) of Princeton University argued against the modern-day presence of the supernatural gifts of the Spirit. He writes of the gifts, "They were distinctively the authentication of the Apostles.... Their function thus confined them to distinctively the Apostolic Church, and they necessarily passed away with it."[3] Countless words of censure and disparagement from other preachers would follow as the twentieth century progressed.

A group established in 1919 and known as The World's Christian Fundamentalist Association passed the following resolution denouncing Pentecostals in 1928:

> Whereas, the present wave of modern Pentecostalism, often referred to as the "tongues movement," and the present wave of fanatical and unscriptural healing which is sweeping over the country today, has become a menace in many churches and a real injury to sane testimony of Fundamental Christians, be it resolved, that this convention go on record as unreservedly opposed to Modern Pentecostalism, including the speaking in unknown tongues, and the fanatical healing known as general healing in the atonement, and the perpetuation of the miraculous sign-healing of Jesus and His apostles, wherein they claim the only reason the church cannot perform these miracles is because of unbelief.[4]

Another organization founded in 1941, the American Council of Christian Churches also refused to affirm or accept Pentecostals. Even though some religious leaders denounced the beliefs and practices associated with Pentecostalism, its momentum was not to be stopped.

In spite of opposition on almost every level, Pentecostal and charismatic expressions of biblical faith exponentially increased, becoming a major force in Christianity since the early days of the twentieth century. Vinson Synan gives an overview of its amazing growth:

By the middle of the twentieth century, the Pentecostals were burgeoning into what some called "the third force in Christendom." Surveys of worldwide Christianity were revealing that three-fourths of all Protestants in Latin America were Pentecostals, that two-thirds of all non-Catholics in Italy were Pentecostals, and that the majority of all Christians in South Africa were Pentecostals. Furthermore, the largest free churches in Russia, Scandinavia, and France were Pentecostal and the growth rates indicated vastly greater growth for the future.[5]

Clearly, this was a work of God that was not built or established on the approval of man or of religious institutions.

Spirit-filled expressions of the Christian faith have also taken on an increasingly influential role in world evangelism and church planting. Mark Noll, who served as Professor of History at Notre Dame and Wheaton remarks, "One of the most momentous developments in the recent history of Christianity must certainly be the emergence of Pentecostalism as a dynamic force around the world."[6] Noll proceeds:

> Pentecostal and charismatic currents have been central in the rapid expansion of Christianity outside the West, with most of the rapidly growing churches in Brazil, Nigeria, Korea, Russia, China, and many other nations either explicitly Pentecostal or heavily influenced by charismatic practices. In these situations, Pentecostal and charismatic forms of Christian faith flourish by directly confronting pagan gods and animistic spirits as well as by imparting the direct immediacy of God's presence.[182] Over the last half century, the charismatic movement in Catholic, Lutheran, Presbyterian, Episcopal, and many other denominations

expanded emphases on healing and other spiritual gifts borrowed from earlier Pentecostalism. Together, the Pentecostal and charismatic emphases on experiencing the grace of God—especially on sensing God through more intimate, less cognitive forms of worship—have influenced Protestants, Catholics, and even some Orthodox all over the world.[7]

It is important to recognize the tremendously rapid changes that have taken place and are occurring around the world. The Center for the Study of Global Christianity estimates that there are now, at the time of this writing, 693,820,000 Pentecostals and Charismatics around the globe. This number represents 27.44 percent of the 2,528,295,000 people who identify as Christians worldwide.[8] Importantly, a significant amount of this growth has taken place outside of North America and Europe, and parallels the growth of the Christian faith in what is sometimes called "the majority world."

Philip Jenkins, a prolific author and the Distinguished Professor of History and Co-Director of the Program on Historical Studies of Religion at Baylor University, writes:

> Christianity has in very recent times ceased to be a Euro-American religion, and is becoming thoroughly global. In 1900, 83 percent of the world's Christians lived in Europe and North America. In 2050, 72 percent of Christians will live in Africa, Asia, and Latin America, and a sizeable share of the remainder will have roots in one or more of those continents.[9]

Not only has a radical demographic shift been happening in the last century concerning where Christians live, but there has also been a significant shift in the beliefs, practices, and spiritual orientation of believers overall.

A rapidly increasing number of Christians around the world have embraced the beliefs, experiences, and practices of Pentecostalism—this includes those who refer to themselves as charismatic. Generally speaking, this means that they recognize not only the reality and importance of the new birth, but also embrace the infilling of the Holy Spirit as described in the book of Acts, including accompanying gifts and operations of the Holy Spirit and divine healing. Philip Jenkins also notes the rapid expansion of charismatics and Pentecostals, and states:

> Since there were only a handful of charismatics and Pentecostals in 1900, and several hundred million today, is it not reasonable to identify this as perhaps the most successful social movement of the past century? According to current projections, the number of charismatic/Pentecostal believers should cross the one billion mark before 2050.[10]

The Charismatic Movement

Around 1960, a dramatic and further development occurred in the Body of Christ. People within various traditional, mainline denominations began having dynamic encounters with the Holy Spirit. This sovereign outpouring of the Holy Spirit was so significant that it commanded the attention of leaders in all denominations over the next many years. Roman Catholics, Episcopalians, Methodists, Lutherans, Presbyterians, Mennonites, and many others had to determine what they were going to do with their members who were receiving the infilling of the Holy Spirit, speaking in tongues, prophesying, praying for the sick, etc.

Responses varied in different denominations and in different churches, ranging from condemnation to acceptance. Some who received this Pentecostal experience, including certain pastors, were able to stay within their existing churches. Many others either chose to leave or were asked to leave, and thousands of independent Charismatic congregations were birthed over the next few decades.

These believers identified with the Pentecostal experience (Acts 2:4), but did not necessarily identify with traditional Pentecostal denominations. They were called Charismatics, based on the Greek word *charismata*, meaning *gift of grace*, and refers to the various gifts given by the Holy Spirit.

Neither space nor time permit for a detailed overview of all that transpired through the working of the Holy Spirit in the rest of the twentieth century. Massive conferences took place, charismatic churches multiplied, traveling teachers and missionaries carried the gospel all around the world, television and radio ministries abounded, and publishing houses produced massive amounts of books and literature. It was truly an explosion of God's power in which multitudes of people experienced His presence, learned His Word, and carried the gospel to others.

I was privileged to come into the things of the Spirit in 1977, and I am thankful for the grace and empowerment that came into my life, enabling me to serve God and His purpose. For more than four decades, I have experienced the presence and operations of the Holy Spirit, including the reality of what the apostle Paul wrote, *"He who speaks in a tongue edifies himself"* (1 Corinthians 14:4). While that specific expression is for personal enrichment, I have also seen outward expressions of the Spirit that benefit others working through my life and through countless friends and coworkers.

Meanwhile in Corinth

The Corinthian church was immature and was prone to misuse the gifts, but Paul did not denounce the gifts or promote their discontinuation. Rather, he coached the believers—some who were erring—to mature and to use the gifts of the Spirit with wisdom, love, and maturity. He told them, *"since you are so eager and ambitious to possess spiritual endowments and manifestations of the [Holy] Spirit, [concentrate on] striving to excel and to abound [in them] in ways that will build up the church"* (1 Corinthians 14:12 Amplified Bible, Classic Edition). Self-edification was not wrong, but when they were gathered together, believers were to seek to edify others.

Paul writes, "I thank God that I speak in tongues more than any of you. But in a church meeting I would rather speak five understandable words to help others than ten thousand words in an unknown language" (1 Corinthians 14:18-19 NLT). The Charismatic Movement was sometimes messy, and excesses and extremes did happen. Some went off on various tangents. But many applied themselves to wisdom, made the necessary adjustments, grew up spiritually, and demonstrated a healthy, balanced, and vibrant expression of the Christian faith.

Toward Greater Unity

Even though certain groups had officially rejected Pentecostals, they were invited in 1943 to be a part of the National Association of Evangelicals (NAE). Vinson Synan writes, "It has been suggested that the admission of the Pentecostal churches into the N.A.E. was the first time in church history that a charismatic movement was accepted into the Church mainstream."[11] Today, the website for the National Association of Evangelicals describes their membership: "Evangelicals are a vibrant and diverse group, including believers found in many churches, denominations and nations. Our community brings together Reformed, Holiness, Anabaptist, Pentecostal, Charismatic and other traditions."[12] While all members may not agree about tongues, healing, or other matters, all member groups do subscribe to the following statement about Jesus, as well as other basic essentials of faith:

> We believe in the deity of our Lord Jesus Christ, in His virgin birth, in His sinless life, in His miracles, in His vicarious and atoning death through His shed blood, in His bodily resurrection, in His ascension to the right hand of the Father, and in His personal return in power and glory.[13]

It was this very Jesus who prayed for His followers in all generations, "May they experience such perfect unity that the world will know that you sent me and that you love them as much as you love me" (John 17:23 NLT).

A Tale of Two Men

Billy Graham and Oral Roberts both rose to national prominence in 1948. Graham was to emerge as the most famous Evangelical preacher in America, while Roberts would become the most popular healing evangelist in the Pentecostal movement. These two men developed a love and friendship that stands as a sterling example of unity and partnership between two major streams within the Christian faith.

Oral Roberts University was founded "upon the power of the Holy Spirit and the authority of Scripture,"[14] and when it was time for the school's dedication ceremony in 1967, Roberts invited Graham to be the speaker for that monumental event. Many years later, a *Charisma Magazine* article reported on their friendship:

> In August of 2009, ORU Founder Oral Roberts reflected on his friendship with Billy Graham. "Billy was the most generous man in the ministry I've ever met. He accepted me as a brother. He said he fell in love with my ministry. I counted him the No. 1 evangelist in the world. We became very close friends."
>
> Upon hearing of Oral Roberts' passing in December 2009, Rev. Graham said, in part: "Oral Roberts was a man of God and a great friend in ministry. I loved him as a brother. We had many quiet conversations over the years."[15]

These two men had different assignments, different church backgrounds, and different perspectives on healing and spiritual gifts. Still, they exhibited kindness, graciousness, and mutual respect as they focused on Jesus Christ and carried out their respective ministries.

Roberts was very proactive in preaching healing and praying for the sick. He states that the Holy Spirit spoke to him and said, "Don't be like other men...be like Jesus and heal the people as He did."[16] He also recounted the first time he prayed for the sick in 1947:

> I was so filled with the power of the Almighty that I seemed to have supernatural strength. It was nearly six o'clock, four hours later, when I finished praying for the last one who needed deliverance. When I left, there was not a doubt that God had called me and was with me for whatever the future would hold. Not only had many been wonderfully healed, but also more people had come to Christ that day than I had seen saved in the past year of pastoral ministry.[17]

As opposed to questioning God's will, Roberts states, "I pray in a positive manner for God to raise a person up because the Word of God teaches us it is God's will for man to have health and to be whole in his entire being."[18]

Graham, on the other hand, was not a healing evangelist or a Pentecostal, yet he expressed respectful views that are, in many ways, Pentecostal-friendly. Graham did not believe that physical healing is for all, yet he relays an inspiring story about his sister-in-law's healing. Having shared certain qualifying thoughts, he writes:

> I do know that God heals under certain circumstances in accordance with His will. My own sister-in-law is an outstanding example. She was dying of tuberculosis. The X-rays showed the seriousness of her condition, but she asked her surgeon father for permission to discontinue medical treatment because she believed God was going to heal her. It was granted, and some godly men and women anointed her with oil and prayed the prayer of faith. Then a new series of X-rays was taken, and to the astonishment of the physicians at the sanatorium she no longer showed any signs of active tuberculosis. Immediately she began to gain weight, and thirty-five years later she is an active Bible teacher, a healthy person. Obviously, she was healed. But note that the healing came, not through someone who had the gift of healing, but through faith.[19]

Graham recognized there were counterfeits and urged caution and discernment, but he writes, "there is no doubt in my mind that there is a gift of healing—that people are healed in answer to the prayer of faith—and that there are other healings, such as healings of relationships.[20]

Regarding healing meetings, Graham had both negative and positive observations:

> I have attended a number of healing meetings. Some sickened me because of the emotional hysteria present. I have also attended healing meetings where the services were conducted decently and in order. At those, I have witnessed the quiet moving of the Spirit of God in a way that could offend no one. In meetings like that, the Spirit used God's servants with special gifts to do His will.[21]

Instead of speaking from hearsay as some are prone to do, it is admirable that Graham spoke from personal and direct observations.

Roberts and Graham had different perspectives about speaking in tongues. Roberts believed that every born-again person could yield to the Holy Spirit and speak to God in what he called "the prayer language of the Spirit."[22] Roberts writes:

> The basic purpose of the baptism of the Holy Spirit is to empower the believer to be a witness of Jesus Christ. It provides an inner power that becomes an outward force to bring the reality of Christ to others. To help release this power, the baptism with the Holy Spirit gives the believer a new tongue with which to praise Him, and with which to edify himself. This is perhaps the most revolutionary experience that can happen to a believer—one who is already a Christian.[23]

Graham accepted that tongues was a gift from God that was for some, but said, "I have difficulty linking the filling of the Holy Spirit to a second baptism and to a necessary accompanying sign, speaking in tongues."[24] He was respectful, though, of friends who told him they spoke in tongues.

> A number of friends have told me that after they had prayed for a long period of time, they suddenly found themselves speaking in an unknown language. For the most part, they have kept it private and have not said everyone else must have the same experience. They have not said that all Christians must speak in tongues as a sign of spiritual maturity. Everyone knew that Corrie ten Boom had spoken in tongues, but she never talked about it and never discussed it. She often rebuked those who did talk about it excessively.[25]

While Graham and Roberts differed on exactly who the gift of tongues was for, they both agreed that tongues, or any other spiritual gift, should never be a source of pride, strife, or division among believers. Graham gives this wise counsel concerning tongues:

> Is this a gift God has seen fit to give you? Don't let it be a source of pride or preoccupation. Become grounded in the whole Word of God. And above all, learn what it means to love others, including believers who may not agree with your emphasis.[26]

In the same vein, Roberts states:

> I know that some of us inadvertently think that we are superior because God has given us the gift of the Holy Spirit and we can speak in the prayer language of the Spirit. Now you've got to get real frank and honest with yourself to admit that. We tend to take some gift and, because it's so great in

our lives, we tend to act like we are superior and those who don't have it in the way we do are inferior. So we divide and hurt and separate from one another. I believe this is a sin! A gift of the Spirit is not our *uniter*, but Christ *himself!*[27]

With that statement, Roberts was emphasizing what many mature Christians understand: It is important to keep Jesus Christ as the center and the main focus of all that we do. Jesus—who He is and what He did—is the basis for our purpose, our partnership, and our fellowship with one another. Neither of these great men took the immature, petty attitude of, "If you don't believe everything exactly the way I do about every point of doctrine, then I can't fellowship with you."

One of the phrases that Roberts was famous for was "Expect a Miracle." Graham's ministry focus was different from that of Roberts, but he acknowledged that in some situations, miracles are still happening today in conjunction with the preaching of the gospel. Graham writes:

And today when the gospel is proclaimed on the frontiers of the Christian faith that approximate the first century situation, miracles still sometimes accompany the advance of the gospel. As indicated by both the prophets Hosea and Joel, as we approach the end of the age we may expect miracles to increase.[28]

Again, stressing "the end of the age," Graham continues:

I believe we will see a dramatic recurrence of signs and wonders that will demonstrate the power of God to a skeptical world. Just as the powers of Satan are being unleashed with greater intensity, so I believe God will allow signs and wonders to be performed.[29]

Graham's gracious spirit was not just evidenced in his relationship with Roberts, but he also sought to build bridges of unity with others in the Pentecostal stream of Christianity. In 1982, Graham accepted an invitation to speak to the students of three different Assemblies of God schools in Springfield, Missouri: Central Bible College, Assemblies of God Theological Seminary, and Evangel University. In his remarks, Graham spoke respectfully of Thomas F. Zimmerman, who was then Superintendent of the Pentecostal denomination, saying that there was "no churchman I love and admire more" than him.[30]

Dr. Mark Hausfeld, former President of the Assemblies of God Theological Seminary describes what happened in the chapel that day as Graham preached to the students, guests, and dignitaries in the Robert H. Spence Chapel at Evangel College (now University) on December 9, 1982:

> I remember the power and clarity of his voice, the excellence of his sermon prep, the anointing upon him, and how I knew I was in the presence of a unique person in Christ. He preached just over 30 minutes and then said, "I need to bring this message to a conclusion, though I have not finished." He brought the sermon to an end and then sat down. When he sat down, in the Chapel balcony a person immediately gave a message in tongues. As soon as the message in tongues finished, the interpretation of the message in tongues followed. The Holy Spirit flowed in the theme of Billy Graham's message. Dr. Thomas Zimmerman said later that day, Billy Graham said to him, "I did not finish my message today, but the Holy Spirit did. Everything that was spoken by the person in the balcony was exactly the points I had remaining in my message, but did not finish." The next week

I saw Billy Graham being interviewed on a Christian TV show. The interviewer asked him, "You minister to so many people, how are you ministered to?" Billy Graham answered, "Last week I spoke at a Christian college in Springfield, Missouri. I was ministered to while at that college." This incredible experience was a memory stone moment in my life and so many others.[31]

If you are like me, you read that with great appreciation for Billy Graham's humility. Some people are quick to criticize anything that is different from their own background or their own previous experiences. Graham looked for the good and sought to affirm it, and he recognized the Holy Spirit at work through different people and through different types of gifts.

While Graham may not have had a ministry of praying for the sick like Oral Roberts, and he may not have been used in the gift of tongues and interpretation like the person in the chapel service in Missouri, no one can dispute the anointing of God that was upon Billy Graham's life to preach the gospel and invite people to respond to Christ's offer of eternal life. Millions were impacted as Graham focused on Jesus and the gift of eternal life He offers.

Perhaps one of the greatest lessons of the twentieth century is that God desires His people to not only have power and gifts but also humility and unity. I believe Gordon Lindsay summarized the heart of God so well and profoundly. Referencing Jesus' prayer in John 17:21, Lindsay writes:

> It is essential that the Body of Christ become one in Spirit, to fulfill that prayer of Jesus. This does not mean that there will not continue to be different churches and groups, nor

that God's people should not be loyal in a special way, to those with whom they are working. But the hour of the competitive spirit, the petty rivalries and the seeking of preeminence is over. We must find a way by which we may recognize all members of the Body of Christ. We must find a means by which the ministry-gifts that God has set in the church may be used for the benefit and blessing of the whole. We must move past the place whereby the men are held together by petty ecclesiastical rules rather than the Golden Rule. We always have denominations and groups, but we dare not allow this to divide the Body of Christ or to build fences that separate God's people from each other.[32]

May all who love Jesus aspire to this standard, regardless of what gifts they have or do not have. We are not to be haughty or think of ourselves as better than others if we have, or think we have, certain gifts. Let us celebrate the gifts of others, seeking only to glorify the Lord Jesus Christ and to advance the gospel and the interests of God in the earth.

Endnotes

1. Bartleman, *How Pentecost Came to Los Angeles*, loc. 815, Kindle.

2. Ibid., loc 960, Kindle.

3. B. B. Warfield, *Counterfeit Miracles* (Seattle, WA: Amazon Digital Services, 2012), 5-6, Kindle.

4. Vinson Synan, *The Holiness-Pentecostal Tradition: Charismatic Movements in the Twentieth Century* (Grand Rapids, MI: Eerdmans, 1997), loc. 2188, Kindle.

5. Ibid., loc. 2291, Kindle.

6. Mark A. Noll, *Turning Points: Decisive Moments in the History of Christianity*, loc. 310, Kindle.

7. Ibid., loc. 312, Kindle.

8. "Status of Global Christianity, 2019," Gordon Conwell Theological Seminary; https://gordonconwell.edu/wp-content/uploads/sites/13/2019/04 /StatusofGlobalChristianity20191.pdf; accessed January 27, 2020.

9. Philip Jenkins, *The Next Christendom: The Coming of Global Christianity* (New York, Oxford University Press, 2011), xi.

10. Ibid., 10.

11. Synan, *The Holiness-Pentecostal Tradition*, loc. 2318, Kindle.

12. "What is an Evangelical," National Association of Evangelicals; https://www.nae .net/what-is-an-evangelical/; accessed January 27, 2020.

13. "Statement of Faith," National Association of Evangelicals; https://www.nae.net /statement-of-faith/; accessed January 27, 2020.

14. "The Vision of ORU," Oral Roberts University; https://oru.edu/news/oru -general-info-media-kit.php; accessed January 27, 2020.

15. Stephanie Hill, "The Unlikely Brotherhood of Oral Roberts and Billy Graham," *Charisma Magazine*; https://www.charismamag.com/spirit/church -ministry/35933-the-unlikely-brotherhood-of-oral-roberts-and-billy-graham; accessed January 27, 2020.

16. Oral Roberts, *The Holy Spirit in the Now I* (Tulsa, OK: Oral Roberts University, 1974), 10.

17. Ibid., 12.

18. Oral Roberts, *101 Questions and Answers on Healing and Salvation* (Tulsa, OK: Oral Roberts University, 1968), 90.

19. Billy Graham, *The Holy Spirit: Activating God's Power in Your Life* (Nashville, TN: Thomas Nelson, www.thomasnelson.com, 1988), loc. 209, Kindle. Used by permission of Thomas Nelson.

20. Ibid., loc. 214, Kindle.

21. Ibid., loc. 211, Kindle.

22. Roberts, *The Holy Spirit in the Now*, 37.

23. Roberts, *101 Questions and Answers*, 72.

24. Graham, *The Holy Spirit*, loc. 225, Kindle.

25. Ibid., loc. 231, Kindle.

26. Ibid., loc. 234, Kindle.

27. Roberts, *The Holy Spirit in the Now*, 51.

28. Graham, *The Holy Spirit*, loc. 217, Kindle.

29. Ibid.

30. "AG Leaders Fondly Remember 'America's Pastor,'" Assemblies of God; https://news.ag.org/en/News/AG-Leaders-Fondly-Remember-America-s-Pastor; accessed January 27, 2020.

31. Mark Hausfeld, Facebook post, February 22, 2018; https://www.facebook.com/mark.hausfeld.5; accessed January 2, 2020.

32. Lindsay, *God's 20th Century Barnabas*, 282.

Present-Day Realities and Applications

CHAPTER SIXTEEN

THE SUPERNATURAL AND ASSOCIATED PITFALLS

Error never shows itself in its naked reality, in order not to be discovered. On the contrary, it dresses elegantly, so that the unwary may be led to believe that it is more truthful than truth itself.

—**Irenaeus of Lyons**

IN my teenage years, a friend of my father showed me what I thought was a really cool "trick." He took an aluminum foil wrapper from a piece of gum, tore off a small piece of the wrapper, and moistened it in his mouth. Then he folded it up, put it in the palm of my hand, and asked me to hold it. Within a few seconds, the little piece of foil became intensely hot, causing me to promptly drop it to avoid getting burnt. I was impressed and fascinated. How did he do that?

Actually, there was nothing "magic" about this trick at all, and he showed me the secret. He had a small pill in his pocket that he had discreetly rubbed between his forefinger and thumb. When he folded up the moist piece of foil and placed it in my hand, residue from that pill—a chemical compound of some kind—began interacting with the aluminum and caused it to become super hot, hot enough to leave a blister on one's hand if not dropped quickly enough.

He gave me several of those small pills in a prescription-type of bottle and told me to enjoy doing the trick for others, but not to reveal the secret. With one of the pills in my pocket, I began performing this at school, and everyone was fascinated with how the foil became scalding hot. People really wanted to know how this happened, and I liked having this special ability and being able to do something that amazed people.

Shun Ego and Sensationalism

While there was nothing sinister about this gag, it provides a bit of insight about what could happen if a person really wanted to have some type of *spiritual* power in order to feed their ego. Scripture tells us such a story in the eighth chapter of Acts as Philip conducted a great evangelistic campaign in Samaria.

As Philip proclaims Jesus to the people, the Bible says that miracles and healings occurred, and that there was great joy in the city (Acts 8:5-8). One of those impacted by this powerful move of God was a man named Simon.

> *A man named Simon had been a sorcerer there for many years, amazing the people of Samaria and claiming to be someone great. Everyone, from the least to the greatest, often spoke of him as "the Great One—the Power of God." They listened closely to him because for a long time he had astounded them with his magic* (Acts 8:9-11 NLT).

Simon comes to faith in Jesus through Philip's preaching, but we soon notice something troubling about his mindset and perspective. Acts 8:13

(NLT) reads, "*Then Simon himself believed and was baptized. He began following Philip wherever he went, and he was amazed by the signs and great miracles Philip performed.*"

Do you see a problem here? Signs and miracles do get attention, but there is no mention of Simon falling deeply in love with Jesus or becoming devotedly committed to the Lord; rather, he only appears to be fascinated by the miracles. Simon had been an egotistical "showman," and unfortunately, those tendencies had not changed. Instead of seeing the miracles as a witness to Jesus, he apparently saw Jesus as a means to miracles.

When Peter and John arrive in Samaria, Simon's misguided motives and perspective came rushing to the surface.

> *As soon as they arrived, they prayed for these new believers to receive the Holy Spirit. The Holy Spirit had not yet come upon any of them, for they had only been baptized in the name of the Lord Jesus. Then Peter and John laid their hands upon these believers, and they received the Holy Spirit.*
>
> *When Simon saw that the Spirit was given when the apostles laid their hands on people, he offered them money to buy this power. "Let me have this power, too," he exclaimed, "so that when I lay my hands on people, they will receive the Holy Spirit!"*
>
> *But Peter replied, "May your money be destroyed with you for thinking God's gift can be bought! You can have no part in this, for your heart is not right with God. Repent of your wickedness and pray to the Lord. Perhaps he will forgive your evil thoughts, for I can see that you are full of bitter jealousy and are held captive by sin."*
>
> *"Pray to the Lord for me," Simon exclaimed, "that these terrible things you've said won't happen to me!"* (Acts 8:15-24 NLT)

There was nothing pure, right, or wholesome about Simon's intentions in his offer to buy power. Simon wasn't seeking the glory of God, nor was he seeking the benefit of others. He had a history of wanting people to admire him and hold him in esteem, and he wanted to use the holy things of God to perpetuate and even increase the very same carnal, ego-based desires.

While I believe these observations about Simon's motives are correct, this is not the specific focus of Peter's harsh rebuke. Peter specifically states, *"May your money be destroyed with you for thinking God's gift can be bought!"* (Acts 8:20 NLT). What specifically drew Peter's ire was Simon's presumption that he could purchase the anointing of the Holy Spirit with cash. J.B. Phillips rightly translates the twentieth verse, *"To hell with you and your money! How dare you think you could buy the gift of God for money!"* Modern readers might think such a bitter reprimand is excessive, but the last time Peter had seen someone operate deceptively regarding the Holy Spirit and finances, Ananias and Sapphira had been struck dead in judgment (Acts 5:1-11). Holy things are not to be trifled with!

Peter would later write about false prophets and teachers, who, "in their greed they will make up clever lies to get hold of your money" (2 Peter 2:3 NLT). The Message version of the Bible renders that verse, *"They're only out for themselves. They'll say anything, **anything**, that sounds good to exploit you."* There is always a danger with any type of power for people to become manipulative and corrupt. Ministers, and all of God's children for that matter, must remember that God gives His gifts for the benefit of others, not for the glorification of the one who has received the gift.

Whatever gifts I have from God, I must recognize those as a holy stewardship entrusted to me that I may glorify Him and serve others. I must never misuse those gifts to abuse, manipulate, or exploit others for my own gratification.

Avoid Gimmicks and "Prophetic Appeals"

Gordon Lindsay was a leading minister and a voice of stability during the great Healing Revival in the middle of the twentieth century. He saw both the glories and the problems of the movement. He witnessed the miraculous power of God that brought blessing to so many, and he grieved over ministers who had great gifts and potential but experienced horrific downfalls because of deception that took them off track. Lindsay issued the following admonition:

> Gimmicks—relics, bones, holy water, indulgences, etc.—cursed the medieval Church. These money-raising devices were designed to appeal to people's ignorance and superstition. Today, too, there are certain preachers who resort to gimmicks to entice people to donate their money. First of all, there should be a clear distinction made between that which is legitimate and that which is not. What we are referring to as gimmicks is the use of articles that purport to have some mysterious power or supposed virtue in them—a sort of charm of fetish—the use of which has no scriptural foundation. These are analogues to the "strange fire," which was offered by Dathan and Abiram, the sons of Aaron, who were divinely appointed priests, but who came under the judgment of God. There is a long list of gimmicks which have been offered to the public. The Reformation had its beginning when Martin Luther became convinced of all the gimmicks the Church used—the relics, the saints' bones,

splinters from the "true cross," etc.—were phony and had no virtue. May God help ministers to abide in the simplicity and purity of the Gospel and not attempt to obtain funds from people with such things.[1]

What is probably more common in recent times than relics are "prophetic appeals" from ministers regarding the "special" blessing that will come upon donors when they give, often a specified amount, in some type of especially anointed offering. Though no tangible gimmicks may be used in some scenarios today, these entire offerings are often based on a bizarre mixture of numerology, some contorted and misapplied Old Testament event, Scripture taken of out context, or simply a special "word from God."

Sometimes a token disclaimer is given that "you can't buy a miracle," but when it comes right down to it, giving a monetary amount to the specially anointed minister as an expression of the donor's faith is the key to unlocking the needed miracle. In some cases, a tangible item is offered, such as a vial of "miracle" water, specially anointed oil, or a prayer cloth of some sort. While these may be offered for free, strong financial appeals will likely follow, or the recipient might be told that to truly "release their faith," or to activate the power in the said item, a financial "seed" should be sown to the ministry providing the anointed item. All such "spiritual" trafficking should be avoided.

Refuse to Manipulate People

Real spiritual power is a sacred trust from Heaven, and it should never be misused or abused. When Kenneth E. Hagin (1917-2003) was entrusted with a healing ministry, he said the Lord admonished him to fulfill his ministry, to be faithful, and then instructed him:

Be sure to give me all the praise and glory for all that is done, and be careful about money. Many of my servants whom I have anointed for this type of ministry have become money-minded and have lost the anointing and ministry I gave them.[2]

Hagin certainly believed in the biblical teaching of tithes and offerings, and encouraged people to be faithful in supporting their local church and giving offerings to other ministries as well, but he said that he was "extremely careful and aboveboard in every dealing that involved money" because "no amount of money is worth jeopardizing the anointing and call of God upon my life."[3] He also said, "I bent over backwards to avoid even the slightest possibility of anyone thinking I was self-seeking."[4]

Financial abuse is just one of the potential problems that can happen when God works supernaturally through an individual. Sometimes people tend to deify persons whom God uses, putting them on a pedestal. For example, when Paul ministered healing to the lame man in Lystra, the crowd's reaction was extreme!

> *When the crowd saw what Paul had done, they shouted in their local dialect, "These men are gods in human form!" They decided that Barnabas was the Greek god Zeus and that Paul was Hermes, since he was the chief speaker. Now the temple of Zeus was located just outside the town. So the priest of the temple and the crowd brought bulls and wreaths of flowers to the town gates, and they prepared to offer sacrifices to the apostles* (Acts 14:11-13 NLT).

We may look at that today and think how silly these pagans were; but in reality, people today are still quick to worship celebrities and put people on pedestals. Children of God should never do this, and servants of God should never let it be done. God did not place us here to receive the adulation of others, nor should we unduly elevate others because of gifts God may have given them, or because of how God works through them.

When Paul and Barnabas realized they were being perceived as gods, they immediately set the record straight. They told them, *"We are merely human beings—just like you!"* (Acts 14:15 NLT). It is good and right to honor spiritual leaders, and actually we should treat *everyone* with honor and respect, but we should never consider others to be superior or infallible. It is true that God might use a person, working through them, to bring healing or other types of blessing to others, but it is not good for anyone involved when we think of others more highly than we should.

Don't Abuse a "Point of Contact"

Sometimes, the term "point of contact" is used to describe when the laying on of hands or the anointing of oil is utilized to minister healing. It is important to remember, though, that it is not the hands or the oil that is doing the healing—God does the healing. If people are not careful, they can turn something that God ordained to be a point of contact for the releasing of their faith into something that borders on, or actually becomes, idolatrous.

A good illustration of this is found in the Old Testament when the children of Israel were experiencing poisonous snake bites in the wilderness. The people cried out to Moses, and Moses cried out to God. Following God's directions, *"Moses made a bronze serpent, and put it on a pole; and so it was, if a serpent had bitten anyone, when he looked at the bronze serpent, he lived"* (Numbers 21:9). The pole or the brass serpent did not heal anyone; rather, it was God who healed the people as they looked in faith according to God's instructions. This was such an effective process that Jesus Himself used this story as a type of His redemptive work: *"And as Moses lifted up the serpent in the wilderness, even so must the Son of Man be lifted up, that whoever believes in Him should not perish but have eternal life"* (John 3:14-15).

What God said and did was good, and it was a blessing to the people. At first, the people responded appropriately and simply obeyed God, but over time, a corrupt and idolatrous mindset set in. The brazen serpent was only meant to be a symbol; God Himself was to be the object and the basis of the people's faith. Over time, the people made the brass serpent on the pole into an idol. Its original purpose had been perverted and distorted, and King Hezekiah destroyed it along with other idolatrous objects.

> *In God's opinion he was a good king; he kept to the standards of his ancestor David. He got rid of the local fertility shrines, smashed the phallic stone monuments, and cut down the sex-and-religion Asherah groves. As a final stroke **he pulverized the ancient bronze serpent that Moses had made**; at that time the Israelites had taken up the practice of sacrificing to it—they had even dignified it with a name, Nehushtan (The Old Serpent)* (2 Kings 18:3-4 The Message).

It seems amazing that the bronze serpent made by Moses—at God's direction—was listed among the idolatrous images from pagan people; but despite its godly origin, it had become an object of idolatrous devotion. Everything God gives is good, but that does not mean that people will not distort it from its original purpose. God-given points of contact, such as the laying on of hands or anointing with oil are good, but always remember to look *through* the point of contact, not *to* the point of contact—always look *to* Jesus.

Don't Limit God

Perhaps Jesus used different methods in ministering healing so people would look more to Him than to one specific mode of operating. Sometimes Jesus laid hands on people, but sometimes He did not. At times He spoke words of healing to people, and in other situations, the healing seems to have been activated by the faith of the one who received it. At times, Jesus cast devils out of people, and in other cases He rebuked the disease. A couple of times Jesus used spit, and one time He even used mud to heal.

In other situations, Jesus instructed people to act—to do something that triggered their healing. Sometimes, there was a combination of methods used. The church in the book of Acts, likewise, utilized different methods. Sometimes the name of Jesus was used, and at times prayer preceded the miracle as in the case of the raising of Dorcas and the healing of Publius' father. The anointing of oil was also prescribed. Unique healings happened through Peter's shadow (Acts 5:15) and through cloths carried from the body of Paul (Acts 19:11-12).

While healing can come through different methods, it is important to always look to God and not to become obsessed with or married to a particular method. In the Old Testament, Naaman, a Syrian military leader who sought healing from leprosy, was furious when Elisha told him to go and dip seven times in the Jordan River (2 Kings 5:1-14). He had expected Elisha to wave his hand over him. Fortunately, after Naaman got over his anger and listened to some sound counsel, he obeyed Elisha and was healed. This makes me wonder how many people may have missed receiving a blessing from God because they had a preconceived idea about how God was supposed to minister to them.

When Jesus Said "No" to Miracles

Some seem to have the idea that Jesus was always eager to perform miracles to prove His divinity, but He was not a magician who did tricks on demand. After feeding the 4,000, religious people came to test Him:

> *When the Pharisees heard that Jesus had arrived, they came and started to argue with him. Testing him, they demanded that he show them a miraculous sign from heaven to prove his authority. When he heard this, he sighed deeply in his spirit and said, "Why do these people keep demanding a miraculous sign? I tell you the truth, I will not give this generation any such sign." So he got back into the boat and left them, and he crossed to the other side of the lake* (Mark 8:11-13 NLT)

In Matthew's account of this, Jesus says before walking away from them: "Only an evil, adulterous generation would demand a miraculous sign, but the only sign I will give them is the sign of the prophet Jonah" (Matthew 16:4 NLT).

Jesus refused to perform miracles when the devil was tempting Him (Matthew 4:1-10), and He also refused to save Himself from crucifixion (Matthew 26:53; 27:40). At different times, Jesus did a miraculous work and then instructed the recipient not to tell anyone about it. One time, Jesus walked into an area where there was a multitude of sick people, and He just healed one person and then walked away. This happened at the pool of Bethesda where there was *"a great multitude of sick people, blind, lame, paralyzed,"* and Jesus healed one man—a lame man—and then *"Jesus had withdrawn, a multitude being in that place"* (John 5:3,13).

We do not know the exact reason why Jesus did everything the way He did, but He did not exploit the miraculous to achieve maximum publicity. He was led by the Holy Spirit, motivated by compassion, and carried out the Father's will in everything.

In one case, we know exactly why no miracles happened. When He preached in his hometown of Nazareth, the people were offended at Him because they had known Him from childhood, and they knew His family (Mark 6:1-6). They couldn't imagine how someone "local" could be the Anointed One.

> And because of their unbelief, he couldn't do any miracles among them except to place his hands on a few sick people and heal them. And he was amazed at their unbelief. Then Jesus went from village to village, teaching the people (Mark 6:5-6 NLT).

It is important to keep miracles in their proper perspective. They were an important part of Jesus' ministry, but they were not His primary purpose in coming to the earth. He came *"to seek and save those who are lost"* (Luke 19:10 NLT) and to die for the sins of the world and to reconcile humankind to God.

As He was facing the cross, Jesus states, "Now my soul is deeply troubled. Should I pray, 'Father, save me from this hour'? But this is the very reason I came!" (John 12:27 NLT). Earlier in John's Gospel, Jesus teaches, "the works which the Father has given Me to finish—the very works that I do—bear witness of Me, that the Father has sent Me" (John 5:36). The miracles Jesus performed then, and the miracles performed now are important; I'm not trying to minimize them. They express the Father's love and they bear witness of Jesus and His gospel. However, it is important to never make what He does more important than who He is.

Don't Make Physical Manifestations the Goal of Ministry

Relative to recent outpourings of the Holy Spirit, some have assumed that outward expressions are something new. However, a study of revival history, especially in the past few centuries, indicates that physical manifestations during times of revival are nothing new at all. In recent centuries, people have responded to God's presence in a number of ways: falling under the power; trembling or shaking; jerking; holy laughter; spontaneous dancing, jumping, running; shouting, weeping crying; visions and/or falling into trances, etc.

While not all revivals have been accompanied by these types of physical manifestations, some certainly have, with the Cane Ridge Revival that began in 1800 being one of the more notable. Noted historian Vinson Synan writes of the occurrences in these Kentucky meetings that had perhaps as many as 25,000 in attendance:

> Their "godly hysteria" included such phenomena as falling, jerking barking like dogs, falling into trances, the "holy laugh," and such wild dances as David performed before the Ark of the Lord. Peter Cartwright reported that in one service he saw five hundred jerking at once. In some services entire congregations would be seized by the "holy laugh," an ecstasy that could hardly be controlled.[5]

Towns and Porter note that "the Cane Ridge revival introduced the element of shouting to revival meetings, so that many were called 'shouting Methodists.'"[6]

As could be expected, physical manifestations in revival and church services have often been a source of controversy and varying opinions.

Some have scathingly denounced all such expressions as fleshly or demonic, deeming them totally inappropriate. Others totally embrace all such manifestations, considering them the crowning sign of God's presence and blessing. Yet others believe that such expressions can be valid and genuine, but call for discernment and wisdom.

It is not uncommon to hear advocates of physical manifestations appeal to Paul's admonition to *"not quench the Spirit"* (1 Thessalonians 5:19). Meanwhile detractors also quote the very same apostle who writes, *"Let all things be done decently and in order"* (1 Corinthians 14:40). Certainly, there is truth and wisdom in both of those passages, but where is the balance? Elmer Towns, a great student of revival history, gives the following sound advice:

> First, don't seek the extraordinary signs of revival, for these unusual expressions are not what revival is about. Second, don't measure the success of a revival by the number or intensity of extraordinary signs; if you do, you'll miss the whole purpose of a revival. Third, seek the Lord, because it is he who revives our hearts. Measure a revival by God himself. Is God present? Focus on what he's doing, not on what people are doing. What has God accomplished? Some see revival as an end in itself, rather than an opportunity to know God. When extraordinary experiences become the goal, revivals become inclusive and sectarian, sometimes even taking on cultic or occult traits. Since the days of Pentecost there is no record of the sudden and direct work of the Spirit of God upon the souls of men that has not been accompanied by events more or less abnormal. It is, indeed, on consideration, only natural that it should be so. We cannot expect an abnormal inrush of Divine light and power, so

profoundly affecting the emotions and changing the lives of men, without remarkable results. As well expect a hurricane, an earthquake, or a flood, to leave nothing abnormal in its course, as to expect a true Revival that is not accompanied by events quite out of our ordinary experience.[7]

Those critical of physical manifestations would do well to remember that people have very different personalities and backgrounds. A conservative, reserved person might be judgmental of a person who is highly expressive, not understanding the battles and challenges that person has faced or the joy he or she now experiences. People who have been delivered from severe illness or tormenting bondage may simply be more effusive in their praise than others. The lame man at the Beautiful Gate responded to his healing by *"walking, leaping, and praising God"* (Acts 3:8). Instead of condemning such a person for being "emotional," it would seem that the more godly response would be to *"Rejoice with those who rejoice"* (Romans 12:15).

At times, people have wrongly judged an individual when God was doing a very special work in his or her life and heart. Consider the case of Hannah, praying at the entrance of the Tabernacle, when she was in the midst of a very sacred time with the Lord.

> *As she was praying to the Lord, Eli watched her. Seeing her lips moving but hearing no sound, he thought she had been drinking. "Must you come here drunk?" he demanded. "Throw away your wine!" "Oh no, sir!" she replied. "I haven't been drinking wine or anything stronger. But I am very discouraged, and I was pouring out my heart to the Lord. Don't think I am a wicked woman! For I have been praying out of great anguish and sorrow." "In that case," Eli said, "go in peace! May the God of Israel grant the request you have asked of him"* (1 Samuel 1:12-17 NLT).

Eli, the high priest, was the religious "expert" in this scenario, and yet he totally misjudged what was happening. He failed to recognize how profoundly God was moving at this moment. The same is true when the people told Bartimaeus to be quiet because he was crying out for Jesus to heal him (Mark 10:46-52). Sometimes we wrongly judge the actions of another person because we fail to understand his or her battles or victories.

Scripture teaches that there are different times and seasons in life (Ecclesiastes 3:1-8), and it stands to reason that people will have different outward expressions at different times. It is also good to keep in mind that the Holy Spirit does not move the same way all the time. The very end of Psalm 46 and the very beginning of Psalm 47 reveal this:

> Be still, and know that I am God... (Psalm 46:10).
>
> Oh, clap your hands, all you peoples! Shout to God with the voice of triumph! (Psalm 47:1).

I have been in services where an atmosphere of celebration and rejoicing prevailed; I have also been in services where people sat in awe and silence at the presence of God. Both were a great blessing to everyone present.

Kenneth E. Hagin describes one of those "Be still and know services," where God's holy presence was powerfully experienced:

> The Holy Ghost so came into the room and filled it with His Presence that nobody moved, nobody said a word. You were afraid to move or speak because a holy awe gripped the crowd. We had no nursery. The babies were in their mothers' arms or asleep on the floor or on a bench. Little children were sitting by their mothers. Yet as we sat in total silence for

an hour and a half, not a baby cried, not a child moved. The Presence of God filled His Temple. Ohhh! You carry that Presence with you for months and months.[8]

Hagin proceeds to share that in one of those types of services, an unsaved man came in and, after sitting in that atmosphere for a period of time, began to tremble under the power of God, made his way to the altar, and surrendered his life to the Lord Jesus. He had heard the gospel at other times, but the power and presence of the Holy Spirit in that holy atmosphere convicted him and drew him to the Savior.

D. Martyn Lloyd-Jones (1899-1981) was a medical doctor turned pastor who served as the minister of Westminster Chapel in London for nearly thirty years. One hundred years after the British Revival of 1859, he preached a series of messages commemorating that event. He states that there are exceptions but notes that there frequently are emotional reactions and other phenomenon that occur during revivals. He asserts, "The phenomenon should not be sought, they should not be encouraged, they should not be boasted."[9]

Lloyd-Jones acknowledges that counterfeits could appear but reasons that "there is nothing more foolish or ridiculous than to dismiss the whole, because of a very small part."[10] Having discussed many aspects and ramifications of revivals and the manifestations that sometimes accompany them, he writes:

> We must not seek phenomena and strange experiences. What we must seek is the manifestation of God's glory and his power and his might. What we must seek is revival. And when that comes it will be so amazing that strange and unusual things may happen, but we shall always know that God is moving amongst us, and we shall be ready to

identify and restrain the false, the spurious, and indeed all which belongs to the evil spirit. Anybody who tries to work up phenomena is a tool of the Devil, and is putting himself into the position of the psychic, and the psychological. No, we must not concentrate upon these things. We must leave it to God, in his sovereign wisdom, to decide whether to grant these occasional concomitants or not. There should be no difficulty in distinguishing between the work of the Spirit, and the work of fanatical men, the work of these unseen forces and powers, or the work of the Devil himself. Let us, therefore, be careful lest we quench the Spirit, and let us keep our eyes fixed upon the glory of God, and the outpouring of his Holy Spirit upon us.[11]

Here are some thoughts relative to physical manifestations:

- Don't make manifestations or the lack of manifestations the main focus. Make Jesus and God's Word the main thing. I know of a minister who prayed for a dozen or more people in a healing line. Everyone "fell" except one. The one person who did not "fall under the power" was healed; no one else was. Faith is what is important, not whether a person falls or not.

- Don't compare yourself or your experience with others. It is impressive to read about the dynamic experiences that people like Finney (a feeling like electricity, waves and waves of liquid love) and Moody (having to ask God to withhold His hand lest he die of joy) had when receiving the infilling of the Holy Spirit. It's great if you "feel" something during the course of your spiritual journey, but remember that walking with God is not about feelings. It's about faith. You don't need to feel spiritually inferior if you don't have as dramatic of an experience as someone else. Spirituality is not about how many goose bumps you may feel.

- The Holy Spirit Himself is perfect, but physical manifestations are processed through the flesh as a person responds to God's presence. Outward actions can reflect an individual's own personality or even learned behaviors that reflect how he or she thinks one is supposed to act in a Spirit-charged environment.

- The sincerity and the spontaneity of the worshipper is key. People should never be pushed, pressured, hyped, or manipulated into acting a certain way to prove they are spiritual. Some physical manifestations can be "put on," or people may act certain ways because of repeated suggestions. Some may act certain ways to garner the attention of others.

- The truths articulated in 1 Corinthians 14 have a wider application than simply with tongues, interpretation, and prophecy. The general principle is that all things that take place in a gathering of believers should be done decently and in order (1 Corinthians 14:40) and should be done to edify the whole body (1 Corinthians 14:12). What might be appropriate at one time or in a certain type of service might not be appropriate at another time or in a different kind of service.

- Discernment and wisdom are important. John teaches, *"Beloved, do not believe every spirit, but test the spirits, whether they are of God; because many false prophets have gone out into the world"* (1 John 4:1). The Spirit of God can prompt many things, but the flesh and even religious spirits can motivate certain behaviors as well. It is important to remember, "*God is not the author of confusion but of peace, as in all the churches of the saints*" (1 Corinthians 14:33).

- If someone's conduct is disruptive and distracting others, it is out of order. The authority of those leading a church service should be respected. A person in attendance should not try to force his or her agenda into the meeting against the consent of those in leadership, even if the person claims that, "The Lord is leading me."

- Never confuse an *effect* of a move of the Spirit with the *purpose* of a move of the Spirit. People may act in various ways (or not) when they are sensing the presence of God, but is the real purpose of God for the person's life being fulfilled? Someone said, "It doesn't matter how high people jump in church if they can't walk straight when they land." When our lives are truly touched by God, the end result should be that we love Him and others more, and we end up living as devoted disciples of the Lord Jesus Christ.

- Historically, physical manifestations in movements are usually more prominent at the front end of revivals and tend to taper off over time. Lloyd-Jones states that, "phenomena tend to disappear as the revival goes on."[12] Wise ministers recognize that there are cycles and seasons of revival, and stay focused on the biblical priorities that are foundational and necessary in every season, such as preaching the gospel, teaching the Word, reaching the lost, and making disciples. These are never obsolete and should always be the mainstay of every movement, not physical manifestations that may come and go.

A good rule of thumb is to always major on the majors. Focus your attention on the major themes of Scripture. Exalt Jesus. Love and reach the lost. Teach the Word. Make disciples.

Don't Neglect Vital Ministry Areas

When God's Spirit moves in a season of revival, it is normal for people to be excited about it. Some become so enamored with the supernatural elements at such a time that they may forget or neglect the other important aspects of successful ministry or the Christian life. In the past four decades of ministry, it has been my observation that those who do well in ministry operate by a combination or blend of graces and abilities. I have never seen anyone prosper and be fruitful in ministry over the long haul just because they had a strong spiritual gift.

Some have experienced an initial season of success because of a certain gift, but poor people skills, a lack of business sense, organizational disarray, or a void in the area of godly character and holiness ultimately undermine their effectiveness and influence. People should not expect the miraculous to make them successful if they are not walking in honesty and integrity or are not exhibiting good ethics or using wisdom. The supernatural is not an excuse—believers must prepare, be diligent, and be responsible in the matters of life.

Endnotes

1. Gordon Lindsay, *The Charismatic Ministry* (Dallas, TX: Christ for the Nations, 2013), 73.

2. Kenneth E. Hagin, *The Midas Touch* (Tulsa, OK: Faith Library Publications, www.rhema.org, 2001), loc. 1476, Kindle.

3. Ibid., loc. 1485, Kindle.

4. Ibid., loc. 1493, Kindle.

5. Synan, *The Holiness-Pentecostal Tradition*, loc. 167, Kindle.

6. Towns and Porter, *The Ten Greatest Revivals Ever*, loc. 79, Kindle.

7. Ibid., loc. 7, Kindle.

8. Hagin, *Plans, Purposes, and Pursuits*, 46.

9. Martyn Lloyd-Jones, *Revival* (Wheaton, IL: Crossway, 1987), loc. 2684, Kindle.

10. Ibid., loc. 2699, Kindle.

11. Ibid., loc. 2706, Kindle.

12. Ibid., loc. 2684, Kindle.

CHAPTER SEVENTEEN

WHEN THE MIRACULOUS DOES NOT OCCUR

Rejoice with those who rejoice, and weep with those who weep.
–Apostle Paul, Romans 12:15

WE love miracles and we rejoice when they occur. However, anyone who has lived very long has also seen situations where a desired miracle does not occur. At such times, a person's faith can be seriously challenged. In Hebrews 11:1-35, we read an outstanding list of heroes of faith who did great exploits for God and experienced great victories, deliverances, and outcomes from God. We celebrate every one of these great testimonies! It is important, though, to continue reading the following verses.

…Others were tortured, not accepting deliverance, that they might obtain a better resurrection. Still others had trial of mockings and scourgings, yes, and of chains and imprisonment. They were stoned, they were sawn in two, were tempted, were slain with the sword. They wandered about in sheepskins and goatskins, being destitute, afflicted, tormented—of whom the

world was not worthy. They wandered in deserts and mountains, in dens and caves of the earth. And all these, having obtained a good testimony through faith, did not receive the promise, God having provided something better for us, that they should not be made perfect apart from us (Hebrews 11:35-40).

Those do not sound like the kinds of results most people want, and yet these people "obtained a good testimony through faith!"

Pastor Gerald Brooks identifies three types of faith in Hebrews 11:

- Triumphant Faith: Faith that results in changed circumstances
- Transformational Faith: Faith that changes the person
- Transcending Faith: Faith that trusts God in spite of negative circumstances

Brooks suggests that 90 percent of teaching on faith is in the first category—the kind of faith that changes a problem. While that faith is one of the three types of faith mentioned in Hebrews 11, Brooks asserts:

We must have faith bigger than life. Our faith cannot be superficial or circumstantial. Our faith must be bigger than today, and bigger than tomorrow. Our faith must be greater than any circumstance we ever deal with. Faith is more about heaven than it is about earth. Our faith takes us beyond this planet.[1]

As humans, we naturally desire to always have positive outcomes, but in the course of most people's lives, it is vital to learn to trust God and receive His grace even when, at times, circumstances do not turn out as we desire.

There is a great miracle recorded in the book of Acts when Peter is supernaturally delivered from prison. Acts 12:5 states that *"constant prayer was offered to God for him by the church"* and the following verses describe God sending an angel to personally escort him out of prison. We even learn that Peter's chains miraculously fell off of his hands and the prison gate supernaturally opened (Acts 12:5-10). Of course, the saints rejoiced greatly when Peter showed up at the house of Mary, the mother of John Mark, where the saints were busy praying for Peter.

We love to feature these kinds of outstanding miracles! They make great testimonies, and they are featured in ministry newsletters and on ministry broadcasts. But it is interesting that right before Luke records Peter's miraculous delivery, which covers fourteen verses, he states in a singular, solitary verse, *"Then he* [Herod] *killed James the brother of John with the sword"* (Acts 12:2).

Consider the contrast here. Much detail is given to Peter's deliverance. We see the saints fervently praying, the rescuing angel on assignment, and the astonishment and wonder of the believers. And yet with James, we get a stark, single sentence stating that Herod killed him. No amplification and no elaboration. There is not even a statement about the church grieving the loss of one of Jesus' top three disciples. There is no mention of how his brother John, the beloved disciple, felt or how his parents, Zebedee and Salome, handled the death of their son.

When Stephen was stoned to death earlier in the book of Acts, we read that *"Some devout men came and buried Stephen with great mourning"* (Acts 8:2 NLT), so Luke did record a tribute in that situation.

I'm certainly not faulting Luke for seemingly rushing over such a significant event as James' death, but I wonder if he was so excited about conveying the details of Peter's miraculous deliverance that he scarcely mentions the death of James. Paul teaches believers to *"Rejoice with those who rejoice, and weep with those who weep"* (Romans 12:15). I want to believe that the church was compassionate and sensitive, and that they wept with the family of James just as much as they rejoiced over Peter's miraculous deliverance. The fact that Luke does not record it certainly does not mean it didn't happen.

Perhaps it is the many years I spent in pastoral ministry, but I have sometimes wondered how John and his parents may have felt when everyone was celebrating and rejoicing over Peter's deliverance from death. I am certain they were thankful, but could they have wondered why that same angel had not shown up to save their son and brother? Our details regarding the story and the surrounding dynamics are limited, but did John or his parents have to deal with any of the following types of tormenting thoughts?

- Didn't God love James as much as he loved Peter?
- When we prayed for James to be delivered, didn't we have enough faith?
- The community of believers cared more for and prayed more diligently for Peter than they did for James.

In addition to dealing with the death of a loved one, surviving family members sometimes have to deal with troubling thoughts that perhaps can tempt them to question the love of God, His goodness, or their own faith. It is important to remember that the Holy Spirit doesn't only perform miracles, He also comforts those who are brokenhearted.

Faith requires that we trust God, but humility requires that we acknowledge we are not omniscient; we don't know everything. Paul includes himself when he writes, *"Now our knowledge is partial and incomplete"* (1 Corinthians 13:9 NLT). If we are going to do well in life, we need to embrace the reality that there are things we do not and may not understand this side of Heaven. I believe this is why Proverbs 3:5 tells us that we need to trust in the Lord with all of our hearts and not lean to our own understanding. Our understanding is limited and can only take us so far, but when we know God's character and goodness, we can trust Him beyond the limitations of our finite minds and our attempts to figure everything out.

Jesus was powerfully anointed by the Holy Spirit and performed many miracles, and yet even He experienced heartache and disappointment. He was personally impacted when King Herod senselessly and cruelly executed Jesus' own cousin, John the Baptist. When Jesus learned of John's death, He wanted to be alone. We can only imagine what Jesus felt, but we know that He experienced the full spectrum of emotions throughout His life. After all, Jesus was made like us in every respect and was tempted like us in every way, except that He was without sin (Hebrews 2:17; 4:15). Matthew's account of Jesus learning about His cousin's death is most insightful:

> *As soon as Jesus heard the news, he left in a boat to a remote area to be alone. But the crowds heard where he was headed and followed on foot from many towns. Jesus saw the huge crowd as he stepped from the boat, and he had compassion on them and healed their sick (Matthew 14:13-14 NLT).*

Jesus had an understandable reaction—He wanted to be alone. But what He did next is remarkable! He saw people in need, and He began healing them.

Jesus did not give up on or turn away from the supernatural, miracle-working power of God because of a significant disappointment. His compassion not only led Him to heal the sick, but then He also fed five thousand people—another miracle (Matthew 14:15-21). The lesson here is that we should not allow a disappointment to keep us from looking for God's compassion and power to be manifested in the future.

Paul experienced many supernatural and miraculous happenings in his life and ministry. Consider the dynamic events Paul experienced:

- Meeting the risen Jesus on the Damascus Road (Acts 9:3-18)
- Elymas the sorcerer is blinded while opposing the gospel (Acts 13:11-12)
- Miracles in Iconium (Acts 14:3)
- The lame man healed in Lystra (Acts 14:8-10)
- The slave girl delivered in Philippi (Acts 16:16-18)
- An earthquake opens the prison in Philippi (Acts 16:25-26)
- Extraordinary healings and miraculous deliverances in Ephesus (Acts 19:11-12)
- Eutychus is raised from the dead in Troas (Acts 20:9-12)
- Unaffected by a viper bite in Malta (Acts 28:3-6)
- Publius and others are healed in Malta (Acts 28:7-9)

Paul even told one church, *"Truly the signs of an apostle were accomplished among you with all perseverance, in signs and wonders and mighty deeds"* (2 Corinthians 12:12). With such a resume of supernatural experiences, some might think that Paul could make miracles happen at will—like flipping on a light switch. Such thinking, though, goes against other information presented in Scripture. There were also times when such things did not occur in Paul's ministry.

For example, Paul knew that Timothy, his close friend and associate, was battling some kind of persistent stomach problem. He advises him,

"*No longer drink only water, but use a little wine for your stomach's sake and your frequent infirmities*" (1 Timothy 5:23). I have heard people say, "Well, if someone today has the gift of healing like the apostles did, he could just go around and heal whoever he wants to." But that's clearly not the case; Paul did not go around arbitrarily and randomly healing everyone. Paul also spoke of another one of his helpers, saying, "*I left Trophimus sick at Miletus*" (2 Timothy 4:20 NLT). In yet another situation, Paul referred to another assistant who was seriously ill and recovered, but Paul took no credit for it; he did not state that he had prayed some kind of miraculous prayer. He writes:

> *Yet I considered it necessary to send to you Epaphroditus, my brother, fellow worker, and fellow soldier, but your messenger and the one who ministered to my need; since he was longing for you all, and was distressed because you had heard that he was sick. For indeed he was sick almost unto death; but God had mercy on him, and not only on him but on me also, lest I should have sorrow upon sorrow. Therefore I sent him the more eagerly, that when you see him again you may rejoice, and I may be less sorrowful. Receive him therefore in the Lord with all gladness, and hold such men in esteem; because for the work of Christ he came close to death, not regarding his life, to supply what was lacking in your service toward me* (Philippians 2:25-30).

Paul simply asserts, "*God had mercy on him.*" In this particular case, Paul states an apparent reason why this sickness occurred—Epaphroditus had not regarded his life, he had not taken care of himself, and he overworked. In the other situations, he does not offer any explanation as to why the person had become sick or why they had not recovered. He did not accuse Timothy or Trophimus of having sin in their lives or of not having faith. He simply did not say why they were sick or why they had not recovered up to that point.

In looking at this objectively, Paul saw some people healed miraculously, and most likely, instantaneously. There were others Paul saw recover gradually, and there were yet others he encouraged to utilize and benefit from medicine. In his private conversations with them, Paul likely encouraged Timothy and Trophimus to continue to trust God.

But here is one thing we know—everyone who ever received divine healing through Paul's ministry eventually died. Everyone Jesus healed and even those He raised from the dead, such as Lazarus, all eventually died. In all of these cases, the Holy Spirit plays another very important role—He is the Comforter! Thank God for what Jesus does for us in this life, but remember what Paul said, *"And if our hope in Christ is only for this life, we are more to be pitied than anyone in the world"* (1 Corinthians 15:19 NLT). Our hope and our faith must transcend whatever happens or does not happen during our life here on earth.

You may be reading this chapter not so much for information but because your heart aches over a disappointing situation you experienced. Please remember that Jesus came to heal the brokenhearted (Isaiah 61:1), and He said, *"Blessed are those who mourn, for they shall be comforted"* (Matthew 5:4). Paul saw many miracles, but he also experienced many struggles and much pain. We thank God for every miracle that happens here on this earth; but we know that ultimately, we have an eternal dwelling place that will be greater than anything we can imagine:

> *And I heard a loud voice from heaven saying, "Behold, the tabernacle of God is with men, and He will dwell with them, and they shall be His people. God Himself will be with them and be their God. And God will wipe away every tear from their eyes; there shall be no more death, nor sorrow, nor crying. There*

shall be no more pain, for the former things have passed away"
(Revelation 21:3-4).

Until that time, we will follow through with the biblical mandate
to rejoice with those who rejoice and weep with those who weep. His
very comforting presence with us is a supernatural provision, and the
indescribable eternity that awaits us is, in itself, miraculous.

Endnote

1. Gerald Brooks, *Snapshots of Faith* (Plano, TX: Gerald Brooks Ministries, 2017),
   86.

CHAPTER EIGHTEEN

PRACTICAL TAKEAWAYS

Wisdom is the right use of knowledge. To know is not to be wise. Many men know a great deal, and are all the greater fools for it. There is no fool so great a fool as a knowing fool. But to know how to use knowledge is to have wisdom.

—Charles Spurgeon

I T is good to be aware of historical information. It is even better if we can know what it means and how to make practical application of that knowledge in our lives. Scripture contains record of the supernatural dealings of God throughout the entirety of God's Word, and history records the power of God in operation from the end of the first century until the present day. But what are some of the vital things we should know and do?

Maintain the Prime Directive

To keep things in perspective, it is important to remember that Jesus never said, "Go into all the world and have revival." Nor did He say, "Go into all the world and work miracles." Our mandate as the church is to

"*Go into all the world and preach the gospel*" (Mark 16:15) and to "*make disciples of all the nations, baptizing them in the name of the Father and of the Son and of the Holy Spirit, teaching them to observe all things that I have commanded you*" (Matthew 28:19-20). Revival and miracles can certainly be part of that, but preaching the gospel and making disciples are the two prime directives that Jesus has given us.

I have seen some who seemed to be more excited about "signs, wonders, and miracles" than they were about Jesus Himself, or about seeing people getting saved and becoming disciples. There is certainly a desire for the supernatural that is healthy (Acts 4:29; 1 Corinthians 12:31), but there can also be an unhealthy obsession with "spiritual thrill seeking." Jesus said that signs would follow believers (Mark 16:17), not that believers would follow signs.

Christians are to have a sense of mission, and that mission involves expressing God's love and truth to those who don't know Him. We should never love signs more than we love God or the people we are endeavoring to reach. We are to be people lovers, allowing God to perform signs as He sees fit to help further His mission, and to help accomplish what He desires in the lives of people He loves.

Remember, Love Never Fails

Not only did Jesus give a Great Commission, He also issued a Great Commandment:

> *A new commandment I give to you, that you love one another; as I have loved you, that you also love one another. By this all will know that you are My disciples, if you have love for one another* (John 13:34-35).

When Tertullian wrote to the rulers of the Roman Empire in defense of Christians, he spoke of their character and their practices. He denounced false accusations made against Christians and said, "It is mainly the deeds of a love so noble that lead many to put a brand upon us. See, they say, how they love one another...how they are ready even to die for one another.... And they are wroth with us, too, because we call each other brethren."[1]

Right in the middle of Paul's most detailed exposition regarding gifts of the Spirit (1 Corinthians 12 and 14) is a towering reminder of the importance of the love of God. Its centrality and its placement is not accidental.

> *Though I speak with the tongues of men and of angels, but have not love, I have become sounding brass or a clanging cymbal. And though I have the gift of prophecy, and understand all mysteries and all knowledge, and though I have all faith, so that I could remove mountains, but have not love, I am nothing. And though I bestow all my goods to feed the poor, and though I give my body to be burned, but have not love, it profits me nothing* (1 Corinthians 13:1-3).

It is good to remember the words of Origen: "The name of Jesus can still remove distractions from the minds of men, expel demons, and also take away diseases. Furthermore, it produces a marvelous meekness of spirit and a complete change of character."[2]

When Origen refers to "meekness of spirit and a complete change of character," it is a powerful reminder of the fruit of the Spirit (Galatians 5:22-23). I recently heard someone say, "It doesn't matter if you speak in tongues if you are mean in English." Being strongly endowed with spiritual gifts is no excuse for a person to be haughty, harsh, or rude.

When Paul says, *"Pursue love, and desire spiritual gifts"* (1 Corinthians 14:1), we are reminded the love and power are not mutually exclusive. We should not endeavor to excel in either area—love or gifts—while neglecting the other.

Do Not Neglect or Devalue the Ordinary Works of the Spirit

It is good to keep in mind the delineation that Jonathan Edwards made. He frequently differentiated between "ordinary" works of the Spirit and "extraordinary" works of the Spirit. If you happen to have strong gifts relative to the "extraordinary" works, or if it is a season of outstanding "signs," that is wonderful. However, you can always focus on doing your part in the "ordinary" workings of the Spirit whether any outstanding manifestations or gifts are occurring at that time or not.

When Edwards assumed his pastorate in Massachusetts, his predecessor told him that they had experienced seasons of outstanding revival 57, 53, 40, 24, and 18 years prior to that time, with the middle three seasons of outpouring being the strongest. Those were seasons of outstanding outpourings of the Holy Spirit with unusual results taking place. Even when Edwards pastored there, they did not have non-stop revival. This is consistent with the oft-observed phenomenon that Spirit-given revivals and special outpourings tend to be cyclical or seasonal in nature.

What are ministers and believers to do when it is not one of those "peak seasons" of spiritual outpourings? This may not be exactly what Paul had in mind when he wrote these words, but his admonition to Timothy seems a very appropriate response: *"Preach the word! Be ready in season and out of season. Convince, rebuke, exhort, with all longsuffering and teaching"* (2 Timothy 4:2). Regardless of the season we are in, whether it is a season of revival or not, whether it is a season of powerful outpouring or not, there are basic Christian responsibilities in which we are all to be diligently engaged.

For example, Luke would have probably never introduced us to Dorcas in the book of Acts had she not been raised from the dead. Certainly we rejoice that God used Peter to perform such an outstanding miracle, but Luke also mentions, *"She was always doing kind things for others and helping the poor"* (Acts 9:36 NLT). Before Peter raised her from the dead, *"The room was filled with widows who were weeping and showing him the coats and other clothes Dorcas had made for them"* (Acts 9:39 NLT). There is such a tendency to put miracles on a pedestal and ignore "basic" works of love and kindness. I believe that Jesus values everything that is done in His name, for His glory.

Antony expresses this whole line of thought so well:

> And it is not fitting to boast at the casting forth of the demons, nor to be uplifted by the healing of diseases: nor is it fitting that he who casts out devils should alone be highly esteemed, while he who casts them not out should be considered nought.... For the working of signs is not ours but the Savior's work.[3]

Right in the middle of the list in 1 Corinthians 12 where Paul is listing such dynamic empowerments of the Spirit such as apostles, prophets, miracles, and healings, he also includes "helps" (1 Corinthians 12:28). Several pastors have related to me that people will sometimes come to them—often people the pastor doesn't even know—and say something like, "Pastor, if you ever need me to preach for you, I'm available."

Some pastors have understandably responded to such offers, "We don't really need any help in the pulpit right now, but we sure could use some help cleaning the building." Most of the time those people disappear very quickly! Some are willing to serve as long as it is in a highly visible position but have no interest in work that is behind the scenes. Sometimes being "spiritual" shows up most vividly in humble, obscure, practical service.

Understand "Legitimate Extremism and Essential Balance"

Donald Gee (1891-1966) was a Pentecostal leader in the twentieth century. His thoughtful and wise teaching earned him the nickname, "The Apostle of Balance." Gee authored more than thirty books, including *Wind and Flame*—it provided an overview of the Pentecostal movement in Great Britain. In the following article, "Extremes Are Sometimes Necessary," Gee brilliantly addresses the delicate tension existing between balance and extremes. The principles he shares are just as relevant today as they were when he wrote them in the mid-twentieth century.

> One of the paradoxes of the truly Pentecostal witness is its emphasis upon the necessity of maintaining a proper balance in doctrine and practice, coupled with a complementary testimony that often urges to extremes in both.
>
> Paul's teaching concerning spiritual gifts is all for balance and moderation—"I will sing with the spirit and I will sing with the understanding also"; We are to avoid giving any impression of being "mad"; "By two, or at the most by three"; God is not the author of confusion, but of peace"; "Let all things be done decently and in order" (1 Cor. 14:15, 23, 276, 33, 40). Yet at the same time he affirms in extreme language

that he speaks with tongues more than they all; expresses a vehement preference for teaching at a ratio of 10,000 to 5; and says "ye may all prophesy" (1 Cor. 14:18, 19, 31).

So many of us are [firmly established] extremists. If we see any ray of truth we push it to such an extreme that our constant pressing of it becomes offensive, vain, and at last erroneous. If we discover any successful line of ministry we run after it to such an extent that it becomes nauseating and exhausted. We are forever missing genuine usefulness by our constant failure to keep well-balanced. In the end men lose confidence in us, our intemperance grieves the Holy Spirit, and we are cast upon the scrap-heap of rejected and unprofitable servants.

But still more of us are in danger of missing a life of power by seeking to walk in monotonous middle-course that never ventures to an extreme at all. Our preaching lacks fire because it always is trying to present both sides of a case at the same time, and our methods are ineffective because they [avoid] any offense against respectability or tradition. We may, if we like, pride ourselves upon our success in avoiding disaster but our safety has been achieved by remaining static. We have made practically no impact upon the community. If it be true that they have never charged us with "madness," it also is true that they never have reported that "God is among us of a truth." Most probably they do not even know of our existence!

We rightly extol the importance of balance; we correctly affirm that the way of truth will not be found in extremes; we justly point out that persistent extremism is suicidal for both men and movements—but we desperately need to recognize that revivals are never launched without someone going to an extreme. Passionate intercession is positively unbalanced; so is much fasting; so is fervent preaching that makes sinners tremble; and feverish itinerating that makes a missionary or an evangelist seem beside himself. We do well to remember that our Lord's Own kinsmen thought that He had gone mad (Mark 3:21); and that He quoted "The zeal of Thine house hath eaten me up" (John 2:17) when He kicked over the table of the money-changers.

The Day of Pentecost so disturbed the emotional balance of the disciples that they seemed like drunken men.... Thirty years later a Roman Governor accused Paul of being mad. The charge was courteously and properly refuted, but let us admit that Festus was no fool. Paul himself testified that at times he was beside himself (2 Cor. 5:13), and his superb sanity of teaching and outlook operated on a heavenly level. There HAS to be an extremism to move things.... Miracles of healing occur when faith refuses to be logical, and blinds itself to arguments, based on plenty of contrary experience and more "balanced" teaching. Indeed we may well inquire whether there is not something extreme in any genuine miracle.

Where, then, lies the way of Pentecostal truth that embraces a legitimate extremism and an essential balance? I can only reply that we need the extremist to start things moving, but we need the balanced teacher to keep them moving in the right direction. We need extremism for a miracle of healing, but we need balanced sanity for health. We need extreme fervor to launch a movement, but we need the repudiation of extremes to save it from self-destruction. Only a wisdom from above can reveal the perfect synthesis. It takes Pentecostal genius to know when and where an extreme doctrine or practice must be modified to a more balanced view; and where, on the other hand, the broad lines of truth must be temporarily narrowed into an extreme emphasis upon one point to ensure a dynamic powerful enough to move things for God. The possession of that uncommon genius marks the God-sent leader who has emerged in truly great periods of revival.[4]

If God Uses You in Extraordinary Ways, Stay Humble

Remember the advice Gregory gave to Augustine of Canterbury when miracles were happening through his ministry: "Whatever gifts you have received relative to doing signs, remember that these powers were not granted for your benefit, but so that others may receive salvation."[5] Likewise, Basil of Caesarea said, "He who receives any of these gifts does not possess it for his own sake but rather for the sake of others...."[6] He also stated, "Since the gift of God is received as a free gift, it is our duty to share it freely and not make it a means of profit for self-gratification."[7]

Unfortunately, many people whom God has used became deceived and thought more highly of themselves than they should have. Whatever gifts God may give us are for the benefit of those we serve and those to whom we are called to minister. If you are gifted to teach, it is for the benefit of those who need to learn. If you are anointed to pray for the sick, it is for their benefit.

Any gift you have received from God is a sacred trust—something you steward for His glory. Guard yourself against pride. It has brought the downfall of many whom God called. D. L. Moody was correct when he said, "We may easily be too big for God to use, but never too small."

Endnotes

1. Tertullian, *Apology*, ed. Alexander Roberts, Sir James Donaldson, and Arthur Cleveland Coxe (Seattle, WA: Amazon Digital Services, 2011), loc. 64, Kindle.

2. Origen, *Origen Against Celsus*, in *The Works of Origen*, ed. Alexander Roberts, Sir James Donaldson, and Arthur Cleveland Coxe (Seattle, WA: Amazon Digital Services, 1885), loc. 10133, Kindle.

3. Athanasius, *Life of St. Antony*, in *The Complete Works of Saint Athanasius*, trans. Philip Schaff (Seattle, WA: Amazon Digital Services, 2016), loc. 5373, Kindle.

4. Donald Gee, "Extremes Are Sometimes Necessary," in *The Voice of Healing* (Dallas, TX: Christ for the Nations, 1953).

5. Gregory the Great, *The Book of Pastoral Rule and Selected Epistles of Pope St. Gregory I (The Great)*, Epistle 28, trans. James Barmby, ed. Paul A. Boer Sr. (Veritas Splendor Publications, 2012), 516, Kindle.

6. Basil, *Ascetical Works*, "The Long Rules," in *The Complete Works of Saint Basil* (Seattle, WA: Amazon Digital Services, 2016), loc. 14787, Kindle.

7. Basil, *Ascetical Works*, "The Morals," in *The Complete Works of Saint Basil* (Seattle, WA: Amazon Digital Services, 2016), loc. 13427, Kindle.

RECOMMENDED READING

THE following list is not a comprehensive bibliography relative to this book. Rather, it is a compilation of a few key resources that are recommended for individuals desiring to study further along the lines of miracles and the supernatural workings of God throughout church history.

Bosworth, F. F. *Christ the Healer*. Grand Rapids, MI: Chosen Books, 2008.

Burgess, Stanley M. *Christian Peoples of the Spirit: A Documentary History of Pentecostal Spirituality from the Early Church to the Present*. New York: New York University Press, 2011.

Burgess, Stanley M. *The New International Dictionary of Pentecostal and Charismatic Movements*. Grand Rapids, MI: Zondervan, 2003.

Gordon, A. J. *The Ministry of Healing: Miracles of Cure in All Ages*. Amazon Digital Services, 1882.

Gordon, A. J. *The Ministry of the Spirit*. Philadelphia, PA: American Baptist Publication Society, 1894.

Graves, Robert W. *Strangers to Fire: When Tradition Trumps Scripture*. Tulsa, OK: Empowered Life Academic, 2014.

Harrell Jr, David Edwin. *All Things Are Possible: The Healing and Charismatic*

Revivals in Modern America. Bloomington, IN: Indiana University Press, 1975.

Hyatt, Eddie L. *2000 Years of Charismatic Christianity: A 21ˢᵗ Century Look at Church History From a Pentecostal/Charismatic Perspective*. Lake Mary, FL: Charisma Media, 2000.

Keener, Craig S. *Gift and Giver: The Holy Spirit for Today*. Grand Rapids, MI: Baker Academic, 2001.

Keener, Craig S. *Miracles: The Credibility of the New Testament Accounts*, Volumes 1 and 2. Grand Rapids, MI: Baker Academic, 2011.

King, J. D. *Regeneration: A Complete History of Healing in the Christian Church*, 3 Volumes. Lee's Summit, MO: Christos Publishing, 2017.

Kydd, Ronald A. N. *Charismatic Gifts in the Early Church*. Peabody, MA: Hendrickson Publishers, 2014.

Lawson, James Gilchrist. *Deeper Experiences of Famous Christians*. Jawbone Digital Services, 1911.

Oliver, Jeff. *Pentecost to the Present: The Holy Spirit's Enduring Work in the Church*. Newberry, FL: Bridge Logos, 2017.

Synan, Vinson. *The Century of the Holy Spirit: 100 Years of Pentecostal and Charismatic Renewal, 1901-2001*. Nashville, TN: Thomas Nelson Publishers, 2001.

Synan, Vinson. *The Holiness-Pentecostal Tradition: Charismatic Movements in the Twentieth Century*. Grand Rapids, MI: Eerdmans, 1997.

Towns, Elmer, and Douglas Porter. *The Ten Greatest Revivals Ever*. Ann Arbor, MI: Servant Publications, 2000.

ABOUT THE AUTHOR

BIBLE teacher and author Tony Cooke graduated from RHEMA Bible Training Center in 1980 and received degrees from North Central University (Bachelor's in Church Ministries) and from Liberty University (Master's in Theological Studies/Church History). Tony's passion for teaching the Bible has taken him to forty-seven states and thirty-three nations.

Other books by Tony include:

- *Life After Death: Rediscovering Life After Loss of a Loved One*
- *In Search of Timothy: Discovering and Developing Greatness in Church Staff and Volunteers*
- *Grace, the DNA of God; Qualified: Serving God with Integrity and Finishing Your Course with Honor*
- *Through the Storms: Help from Heaven When All Hell Breaks Loose*
- *Your Place on God's Dream Team: The Making of Champions*
- *The Work Book: What We Do Matters to God*
- *Lift: Experiencing the Elevated Life.*

Various titles have been translated and published in eight other languages.

Tony and his wife, Lisa, reside in Broken Arrow, Oklahoma, and are the parents of two children.

www.tonycooke.org

The Harrison House Vision

Proclaiming the truth and the power
of the Gospel of Jesus Christ with excellence.
Challenging Christians
to live victoriously,
grow spiritually,
know God intimately.

Connect with us on

f Facebook @ HarrisonHousePublishers

and ⊡ Instagram @ HarrisonHousePublishing

so you can stay up to date with news

about our books and our authors.

Visit us at **www.harrisonhouse.com**

for a complete product listing as well as

monthly specials for wholesale distribution.